Library of
Davidson College

MARX'S ECONOMICS
A DUAL THEORY OF VALUE
AND GROWTH

MARX'S ECONOMICS
A DUAL THEORY OF VALUE
AND GROWTH

Michio Morishima

MARX'S ECONOMICS
A DUAL THEORY
OF VALUE AND GROWTH

CAMBRIDGE
AT THE UNIVERSITY PRESS
1973

Published by the Syndics of the Cambridge University Press
Bentley House, 200 Euston Road, London NW1 2DB
American Branch: 32 East 57th Street, New York, N.Y. 10022

© Cambridge University Press 1973

Library of Congress Catalogue Card Number: 72–83591

ISBN: 0 521 87473

Printed in Great Britain
at the University Printing House, Cambridge
(Brooke Crutchley, University Printer)

Michio Morishima

MARX'S ECONOMICS
A DUAL THEORY
OF VALUE AND GROWTH

CAMBRIDGE
AT THE UNIVERSITY PRESS
1973

Published by the Syndics of the Cambridge University Press
Bentley House, 200 Euston Road, London NW1 2DB
American Branch: 32 East 57th Street, New York, N.Y. 10022

© Cambridge University Press 1973

Library of Congress Catalogue Card Number: 72-83591

ISBN: 0 521 87473

Printed in Great Britain
at the University Printing House, Cambridge
(Brooke Crutchley, University Printer)

Contents

Preface	page vii
Introduction	1

PART I. The Labour Theory of Value

1 Dual definition of value	10
2 Hidden assumptions	21
3 Quantitative determination of relative value	28
4 Value, use-value and exchange-value	36

PART II. The Theory of Exploitation

5 Surplus value and exploitation	46
6 The rate of profit	56

PART III. The Transformation Problem

7 The static transformation problem	72
8 The aggregation problem	87

PART IV. The Reproduction Scheme

9 Simple reproduction	105
10 Extended reproduction	117
11 The reserve army and the falling rate of profit	129
12 The dynamic transformation problem	145

PART V. Capital and Value

13 The turnover of capital	164
14 The labour theory of value revisited	179
Index	197

Contents

Preface *page* vii

Introduction 1

Part I. The Labour Theory of Value
1 Dual definition of value 10
2 Hidden assumptions 21
3 Quantitative determination of relative value 28
4 Value, use-value and exchange-value 36

Part II. The Theory of Exploitation
5 Surplus value and exploitation 46
6 The rate of profit 56

Part III. The Transformation Problem
7 The static transformation problem 72
8 The aggregation problem 87

Part IV. The Reproduction Scheme
9 Simple reproduction 105
10 Extended reproduction 117
11 The reserve army and the falling rate of profit 129
12 The dynamic transformation problem 145

Part V. Capital and Value
13 The turnover of capital 164
14 The labour theory of value revisited 179

Index 197

Preface

In this book Marx's economic thought is reviewed in the light o the present-day advanced level of economic theory. His economics in fact covers many branches of social science, so that it is too large a subject to be dealt with by a specialized mathematical economist; I therefore confine myself to discussing only its core, that is his general equilibrium model, which has two main constituents: the theory of value and the theory of reproduction. I am satisfied with this partial approach because my purpose in this book is not to recapitulate his economics but to give it rigorous expression, so that we can discuss Marx in the same way as, for example, Walras. (However, it must be added that this book is not difficult mathematically, although its reasoning is rigorous.) Marx's theory of growth when so formulated may be compared with the neoclassical theory of growth examined in chapters I-V of my *Theory of Economic Growth* (Oxford, 1969). Thus this book is intended, on the one hand, to make its own contributions to Marxian economics and, on the other, to form a trilogy on growth together with *Theory of Economic Growth* and *Equilibrium, Stability and Growth* (Oxford, 1964); these three books may be taken, in the reverse order of publication, as the introduction, the text and the mathematical appendix, respectively, of such a trilogy.

I have so far published three articles with a flavour of Marxian economics. One, which was written with Dr F. Seton and published in *Econometrica*, 1961, deals with the labour theory of value and the aggregation of outputs in terms of values, while the other two, published in *Metroeconomica*, 1956 and *Econometrica*, 1960, are concerned directly or indirectly with Marx's theory of reproduction. They are the bases from which I started to tackle the problem. In fact, the first half of this book may be regarded as an elaboration of the Morishima–Seton paper, and the second half as an introduction to my 1960 *Econometrica* paper. I must acknowledge here that Dr Seton's contribution to the 1961 paper was particularly significant, because I was not very familiar with Marxian economics when we wrote it in 1957.

With much help from Professor Okishio's books (unfortunately,

PREFACE

all in Japanese), I had gathered almost all the material for this book by September 1968. The first mimeographed version was available early in January 1971, and has subsequently circulated among students and specialists as notes to my lectures 'Marx in the light of contemporary economic analysis' at the London School of Economics. During this rather long gestation period new additions to the literature have appeared, such as A. Brody, *Proportions, Prices and Planning* (Budapest, 1970), and Professor Samuelson's article in the *Journal of Economic Literature*, 1971. Although this final version deals with the problems which they have raised, particularly those discussed in the latter, it is substantially the same as the original lecture notes, except that it is enriched by many quotations from Marx's *Capital*, Progress Publishers, Moscow (vol. I, 1965, vol. II, 1967 and vol. III, 1966).

In addition to the acknowledgements so far mentioned, one has to be made to Professor Joan Robinson, who read an earlier draft of this book and gave me comments. A long discussion which I had with her in Osaka on the transformation problem was stimulating and timely. Other acknowledgements are due to Professors M. Tanaka (Kyoto), Y. Takasuka (Hitotsubashi) and T. Sakurai (Mushasi), who were in London while I was working on this book, and to Dr A. Zauberman of the L.S.E. These specialists on Marx and Soviet economics gave me much useful information. I have also benefited by a number of helpful comments and suggestions from members of the seminars in many British and Italian universities where I was given the opportunity to read some parts of the book, and also from those who attended my lectures.

I owe immense stylistic improvements to the editorial officers of the Press, and Miss Luba Mumford typed versions of the whole manuscript.

August 1972   M. M.

Introduction

It is our great misfortune that economists have for a long time been divided between the 'orthodox' and Marxian camps as a result of cliquishness; each school has lost touch with the other and has become inbred. In Japan, for example, Marxian economists have formed an association called Keizai Riron Gakkai (Economic Theoretical Association) in opposition to the Riron Keizai Gakkai (Theoretical Economic Association) of non-Marxists. In spite of the similarity of the names of the societies, no fruitful conversation has ever been held between them. They are at daggers drawn and describe each other as a society for reactionaries and a society for economists with lower I.Q.s.

This has been the tradition since Marx. However, we may notice a significant difference between the quarrels of the 1870s and those of the 1970s. It is true that Marx attacked many of his predecessors, but in his criticism he used the same language as they had used. Although he began his life as a philosopher, he later became fascinated by classical economics, which might be considered the mathematical economics of his time, and remodelled its tools and apparatus in order to construct his own economics. The fact that he was one of the authorities on classical economics made it possible for a dialectic development to take place between Marxian and traditional economics. It is indeed a pity that contemporary Marxists have lost the spirit of Marx in this respect.[1]

On the other hand orthodox economists, too, are in the wrong, not only in segregating Marxists but also in undervaluing Marx, who should in my opinion be ranked as high as Walras in the history of mathematical economics. It has rarely been pointed out that the general equilibrium theory was formulated independently and simultaneously by Walras and Marx, whereas it has often been mentioned that the utility theory of consumer's behaviour was discovered independently and simultaneously by

[1] Recently a number of East European economists have started to think in terms of the same terminology as Western economists commonly use. This is a change to be welcomed. See for example A. Bródy, *Proportions, Prices and Planning* (Budapest, 1970), 194 pp. For the recent currents of economic thought in the Soviet bloc, see A. Zauberman, *Aspects of Planometrics* (London: Athlone Press, 1967), 318 pp.

Walras, Jevons and Menger. It was in 1874 that Walras' *Eléments d'économie politique pure* was first published; whilst it was early in the 1860s that Marx began to investigate the problem of 'reproduction and circulation of the aggregate social capital'. The fact that Marx's work was only published after his death – by Engels, in volumes II and III of *Capital* in 1885 and 1894 respectively – does not affect the greatness of his achievement at all. Indeed, Marx's theory of reproduction and Walras' theory of capital accumulation should be honoured together as the parents of the modern, dynamic theory of general economic equilibrium.

However, unlike Walras but like Hicks, Marx constructed a two-stage general equilibrium theory. It has often been pointed out that Walrasian miscroscopic equilibrium theory is rather sterile, since it is too general and complicated to be able to derive definite conclusions. To get rid of this weakness Hicks developed an aggregation theory and reduced the general microeconomic equilibrium system to a macroeconomic system with a few variables and equations. One of the main purposes of Hicks' *Value and Capital* was to confirm or refute Keynesian propositions from the viewpoint of general equilibrium theory. By assuming that prices of all commodities change proportionately, Hicks treated all commodities as if they were a single commodity; he thereby obtained a three-equation system, consisting of the demand-supply equations for commodities, bonds, and money, by which the Keynesian theses were tested.[2]

Marx was in a similar position. He also wanted to derive some definite laws of movement for capitalist society and therefore needed a method of aggregation which would enable him to avoid the pure, general but powerless Walrasian conclusion: Everything depends on everything else. But Marx was satisfied with neither the Hicksian method of taking relative prices as weights of aggregation, nor Keynes' solution of measuring aggregate output, aggregate consumption and so on in terms of wage-units, because the weights used in these methods of aggregation would fluctuate, depending on market conditions. Marx, unlike Hicks and Keynes, wanted to establish economic laws of a very long-run nature, such as 'the law of the tendency of the rate of profit to fall', 'the law of population peculiar to the capitalist mode of production', 'the general law of capitalist

[2] J. R. Hicks, *Value and Capital* (Oxford University Press, 1946).

accumulation', and so forth, so that he had to base his macro-model on more stable and more solid aggregates. It is my opinion that the labour theory of value plays a most important part in Marx's economics, since it provides a system of constants, in terms of which his microeconomic model may be aggregated into a two-departmental macroeconomic model, under a number of assumptions.

It is no exaggeration to say that before Kalecki, Frisch and Tinbergen no economist except Marx, had obtained a macro-dynamic model rigorously constructed in a scientific way. His micro-model, the foundation of his macro-model, might on the other hand, as I have mentioned, be compared with Walras' general equilibrium model of capital formation and credit. These are the most elaborate models we have ever had, though Walras' is more detailed than Marx's in the analysis of consumer demand for commodities. This last point has often been reckoned as one of the defects of Marx's theory, but it must be remembered that only by drastically simplifying the aspect of consumers' choice was he able successfully to derive definite dynamic laws concerning the working of his sytem through time. It was a very practical bargain, which has become popular among us since Keynes' *General Theory*. Hicks accepted the same exchange in his *Theory of the Trade Cycle*. Leontief, in his short-run theory, even regarded consumption as constant. Thus many contemporary economists believe that it is more important to obtain a theory which can describe dynamic movements of the economy, rather than one which can elaborate consumers' preference. This is exactly the choice which Marx made.

Moreover, Marx's theory of reproduction is very similar to Leontief's input–output analysis. (Or more correctly, we should say conversely that Leontief reproduced Marx as well as Walras in a pragmatic way.) And as we shall see later, Marx's theory contains in itself a way to the von Neumann Revolution; although he will have lost some of his properties during the Revolution, after it he will be honoured as one of the authors of the Marx–von Neumann model, in which, if we wish, we can allow for consumers' choice as I have done in my *Equilibrium, Stability and Growth*. Thus Marx is still active on the frontier of our science. One of his tools has recently been rediscovered and named the factor–price frontier – one of the most fundamental concepts of present-day growth theory. His idea of the dual duality, one duality between physical and value systems and the other between physical and price systems, has now been acknowledged by all economists as the first principle of all societies producing commodities for exchange, though it has to be simplified into a single duality between physical outputs and prices. The concept of the value-composition of capital, which Marx utilized in aggregating industries and in constructing his breakdown thesis, is no more than the Marxian counterpart of the capital–labour ratio, which has been found most useful in the analysis of growth. These would be enough examples to recommend Marx as a purely academic economist for one of the very few chairs with the highest authority.

Unfortunately, however, it will be found that Marx has to lose much, even his most precious properties, in order to be legitimated by orthodox economists. Marx's labour theory of value and his theory of exploitation are, in spite of repeated criticisms by his opponents, highly suggestive and economically meaningful under some conditions. Nevertheless, they must be victims of the von Neumann Revolution; in fact, as we shall see, von Neumann's new treatment of capital goods and his criterion for the choice of techniques are found to conflict with the uniqueness of the actual value system, which is an unavoidable requisite for a system of weights to be able to serve as aggregators. It is true, as we shall also see, that the value theory and the exploitation theory may be revised in terms of the optimum values so as to survive the Revolution. But such revisions assume homogeneous labour; otherwise the value theory, either in the optimum or in the actual form, may be inconsistent with any uniform rate of exploitation.

Another victim is provided by his theory of the breakdown of the capitalist mode of production. It is evidently the essence of Marxism, but it was only briefly discussed by Marx himself; so that he might not be too surprised to hear that counter-examples have been found later. It must also be emphasized, on the other hand, that despite the counter-examples more work needs to be done in this largely unexplored area. As mathematical growth theory has become involved in the Rostovian take-off problem, it must be concerned with the Marxian breakdown problem too, and many interesting findings may be expected.

It will take a long time for these Marxian concepts to re-establish their legitimacy; perhaps they will never be able to acquire full citizenship in scientific economics. Nevertheless, they are attractive and worth speculating about. It is no wonder that some economists cannot agree that they should be abandoned. Those who are interested in these subjects will continue to form a subgroup for investigating such special and yet illegitimate topics. Marxian economics may continue to exist in this way after all the valid achievements of Marx have been commonly accepted by economists, and the division between valid Marxian economics and orthodox theory has been removed.

Thus our approach to Marx is somewhat different from the so-called Marxian economics, now stylized by both Marxists and non-Marxists. We make Marx stand out not only for his own sake, but against the economic theory of our time. Our aim is to recognize the greatness of Marx from the viewpoint of modern advanced economic theory and, by so doing, to contribute to the development of our science. We do not discuss Marx in relation to his predecessors, such as Smith, Ricardo and Quesnay; we pay no attention to the development of Marxian economics after Marx. We neglect even his works other than the three volumes of *Capital*, and confine ourselves to assessing, according to the standards of contemporary economic theory, his contributions in that book to the following major topics of traditional Marxian economics: (1) the labour theory of value, (2) the theory of exploitation, (3) the transformation problem, (4) reproduction, (5) the law of relative surplus population, (6) the falling rate of profit, and (7) the turnover of capital.

In part I the classical labour theory of value is rigorously mathematized in a familar form parallel to Leontief's intersectoral price–cost equations. The hidden assumptions are all revealed and, by the use of the mathematics of the input–output analysis, the comparative statical laws concerning the behaviour of the relative values of commodities (in terms of a standard commodity arbitrarily chosen) are proved. There is a duality between physical outputs and values of commodities, which is similar to the duality between physical outputs and competitive prices. It is seen that the labour theory of value may be compatible with the utility theory of consumers' demands or any of its improved variations.

Part II discusses a fundamental theorem concerned with the rate of profit, after it explains Marx's theory of exploitation. The Morishima–Seton–Okishio theorem states that the equilibrium rate of profit is positive if and only if the rate of exploitation is positive.[3] This is one of the theorems which Marx wanted to establish in *Capital*. It may be considered as the heart and soul of Marxian philosophy, since it implies that exploitation is necessary for the continued existence of a capitalist economy, because it cannot survive if the equilibrium rate of profit is not positive. The theorem is proved by using the concepts of the factor–price frontier and the exploitation frontier. Since the factor–price frontier is a topic at the forefront of contemporary economic theory, the theorem may be of great interest, even if we confine ourselves to considering only its analytical aspects.

Marxian economics, unlike traditional economics, has developed two different systems of accounting, one in terms of prices and the other in terms of values. If there were no exploitation, they would be identical. But in any capitalist economy where exploitation exists, the 'law of value' does not present itself in its pure and simple form; values and prices may differ from each other. The transformation problem is therefore concerned with the conversion of accounts in terms of value into accounts in terms of price. Chapter 7, part III is concerned with the problem of converting the values of commodities into their production prices, whereas the problem of converting the rate of surplus value into the rate of profit is the subject of chapter 6, part II. Our discussion of the transformation problem brings forth, in addition to the main results aimed at,[4] a by-product which is

---

[3] M. Morishima and F. Seton, 'Aggregation in Leontief Matrices and the Labour Theory of Value', *Econometrica*, 1961; N. Okishio, 'A Mathematical Note on Marxian Theorems', *Weltwirtschaftliches Archiv*, 1963.

[4] It has been a tradition among critics of Marx since Böhm-Bawerk to point out contradictions between volumes I and III or to conclude that Marx was wrong in the transformation problem. The tradition has recently been reinforced by using modern techniques of mathematical economics. (See P. A. Samuelson, 'Understanding the Marxian Notion of Exploitation: A Summary of the So-Called Transformation Problem Between Marxian Values and Competitive Prices', *Journal of Economic Literature*, vol. IX, no. 2, June 1971, pp. 399–431.) My discussion of the transformation problem in this book, the original version of which was available in a mimeographed form before the publication of Samuelson' paper, is very different from his in its conclusions, in spite of the surprising similarity in the mathematics used. (For example, he has also obtained the exploitation frontier as well as the factor–price frontier.) I am very much more sympathetic than he is. This is

more important than the main products, although Marx was not fully aware of it. This is the finding that the aggregation condition that industries which are similar in the value-composition of capital can be aggregated safely into one hybrid sector, a 'department', is a corollary of the transformation problem, offering the basis for Marx's two-departmental growth theory. Chapter 8, in which the aggregation condition is established, is an important chapter forming a bridge between Marx's micro-theory of price determination and his macro-theory of output determination.

Part IV deals with Marx's theory of economic growth. We follow Marx in starting by analysing the state of simple reproduction. When the system satisfies Marx's aggregation conditions, various elementary sectors (or industries) can be aggregated into two major departments, producing consumption and capital goods respectively. This simple macro-theory of stationary states is then generalized into the theory of extended reproduction which is Marx's growth theory. It is seen that his model performs badly because he assigned different and asymmetric roles to the capitalists of departments I and II in the accumulation of capital. But with some revisions the model is found to generate a dynamic path which is unstable, as it diverges from the balanced equilibrium growth path, unless it is already on the balanced growth path at the outset.

As soon as we derive such an unstable path, we can easily discuss Marx's theory of relative surplus population, on which the theorem of the breakdown of the capitalist mode of production is based. Its uniqueness is clear when it is compared with the neo-classical theory. It removes the postulate of full-employment and full-capacity growth and maintains the necessity of monotonic or cyclic accumulation of the reserve army of the labour force. It is not difficult to find counter-examples to Marx; but nevertheless it is true that the cases alleged by him are possibilities that are missed or suppressed by neo-classical economists. Finally, the last part of chapter 11 is devoted to a correct proof of the law of the tendency of the rate of profit to fall.

Part V is mainly devoted to an appraisal of Marx's achievements. In chapter 14 we criticize the labour theory of value in its

an interesting example of the non-univalence of the correspondence between economics and mathematics.

relation to (i) the heterogeneity of labour, (ii) joint production, and (iii) the problem of choice of techniques. Once one of these three is admitted, the labour theory of value is seen to get into difficulties. This means that, rigorously speaking, we cannot admit Marx unless he is prepared to abandon the labour theory of value. At first sight this may seem to be a most drastic proposal, which Marxian economists could not accept; but Marxian economics without the labour theory of value is in fact found to be as conceivable as Walrasian economics without utility theory, for the following reasons. Firstly, it must be remembered that we understand the labour theory of value as a theory of aggregation, reducing the number of sectors to a manageably small number. We understand this aggregation theory as a pragmatic theory which is applicable in some cases and inapplicable in others, as Hicks' theory of a group of commodities is in his *Value and Capital*. We must avoid it because we want to obtain a rigorous general theory, but we admit that it is a useful theory if it is carefully applied. Secondly, by virtue of the recent development of multi-sectoral growth analysis we are now very much richer in the techniques of dynamic analysis than was Marx. In the future it may be possible to derive fruitful conclusions from the Marxian multi-sectoral growth model by using such new techniques; if so, aggregation may be avoided and the role of the labour theory of value will become less important.

In chapter 13, before making these critical comments, we show that Marx's theory of reproduction was the prototype for the contemporary theory of economic growth. In fact his theory is comparable with von Neumann's theory, which is the most satisfactory dynamic economic theory we are now provided with. It is indeed a great surprise to find that many of von Neumann's novel ideas were clearly stated in *Capital*. Furthermore, Marx's work in this field was done independently of the labour theory of value and can easily be developed into the Marx–von Neumann theory of general dynamic equilibrium. The conclusion is, therefore, that irrespective of our ideologies or political views, we all owe the foundation of dynamic general equilibrium theory, the core of economic theory, to Marx.

This appraisal may be compared with that made by O. Lange nearly forty years ago. He compared Marxian economics and modern economic theory as follows: 'Marxian economics can work the economic evolution of capitalist society into a consistent theory from which its necessity is deduced, while "bourgeois" economists get no further than mere historical description. On the other hand, "bourgeois" economics is able to grasp the phenomena of the every-day life of a capitalist economy in a manner that is far superior to anything the Marxists can produce.'[5] However Lange never compared Marx's analytical dynamic theory, rather than his historical and sociological theory of economic evolution, directly with its counterparts in modern economic theory. If he had compared them, he might have conceded the superiority of Marxian economics over modern economics in dynamic analysis. In spite of the existence of Frisch's, Tinbergen's and Kalecki's macro-dynamics and von Neumann's growth theory, the interest of the majority of orthodox economists was confined to static or short-run problems at the time when Lange's comparison was made. It was only after the war that the theory of growth became the main subject of orthodox economics. It took nearly ninety years for orthodox economists to overcome the initial advantages of Marxian economics in the field of dynamics. Now it is proposed to integrate the growth theories of the two schools into the Marx–von Neumann theory, and a new stage of development is about to start.

[5] O. Lange, 'Marxian Economics and Modern Economic Theory', *Review of Economic Studies*, June 1935, p. 191.

PART I
The Labour Theory of Value

CHAPTER I
Dual definition of value

In Marx's economics the labour theory of value has two functions: (i) to explain the equilibrium prices (or the exchange values) of commodities, around which actual prices fluctuate over time, and (ii) to provide aggregators, or weights of aggregation, in terms of which a large number of industries (or primitive sectors) are aggregated into a small number of 'departments'. Marx devoted many pages of *Capital* to the first problem, but was not explicit about, or was unaware of, the second point. Nevertheless, it is true that Marx aggregated industries into departments in terms of values, and I believe Marx would have elaborated his value theory as an aggregation theory if he had had a chance to read Keynes' *General Theory*.

Most of the followers and antagonists of Marx discussed only the first aspect of the labour theory of value. But I believe that the second aspect is more important. As is well known, Marx may be contrasted with Keynes who aggregated commodities in terms of their market wage-prices (i.e. market prices in terms of labour) to measure aggregates such as income, consumption and so on. He emphasized that market prices were easily changed from time to time by casual causes; so if market prices are used as aggregators, the components of an aggregate will have different weights from time to time, depending on the prevailing conditions in the market. Marx wanted a more solid basis for his macroeconomics and so adopted values as aggregators because they were more fundamental than prices; he thought that values could be determined by technology alone and hence were not influenced by changes in wages and prices in the market, as long as the methods of production chosen remained unaffected.[1]

[1] In the so-called 'neo-classical' model with smooth production functions, a small change in wages and prices gives rise to a change in capital-input and labour-input coefficients, which in turn gives rise to a change in values. Therefore we cannot say

DUAL DEFINITION OF VALUE

In Marx's *Capital* there seem to be two definitions of value, which are:

(i) 'All that these things now tell us is, that human labour-power has been expended in their production, that human labour is embodied in them. When looked at as crystals of this social substance, common to them all, they are – Values.' (*Capital*, vol. I, p. 38.)

(ii) 'We see then that that which determines the magnitude of the value of any article is the amount of labour socially necessary, or the labour-time socially necessary for its production.' (I, p. 39.)

At first sight these may look like identical definitions, and Marx actually regarded them as synonymous. They are, however, found to be different views of value, their equivalence being established only if a rigorous proof is provided.

Consider a society where corn and compost are produced. In order to produce one unit of corn (commodity 1), a_{11} units of corn, a_{21} units of compost (commodity 2) and l_1 hours of labour are needed. Let the value of corn by λ_1 and that of compost λ_2. According to the first definition, the value of corn is defined as the total amount of labour (in terms of hours) embodied or materialized in one unit of corn. As the a_{11} units of corn and a_{21} units of compost consumed in the production of one unit of corn contain $a_{11}\lambda_1$ and $a_{21}\lambda_2$ hours of labour and, in addition, l_1 hours of labour are directly consumed in the process of the production of corn, in one unit of corn hours of labour amounting to[2]

$$\lambda_1 = a_{11}\lambda_1 + a_{21}\lambda_2 + l_1$$

are materialized or crystalized.

On the other hand, according to Leontief's input–output analysis one unit of the net output of corn is obtained by producing q_1 units of gross output of corn and q_2 units of gross output

that values are more rigid than prices. Thus, even if Marx had hit on the idea of a smooth production function he would have rejected it, as he wanted to establish values as more stable variables which would be independent of small short-run changes in wages and prices.

[2] This equation was explained by Marx as follows: 'The labourer adds fresh value to the subject of his labour by expending upon it a given amount of additional labour, no matter what the specific character and utility of that labour may be. On the other hand, the values of the means of production used up in the process are preserved, and present themselves afresh as constituent parts of the value of the product; the values of the cotton and the spindle, for instance, re-appear again in the value of the yarn. The values of the means of production is therefore preserved, by being transferred to the product.' (I, p. 199.)

of compost, so that $l_1 q_1$ hours of labour are employed in the corn industry and $l_2 q_2$ in the compost industry. The labour-time socially necessary for producing one unit of corn is given as

$$\mu_1 = l_1 q_1 + l_2 q_2,$$

which is the value of corn according to the second definition.

Thus the mathematical expressions of the two definitions of value are quite distinct, despite the *prima facie* similarity of the literal definitions. Therefore we must decide whether $\lambda_1 = \mu_1$ or not. We are thus confronted, at the beginning of Marxian economics, with a very modern problem of the duality between the value determination system and the input-output system, which has recently become familiar among orthodox economists through mathematical investigations into Leontief's input-output system.

The problem is now dealt with in a more general way. Consider a closed economy producing m commodities, the first n of them being capital goods (or means of production), and the remaining $m-n$ being wage or luxury goods. We assume in the following,

(*a*) that to each industry there is available one and only one method of production, so that there is no problem of 'choice of techniques';

(*b*) that each industry produces one kind of output, without any by-product, so that there are no 'joint production problems';

(*c*) that there are no primary factors of production other than labour; labour is measured in terms of unskilled or abstract labour, so that there is no problem of 'heterogeneous concrete labours';

(*d*) that all capital goods have the same span of life, which is taken as unity, so that there are no fixed capital goods in the proper sense left over to the next period for further production after having been used in the current period;

(*e*) that all commodities have the same period of production, which is taken as one unit of time;

(*f*) that each production process is of the point-input-point-output type; inputs are made at the beginning of the production period and outputs are obtained at the end of the period, so that labour is used only once in each production period.[3]

[3] Assumption (*f*) implies that at the beginning of the period capitalists must have a wage fund which is equal to the wage bill. In the other extreme case of wages

DUAL DEFINITION OF VALUE

All these assumptions, which are deliberately made, play important roles in the construction of the prototype of the labour theory of value. In particular, assumptions (d), (e) and (f) imply that all capitals, constant and variable, are turned over identically. One might think that this is a serious abstraction from reality. But it is an abstraction adopted by von Neumann and enables us not only to simplify the analysis but also to resolve many problems of capital theory. Marx too thought that these assumptions were very unrealistic; accordingly he took some account of the differences in the turnover of various capitals. Although his analysis of 'the turnover of capital', 'the working period' and 'the time of production' developed in volume II, part II of *Capital* is not identical with von Neumann's, they are not very different from each other. Marx's model, if it is put at the beginning in a form which satisfies assumptions $(a)-(f)$, can easily be converted into a von Neumann-like model. In the final chapter of this book, where the labour theory of value is revisited, the implications and effects of $(a)-(f)$ are all examined and von Neumann generalizations are made to the prototype; alternative techniques of production and joint products are allowed for and the reducibility of all sorts of labour to the homogeneous 'human labour in the abstract' is discussed. Until then, we are satisfied with dealing with the abstract economy.

Let a unit of commodity i be produced by a_{ji} units of capital good j ($j = 1, ..., n$) and l_i units of labour. a_{ji}s are measured in terms of the respective natural physical units (say, in 2 tons of coal per one bulldozer) and l_is by the duration of labour or in labour-time. The production process of commodity i is characterized by a vector $(a_{1i}, a_{2i}, ..., a_{ni}, l_i)$, the input of goods and labour in these amounts at a point of time bringing forth a unit of commodity i after the lapse of a production period. The amount of labour embodied in one unit of commodity i, denoted by λ_i, is defined as the sum of the amount

being paid at the end of the period, the wage fund is zero, in spite of the wage bill being still positive. Thus even in the simplest case of the point–input–point–output production processes of one period of production, the wage fund may differ from the wage bill. I have called the economy with the point–input–point–output processes the Marx–von Neumann economy if wages are paid at the beginning of the period and the Walras–von Neumann if they are paid at the end. See my *Equilibrium, Stability and Growth* (Oxford, 1964), ch. 5.

of direct labour and the amount of labour embodied in other factors of production used directly in producing a unit of commodity i. Evidently a_{1i} units of capital good $1, \ldots, a_{ni}$ units of capital good n embody $a_{1i}\lambda_n, \ldots, a_{ni}\lambda_n$ units of labour, which together with the direct labour used, l_i, determine the total labour embodied in commodity i, such that

$$\lambda_i = a_{1i}\lambda_1 + \ldots + a_{ni}\lambda_n + l_i.$$

We thus have a value-determination equation for each commodity, so that we have m equations altogether.[4] For example, in the special case of two capital goods and one wage good, they are written as

$$\lambda_1 = a_{11}\lambda_1 + a_{21}\lambda_2 + l_1,$$

$$\lambda_2 = a_{12}\lambda_1 + a_{22}\lambda_2 + l_2,$$

for capital goods, and

$$\lambda_3 = a_{13}\lambda_1 + a_{23}\lambda_2 + l_3$$

for the wage good. The two equations for capital goods jointly determine the two unknown values of capital goods, λ_1 and λ_2, simultaneously, and these in turn determine the value of the wage good λ_3, by virtue of the last value equation for the wage good. It is seen that no single sector can independently determine the value of its product, except in the trivial case of the system being completely decomposable into sectors (i.e. the case of $a_{ij} = 0$ for all i, j such that $i \neq j$). Values are thus determined socially. But it must be noted that they are determined only by

---

[4] One might think that when the methods of production employed in period t are different from those which have been employed in period $t-1$, the λ's appearing on the left-hand side of the equations should be distinguished by subscript t from those on the right-hand side with $t-1$. However, in this case, those commodities which have been produced by the old methods of production and are used as factors of production in period t have to be re-evaluated at the new values, i.e. the amounts of labour that are required to produce these commodities by the new methods of production prevailing in period t, so that the same λ's appear on both sides of the value-determining equations. As has been pointed out by Okishio, Marx wrote: 'The labour-time socially necessary is that required to produce an article under the normal conditions of production, and with the average degree of skill and intensity prevalent at the time.' (I, p. 39.) 'The value of every commodity – thus also of the commodities making up the capital – is determined not by the necessary labour-time contained in it, but by the *social* labour-time required for its reproduction.' (III, p. 141; italics by Marx.) See N. Okishio, *Shihon-sei Keizai no Kiso-riron* (The Fundamental Theory of the Capitalist Economy) (Sobun-sha, 1965), p. 14.

technological coefficients, a_{ij}s and l_is; they are independent of the market, the class-structure of the society, taxes and so on. Marx wanted to explain economic phenomena by using this materialistic concept. 'It becomes plain, that it is not the exchange of commodities which regulates the magnitude of their value; but, on the contrary, that it is the magnitude of their value which controls their exchange proportions'. (I, p. 63.)

In the general case of n capital goods and $m-n$ wage or luxury goods, the above equations are written more conveniently, in matrix form, as

$$\Lambda_\mathrm{I} = \Lambda_\mathrm{I} A_\mathrm{I} + L_\mathrm{I}, \tag{1}$$

$$\Lambda_\mathrm{II} = \Lambda_\mathrm{I} A_\mathrm{II} + L_\mathrm{II}, \tag{2}$$

where

$$A_\mathrm{I} = \begin{bmatrix} a_{11} & \cdots & a_{1n} \\ \vdots & & \vdots \\ a_{n1} & \cdots & a_{nn} \end{bmatrix}, \quad A_\mathrm{II} = \begin{bmatrix} a_{1n+1} & \cdots & a_{1m} \\ \vdots & & \vdots \\ a_{nn+1} & \cdots & a_{nm} \end{bmatrix},$$

$$L_\mathrm{I} = (l_1, \ldots, l_n), \quad L_\mathrm{II} = (l_{n+1}, \ldots, l_m),$$

$$\Lambda_\mathrm{I} = (\lambda_1, \ldots, \lambda_n), \quad \Lambda_\mathrm{II} = (\lambda_{n+1}, \ldots, \lambda_m).$$

As are referred to as capital coefficient matrices, Ls as labour-input coefficient vectors, and Λs as value vectors. Note that A_I is square and A_II rectangular; Ls and Λs are row vectors.

According to the second definition, the value of a commodity is the total amount of labour necessary to produce a unit of that commodity with the method of production prevailing in the society. In order to produce a unit of capital good 1, say, $a_{11}, \ldots, a_{n1}$ units of capital goods $1, \ldots, n$ are required. These capital goods must be produced, which in turn requires the production of further capital goods, and so forth. Thus an increase of one unit of output of capital good 1 gives rise to multiplier effects on outputs of capital goods $1, \ldots, n$. To obtain the total amounts of capital goods, $x_1^1, \ldots, x_n^1$, which are required after taking all repercussions into account for the production of a unit of capital good 1, we must solve the input–output equations:

$$\left. \begin{aligned} x_1^1 &= a_{11} x_1^1 + \ldots + a_{1n} x_n^1 + 1, \\ x_2^1 &= a_{21} x_1^1 + \ldots + a_{2n} x_n^1 + 0, \\ \vdots & \quad \vdots \quad\quad\quad\quad \vdots \quad\quad \vdots \\ x_n^1 &= a_{n1} x_1^1 + \ldots + a_{nn} x_n^1 + 0, \end{aligned} \right\} \tag{3.1}$$

and the total amount of labour necessary to produce one unit of capital good 1 is given by

$$\mu_1 = \sum_{j=1}^{n} l_j x_j^1. \quad (4.1)$$

As it takes one period of time to produce any of these commodities, inputs, $\Sigma a_{jj} x_j^1$, $i = 1, \ldots, n$, are made at the beginning of the period and outputs, x_i^1, $i = 1, \ldots, n$, are only available at the end of the period. Therefore in the actual process of production industries use the necessary amounts of capital goods, which are replaced at the end of the production process. The parts of outputs which remain after the replacement are called *net* outputs; in the present case we have only one unit of net output of capital good 1.

Similarly, the value of capital good 2 is determined by

$$\left.\begin{aligned} x_1^2 &= a_{11} x_1^2 + \ldots + a_{1n} x_n^2 + 0, \\ x_2^2 &= a_{21} x_1^2 + \ldots + a_{2n} x_n^2 + 1, \\ &\vdots \qquad \vdots \qquad \vdots \\ x_n^2 &= a_{n1} x_1^2 + \ldots + a_{nn} x_n^2 + 0, \end{aligned}\right\} \quad (3.2)$$

as

$$\mu_2 = \sum_{j=1}^{n} l_j x_j^2. \quad (4.2)$$

Also, we have similar $n-2$ sets of equations for the remaining capital goods, $3, \ldots, n$. These, together with (3.1) and (3.2), give n sets of input–output equations, which may *en masse* be put in the following concise expressions:

$$X_\mathrm{I} = A_\mathrm{I} X_\mathrm{I} + I, \quad (3)$$

where I is the $n \times n$ identity matrix, as usual, and

$$X_\mathrm{I} = \begin{bmatrix} x_1^1 & x_1^2 & \ldots & x_1^n \\ \vdots & \vdots & & \vdots \\ x_n^1 & x_n^2 & \ldots & x_n^n \end{bmatrix}.$$

Once the outputs $x_1^i, \ldots, x_n^i$ (the ith column of X_I) required for the production of one unit of capital good i are determined, its value by the second definition is calculated analogously to (4.1) or (4.2) above. Or the value vector of capital goods is calculated as

$$M_\mathrm{I} = L_\mathrm{I} X_\mathrm{I}, \quad (4)$$

DUAL DEFINITION OF VALUE

where $M_{\mathrm{I}} = (\mu_1, \mu_2, ..., \mu_n)$ is the value vector of capital goods by the second definition, which for consistency of the two definitions should be equal to Λ_{I}, the value vector by the first definition, as will be seen below.

For wage and luxury goods there are two processes of production. The capital goods necessary for the replacement of the stocks of capital goods used are produced in the first process, while in the second process capital goods are combined with labour to produce wage or luxury goods. Capital goods, $1, ..., n$, of the amounts $a_{1i}, ..., a_{ni}$, respectively, are required per unit of wage or luxury good i $(i = n+1, ..., m)$, so that for the purpose of replacement capital goods must be produced in the amounts, $x_1^i, ..., x_n^i$, determined by the following equations, in order to provide the wage or luxury-good industry with net outputs of capital goods in the amounts which are just enough for the repayment:

$$\left.\begin{aligned} x_1^i &= a_{11} x_1^i + ... + a_{1n} x_n^i + a_{1i}, \\ x_2^i &= a_{21} x_1^i + ... + a_{2n} x_n^i + a_{2i}, \\ &\vdots \qquad \vdots \qquad \vdots \qquad \vdots \\ x_n^i &= a_{n1} x_1^i + ... + a_{nn} x_n^i + a_{ni}. \end{aligned}\right\} \quad (5.\mathrm{i})$$

In this first process of production $\sum_{j=1}^{n} l_j x_j^i$ workers are employed, and in the second process industry i combines l_i workers with the appropriate amounts of capital goods; therefore the total labour necessary for producing one unit of wage or luxury good i amounts to

$$\mu_i = \sum_{j=1}^{n} l_j x_j^i + l_i, \qquad (6.\mathrm{i})$$

which gives the value of good i by the second definition.

We have (5.i) and (6.i) for each of the wage and luxury goods, so that we have altogether $m-n$ such sets of equations. They can be written, in matrix notation, as

$$X_{\mathrm{II}} = A_{\mathrm{I}} X_{\mathrm{II}} + A_{\mathrm{II}}, \qquad (5)$$

$$M_{\mathrm{II}} = L_{\mathrm{I}} X_{\mathrm{II}} + L_{\mathrm{II}}, \qquad (6)$$

where

$$X_{\mathrm{II}} = \begin{bmatrix} x_1^{n+1} & x_1^{n+2} & ... & x_1^m \\ \vdots & \vdots & & \vdots \\ x_n^{n+1} & x_n^{n+2} & ... & x_n^m \end{bmatrix}, \quad \text{an } n \times (m-n) \text{ matrix,}$$

and $M_{II} = (\mu_{n+1}, ..., \mu_m)$.

Although the value formulas (1) and (2) are utterly different from (4) and (6), it is not difficult to establish the equivalence of the two definitions. First, postmultiply (1) by X_I, and transfering the first term on the right-hand side to the left we have

$$\Lambda_I(X_I - A_I X_I) = L_I X_I.$$

The part in parentheses is equal to I because of (3); therefore we obtain $\Lambda_I = L_I X_I$, establishing the identity of the values of capital goods by the two definitions, $\Lambda_I = M_I$.

Secondly, adding (1) postmultiplied by X_{II} to (2) and rearranging the terms, we have

$$\Lambda_{II} + \Lambda_I X_{II} - \Lambda_I(A_I X_{II} + A_{II}) = L_I X_{II} + L_{II}.$$

By (5) the part in parentheses is X_{II}, so that the third term on the left-hand side offsets the second term. Also, from (6), the right-hand side equals M_{II}. Hence the above equation implies $\Lambda_{II} = M_{II}$. Thus the two definitions are identical for wage and luxury goods too.[5]

In spite of this argument, which justifies Marx's presumption, the labour theory of value might be criticized on the grounds that values, unlike prices, are not observable and are not determined by any institution; it might be felt that science should avoid such metaphysical concepts. The identity between the two definitions of value, however, enables us to avoid criticisms of this sort. Value is not a mythical concept, but one which can claim citizenship in the modern, rigorous science of economics. It is clear from the second definition of value that values are not more than the employment multipliers discussed by Kahn and later by Keynes, which can be calculated from Leontief's input–output

[5] By solving the relevant equations explicitly, we can more directly and more mechanically derive the same results. First we have from (1)

$$\Lambda_I = L_I(I - A_I)^{-1}$$

which is equal to M_I, obtained by eliminating X_I from (3) and (4). Secondly, substituting for Λ_I from the above equation, we obtain from (2)

$$\Lambda_{II} = L_I(I - A_I)^{-1} A_{II} + L_{II}$$

which is equal to M_{II}, obtained by eliminating X_{II} from (5) and (6).

table, while the first definition imputes the total increase in employment caused by an increase in output to the factors of production utilized. Thus it is seen that there are modern concepts behind the classical labour theory, 'physical interdependence' and 'valuation', between which there holds a duality theorem establishing the identity of the two aspects of the economy.

We may expatiate on this view as follows. Let y be a column vector of *net* outputs of capital goods and z a column vector of outputs of wage or luxury goods. National product (or national income) in terms of value amounts to

$$\Lambda_\mathrm{I} y + \Lambda_\mathrm{II} z. \tag{7}$$

If the stocks of capital goods are kept intact, net outputs of capital goods, y, bring forth gross outputs of capital goods of the amounts $X_\mathrm{I} y$, and outputs of wage or luxury goods, z, induce outputs of capital goods of $X_\mathrm{II} z$, because of (3) and (5) respectively; so that total employment (in labour-time) in the capital good industries amounts to $L_\mathrm{I}(X_\mathrm{I} y + X_\mathrm{II} z)$, which together with the employment in the wage and luxury-good industries, $L_\mathrm{II} z$, gives total employment in the economy as

$$L_\mathrm{I} X_\mathrm{I} y + L_\mathrm{I} X_\mathrm{II} z + L_\mathrm{II} z = M_\mathrm{I} y + M_\mathrm{II} z \quad \text{(by the definition of } M\text{s)}$$
$$= \Lambda_\mathrm{I} y + \Lambda_\mathrm{II} z \quad \text{(by the equivalence of } M\text{s and } \Lambda\text{s),} \tag{8}$$

that is, the value of national product equals total employment. (It is interesting to see that a direct corollary of this equality is Keynes' principle of effective demand, which implies that employment is expanded only by increasing national income.) Furthermore, it is seen that the value of national income equals the value of capital consumed *plus* the direct employment needed to produce net outputs of capital goods y and wage and luxury goods z, as we have

$$\Lambda_\mathrm{I} y + \Lambda_\mathrm{II} z = (\Lambda_\mathrm{I} A_\mathrm{I} y + \Lambda_\mathrm{I} A_\mathrm{II} z) + (L_\mathrm{I} y + L_\mathrm{II} z) \tag{9}$$

because of the definitional equations (1) and (2). Therefore it follows from (8) and (9) that the value of capital utilized (the part in the first parentheses on the right-hand side of (9)) is equal to the difference between total employment (the left-hand side of (8)) and the direct employment for y and z (the part in the second parentheses of (9)). Thus the accounting in terms of value is 'observable', since it is no more than the calculation in terms of employment. It is now concluded that in an economy where assumptions $(a)-(f)$ hold, values can be calculated unambiguously if necessary empirical data are available.

CHAPTER 2
Hidden assumptions

Thus we have two alternative systems of determination of values. Both of them must give the same economically meaningful solutions, with all values being positive or at least non-negative. Marx did not establish the positiveness of values, but instead took it for granted. However the non-negativeness of material and labour input coefficients does not necessarily by itself imply the positiveness of values, so that there must be some hidden assumptions behind Marx, which ensure the meaningfulness of the labour theory of value.[1] By revealing them, the theory is made more informative.

The value-determining equations may give negative solutions unless some additional conditions are satisfied. This statement may at first sight seem very surprising, because it is impossible for the production of a commodity to require a negative amount of labour-time. One may naturally (and reasonably) query once again whether the solutions to the value equations (1) and (2) in chapter 1 really coincide with the labour-time required for the production of commodities; and by a more searching investigation we find that there are exceptional cases in which (1) and (2) give meaningless solutions differing from the 'values'. However, as will be seen below, exceptions are fortunately harmless, since they happen only when the production of a unit of net output of a commodity is technologically infeasible. It is obviously meaningless to enquire about the labour-time required to produce a commodity when it is in fact infeasible to produce a unit of it, although even in such cases we may solve equations (1) and (2) in chapter 1 with respect to the 'value' vector Λ, to obtain nonsensical solutions. This is the exposure of the trick.

[1] Consider an economy producing two goods, A and B. 5 units of A, 6 units of B and 1 unit of labour are required to produce 10 units of A, while 4 units of A, 7 units of B and 1 unit of labour are needed for 10 units of B. The value equations are:
$$\lambda_1 = 0.5\lambda_1 + 0.6\lambda_2 + 0.1,$$
$$\lambda_2 = 0.4\lambda_1 + 0.7\lambda_2 + 0.1$$
and the solutions are $\lambda_1 = -1$ and $\lambda_2 = -1$.

The condition for non-negative Leontief prices was first applied to Marx's value system by N. Okishio. See his *Sai-seisan no Riron* (Theory of Reproduction) (Sobunsha, 1957).

We begin, therefore, by assuming that society is provided with a technology by which it can produce any good. It is assumed that the $n \times n$ input-coefficient matrix of capital-good industries A_I is *productive*, in the sense that there exists a positive vector x^0 such that $x^0 > A_I x^0$; then every capital good industry in the society can simultaneously produce positive net outputs when they are operated at the levels x^0. It will be seen that, given other unrestrictive assumptions, the productiveness of the capital-good industries is necessary and sufficient for any sort of goods to be producible within the society. Thus one of the most basic assumptions of Marx must be that the technology has already been developed to such a level that production processes which are 'productive' are available to the capital-good industries of the society.

It is not difficult to see that 'productiveness' is necessary and sufficient for the society's self-containedness in production. Suppose A_I is productive; then there is an $x^0 > 0$ such that for any given net output vector, $f \geqslant 0$, of the capital-good industries we have
$$tx^0 > A_I tx^0 + f,$$
for a sufficiently large scalar t. (This means that by operating the processes of the capital-good industries at very high levels tx^0, it is possible to produce net outputs exceeding the prescribed output, f.) Let $x^1 = A_I tx^0 + f$, then $tx^0 > x^1$. Therefore,
$$x^1 \geqslant A_I x^1 + f$$
because $A_I \geqslant 0$. Next, let $x^2 = A_I x^1 + f$, then
$$x^2 \geqslant A_I x^2 + f.$$

Repeating this procedure, we have a monotonically decreasing sequence, $tx^0, x^1, x^2, \ldots$, which is bounded from below by $f \geqslant 0$, so that it has a non-negative limiting vector x at which we have
$$x = A_I x + f. \tag{1}$$

Conversely, if (1) has a non-negative solution x for any non-negative, non-zero f, then it is evident that a positive solution x^0 is associated with a positive f^0, because $x^0 = A_I x^0 + f^0 > 0$ as $f^0 > 0$. Therefore,
$$x^0 > A_I x^0,$$
that is, A_I is productive.

Let us now specify f such that the ith element of f is unity, all others being zero. Then the solution vector x^i for (1) corresponding to this f gives the gross outputs of capital goods which are needed to produce one unit of net output of commodity i. If x^i is non-negative the production is feasible, whilst if some or all elements of x^i are negative it is infeasible. When A_I is productive x^i is non-negative as has been seen above, and hence it is technologically feasible to produce one unit of net output of commodity i by producing all the necessary capital goods within the society. As x^i is non-negative, the amount of labour, Lx^i, directly required for the production of x^i (i.e. the value of commodity i) may be meaningfully calculated and is non-negative.

Next we may specify f such that it equals the vector of capital-input coefficients of a wage or luxury-good industry i. As before, the solution vector for (1) corresponding to this f is denoted by x^i, which is again non-negative because A_I is productive and f is non-negative. Hence production is feasible, and it is meaningful to calculate the labour-time which is necessary directly or indirectly to produce one unit of the wage or luxury commodity i. Evidently the value of commodity i, $Lx^i + l_i$, is non-negative, as L, x^i and l_i are all non-negative.

Next, we show that the productiveness of the capital-good industries is necessary (but not sufficient) for the viability of capitalist society. It is evident that capitalist society is not sustainable unless its sectors can simultaneously yield positive profits. This means that there must be a system of prices and wage rates $(p_1, p_2, ..., p_m, w)$ at which the cost of a production process is evaluated as being less than the price of its output:

$$p_\text{I} > p_\text{I} A_\text{I} + w L_\text{I} \quad \text{for capital goods,} \qquad (2)$$

$$p_\text{II} > p_\text{I} A_\text{II} + w L_\text{II} \quad \text{for wage and luxury goods,} \qquad (3)$$

where p_I represents the (row) vector of prices of capital goods, $(p_1, ..., p_n)$ and p_II the (row) vector of prices of wage and luxury goods, $(p_{n+1}, ..., p_m)$. As $w \geq 0$, (2) implies

$$p_\text{I} > p_\text{I} A_\text{I} \qquad (4)$$

but not *vice versa*, of course.[2] Therefore, (4) is necessary (but not sufficient) for the possibility of simultaneous profitability of the

[2] In fact, if w is high enough, there are some industries which cannot earn positive profits.

industries; and it is seen that a positive price set p_I satisfying (4) exists if and only if the productiveness of the capital-good industries is postulated.

Let g be any positive row vector, and consider

$$y = yA_\text{I} + g. \tag{5}$$

As A_I is productive, the input–output equation (1) has a non-negative, non-zero solution x, for the column vector f being non-negative, non-zero. By premultiplying (1) by y, we have

$$yx = yA_\text{I}x + yf,$$

and by postmultiplying (5) by x,

$$yx = yA_\text{I}x + gx.$$

Hence $$yf = gx.$$

We may take the ith component of f as one, the others being zero, so that $yf = y_i$. On the other hand, gx is always positive because all components of g are positive, and x is non-negative, non-zero. Thus $y_i > 0$ for all $i = 1, \ldots, n$; at these y_is we have

$$y > yA_\text{I} \tag{6}$$

by subtracting $g > 0$ from (5).

Conversely, suppose (6) holds for some $y > 0$. (6) is equivalent to the expression
$$y' > A_\text{I}'y',$$

where A_I' stands for the transposed matrix of A_I and y' for the transposed vector of y. Thus A_I' is 'productive'; therefore, by the same argument as above, A_I' has a positive vector z such that

$$x > zA_\text{I}'.$$

Hence for z' (the transposed vector of z) > 0,

$$z' > A_\text{I}z',$$

which implies that A_I is 'productive'. Thus the productiveness of A_I implies that of A_I' and vice versa.

This mathematical argument proves the existence of a positive price set p_I fulfilling inequality (4), if and only if the input-coefficient matrix A_I of the capital-good industries is productive. However, this is not sufficient to establish the possibility that capitalist society may be viable; a further condition is required. Nevertheless, it is important to see that this necessary condition for the possibility of capitalism being viable is identical with the necessary and sufficient condition for the meaningfulness of the labour theory of value, which establishes the non-negativeness of the 'values' of commodities. The further condition required for viability to be possible will be seen, in chapter 5 below, to be identical with the condition that the real-wage rate must be set at such a level that workers are exploited by capitalists.

We may now outline Marx's approach. First he postulates the productiveness of capital-good industries, by which the labour theory of value is made meaningful and without which the capitalist system cannot be maintained. Next he introduces in his theory of exploitation an additional postulate, which restricts the rate of real wages so as to make it possible for capitalist society to be viable. He then asks under what conditions of prices and wage rate the society is really viable, in the sense that each industry yields positive profits; and he finds that it is so at the equilibrium prices and the equilibrium wage rate. Finally he shows that even if the prices and wage rate are set at their respective equilibrium values, so that there is no conflict on the valuation side, there are other reasons for the inviability of capitalist society on the physical (or input–output) and employment side; that is to say, the system as a whole may be partially or completely unstable, so that it is confronted with the possibility (or necessity as Marx believed) of breakdown. From the point of view of contemporary economic theory, his theory of extended reproduction and of the reserve army may be considered as a pioneering attempt to find the saddle-point property of growth equilibrium.

We shall devote the rest of this chapter to showing that all the values of commodities become positive if some additional assumptions are made.[3] First of all, it is evident that the values of all commodities are positive if labour is indispensable for the production of any single capital good, i.e. L_I is strictly positive. It seems that Marx assumed this. But we may weaken the assumption into $L_I \geq 0, \neq 0$, if the mere non-negativeness of A_I is

---

[3] The following discussion is not difficult, though it is purely mathematical. Those who do not like mathematics may avoid it without much loss in their understanding of Marx's value theory.

strengthened into indecomposable non-negativeness, which is defined as follows.

Partition capital goods industries $(1, 2, ..., n)$ into two subgroups $(1, ..., k)$ and $(k+1, ..., n)$. If either of them can produce its own outputs without using outputs of the other subgroup as inputs, then it is said to be an independent subgroup. The entire group $(1, ..., n)$ is said to be indecomposable if there is no independent subgroup.

Now let A_I be partitioned arbitrarily into

$$A_I = \begin{bmatrix} A_{11} & A_{12} \\ A_{21} & A_{22} \end{bmatrix}$$

with A_{11} and A_{22} being square. Correspondingly, the output vector of capital goods x_I is partitioned into

$$x_I = \begin{bmatrix} x^1 \\ x^2 \end{bmatrix}.$$

When all capital-goods industries in the first subgroup produce their own products at some positive rates $x^1 > 0$, then the indecomposability implies that they must use some goods in the second group, so that $A_{21} x^1 \neq 0$. Therefore at least one element of A_{21} must be positive; that is to say, A_I cannot be transformed by permutations of the same rows and columns into the form

$$\begin{bmatrix} A_{11} & A_{12} \\ 0 & A_{22} \end{bmatrix}.$$

We can now show that if A_I is non-negative, indecomposable and productive, then the solution x to the input–output equation (1) is strictly positive for all $f \geq 0$, $\neq 0$. To see this, we suppose that some of the elements of f are zero, and partition (1) as

$$\begin{bmatrix} x^1 \\ x^2 \end{bmatrix} = \begin{bmatrix} A_{11} & A_{12} \\ A_{21} & A_{22} \end{bmatrix} \begin{bmatrix} x^1 \\ x^2 \end{bmatrix} + \begin{bmatrix} f^1 \\ 0 \end{bmatrix}. \quad (7)$$

where $f^1 > 0$. As $A_I \geq 0$ and $x \geq 0$, we have $x^1 > 0$ and $x^2 \geq 0$.

Now suppose some of the elements of x^2 are zero. We reclassify x into two groups, such that positive members of the old second group and all members of the old first group are members of the new first group, and the others (i.e. zero members of the old second group) are members of the new second group. After this re-classification the equation can be written in the form (7), with $x^1 > 0$, $x^2 = 0$, and $f^1 \geq 0$, $\neq 0$. The indecomposability of A_I implies $A_{21}x^1 \neq 0$; therefore some of the elements of x_2 must be positive. This is a contradiction; so no elements of x can be zero.

We can now clearly state the assumptions for the positive 'values':

(i) The matrix of the capital-input coefficients of capital good industries A_I is non-negative, indecomposable, and productive, while the vector of the labour-input coefficient L_I is non-negative and non-zero.

(ii) The capital and labour-input coefficient matrix $\begin{bmatrix} A_\mathrm{II} \\ L_\mathrm{II} \end{bmatrix}$ of wage and luxury industries is non-negative and non-zero for each column. Assumption (i) implies, in addition to the indecomposability and productiveness of capital good industries, that labour is indispensable to one of the capital goods industries. Assumption (ii) implies that wage and luxury-goods industries may dispense with labour, but every industry in these groups must use some inputs (i.e. either some capital goods or labour or both).

It is now easy to prove the positiveness of values. In order to obtain the value of the ith capital good, we specify as before f of (1) such that the ith component of f is unity, all others being zero. As we have just seen, by virtue of the indecomposability and productiveness of A_I, a strictly positive solution x to (1) corresponds to the specified f. This x is premultiplied by L_I to give the value of capital good i which is positive, as x is positive and L_I is non-negative, non-zero.

To obtain the value of a wage or luxury good i, f is set such that it equals the vector of the capital-input coefficients of the wage or luxury good i; the f may be zero, or non-negative, non-zero. If it is zero, the corresponding solution x to (1) is of course zero, but the value of the wage or luxury good i,

$$\lambda_i = \sum_{j=1}^{n} l_j x_j + l_i \qquad (8)$$

is positive since $l_i > 0$ by assumption (ii). If f is non-zero, then the corresponding x_js are all positive by the indecomposability and productiveness of A_I; hence $\lambda_i > 0$, irrespective of whether l_i is positive or zero, because the first term of the right-hand side of (8) is positive, since L_I is non-negative and non-zero.

CHAPTER 3

Quantitative determination of relative value

After the determination of the absolute values of 'values', Marx took a particular commodity (say, capital good 1) as the standard commodity (or 'value numeraire'), in terms of which the value of every other commodity was expressed. The ratio of the value of commodity i to the value of the standard commodity, λ_i/λ_1, which Marx called 'relative value', expresses a definite quantity of the standard commodity, q, which is equivalent, in 'value', to one unit of commodity i; that is to say, $\lambda_i = q\lambda_1$, which means that the same quantity of value substance (congealed labour) is embodied in one unit of commodity i and q units of the standard commodity. 'The two commodities [of these quantities] have each cost the same amount of labour or the same quantity of labour-time.' (I, p. 53.)

Let us consider an imaginary society of simple non-capitalistic production (i.e. Marx's 'simple commodity production') composed of individuals who exchange with each other their products, which are produced by means of production owned by themselves. In such a society there are no capitalists and hence no exploitation of workers by them; prices or exchange ratios between commodities must in the state of equilibrium be equal to the relative values, provided the primary factors of production other than labour are all free. It is true that the actual exchange ratios in the market may differ from the relative values. For example, when it takes one hour to hunt a deer and two hours of equally simple labour to hunt a beaver, the exchange ratio of deer to beaver may be greater or smaller than 2 (the relative value of beaver to deer), depending on whether deer is relatively more abundant or more scarce in the market than beaver. But such deviations do not last for long, because if the exchange ratio of deer to beaver exceeds 2, then there will be more beaver and less deer hunting, because the former is more profitable than the latter; and *vice versa*. Therefore the market price will ultimately be settled at the equilibrium exchange ratio, which is equal to the relative value.

The relative values, as well as the absolute 'values', are completely determined by the technological coefficients A_I, L_I and

A_{II}, L_{II}. Thus as far as the equilibrium prices are concerned, marginal utilities have no role in their determination, at least in society with simple commodity production. In the long-run the marginal utilities adapt themselves to the costs of production, but not the other way round. Instead of studying comparative statical laws of price changes with respect to a shift in demand, such as those discussed by Walras, Hicks, Samuelson and others, it was natural for Marx to investigate the effects of a change in a production coefficient on the relative values.

Marx knew that the labour-time necessary for the production of commodities would vary with every change in the productiveness of labour. He examined 'the influence of such changes on the quantitative aspect of the relative expression of value'. (I, p. 53). Unfortunately, however, he did not consider the problem properly as an inter-industrial problem, although he was examining the effects of a change in a labour-input coefficient, l_i, or a capital-input coefficient, a_{ik}, so that he could only obtain the following four results, which are tautological and therefore self-evident:

(a) The relative value of commodity i, i.e. its value expressed in terms of commodity 1, rises and falls directly with the value of i, the value of 1 being supposed constant.

(b) If the value of commodity i remains constant, its relative value expressed in commodity 1 rises and falls inversely with the value of commodity 1.

(c) If the values of all commodities rise or fall simultaneously and in the same proportion, their relative values will remain unaltered.

(d) When the values of commodities i and 1 change at different rates or in opposite directions, we have different effects on the relative value of i, which can be deduced from the previous results (a) and (b) as a combination of them. (See I, pp. 53–4.)

A change in a technological coefficient, either l_i or a_{ik}, influences both λ_i and λ_1, so that neither of Marx's rules (a) or (b) is applicable. He cannot apply his rule (d) either, because he does not know the rates at which the values of commodities i and 1 change, so that the proportions in which rules (a) and (b) are combined are unknown to him. These proportions are found only by analysing the effects of a change in a coefficient, l_i or a_{ik}, of the value-determination equations on the solutions to them.

The problem is intrinsically mathematical but not very difficult. Marx failed to attack the problem properly and obtained only the trivial results just mentioned, because of his lack of mathematics. To us, however, it is not difficult to solve the problem with definite results, particularly because we can use the mathematics recently developed in relation to Leontief's input–output analysis.

In addition to the technological conditions for positive values given in the last chapter we assume in the following, for the sake of simplicity, that each industry has a positive labour-input coefficient. Then it is seen that if the labour-input coefficient of industry i decreases, those of all other industries and the capital-input coefficients of all industries remaining unchanged, then the relative value of commodity i in terms of the standard commodity 1 decreases proportionately more than that of any other commodity j. This proposition is true for any commodity i, irrespective of whether it is a capital good or a wage or luxury good.

We are first concerned with the case where i is a capital good, so that $i \leqslant n$. Let us begin by showing that a decrease in l_i causes a decrease in the absolute 'values' of all capital goods. Differentiating the value-determination equations of capital-goods industries with respect to l_i, we get

$$\begin{aligned}\frac{\partial \lambda_1}{\partial l_i} &= a_{11}\frac{\partial \lambda_1}{\partial l_i} + \ldots + a_{n1}\frac{\partial \lambda_n}{\partial l_i} + 0, \\ &\vdots \\ \frac{\partial \lambda_i}{\partial l_i} &= a_{1i}\frac{\partial \lambda_1}{\partial l_i} + \ldots + a_{ni}\frac{\partial \lambda_n}{\partial l_i} + 1, \\ &\vdots \\ \frac{\partial \lambda_n}{\partial l_i} &= a_{1n}\frac{\partial \lambda_1}{\partial l_i} + \ldots + a_{nn}\frac{\partial \lambda_n}{\partial l_i} + 0, \end{aligned} \quad (1)$$

or, in matrix form,
$$\frac{\partial \Lambda_\mathrm{I}}{\partial l_i} = \frac{\partial \Lambda_\mathrm{I}}{\partial l_i} A_\mathrm{I} + k_\delta, \quad (1)$$

where k_δ is a row vector $(\delta_{1i}, \delta_{2i}, \ldots, \delta_{ni})$ with Kronecker's δs as its components, so that its ith component is unity, while the others are zero.[1] The equation (1) is now combined with the equation (1) in the last chapter, i.e.

$$x = A_\mathrm{I} x + f, \quad (2)$$

---

[1] The Kronecker delta is the function δ_{ji} of two variables j and i defined by $\delta_{ji} = 1$ if $j = i$, and $\delta_{ji} = 0$ if $j \neq i$.

where f is a column vector of non-negative components (not all zero), so that we may take a component, say the jth, as unity and all others are zero. It has been seen that the vector x corresponding to such an f is strictly positive, since it is assumed that the non-negative matrix A_I is productive and indecomposable. Postmultiplying (1) by x, premultiplying (2) by $\partial \Lambda_\mathrm{I}/\partial l_i$ and eliminating the common terms from both equations, we obtain

$$k_\delta x = \frac{\partial \Lambda_\mathrm{I}}{\partial l_i} f.$$

Because k_δ and f are specified such that the ith and the jth components are unity, others being zero, we get $k_\delta x = x_i$ (the ith component of x) and $\partial \Lambda_\mathrm{I}/\partial l_i f = \partial \lambda_j/\partial l_i$ (the jth component of $\partial \Lambda_\mathrm{I}/\partial l_i$). Hence $x > 0$ implies $\partial \lambda_j/\partial l_i > 0$ for all j, which means that the labour-input coefficient l_i and all the absolute values λ_j, $j = 1, ..., n$, vary in the same direction.

We now prove the proposition by *reductio ad absurdum*, and suppose the contrary of the conclusion; that is, that there is, other than commodity i, a commodity j whose value falls at the greatest rate. Let us denote the values after the change by $\lambda_1^*, ..., \lambda_n^*$. If commodity j is a capital good, we have

$$\lambda_j = a_{1j}\lambda_1 + ... + a_{nj}\lambda_n + l_j \quad (j \leqslant n) \tag{3}$$

before the change, and

$$\lambda_j^* = a_{1j}\lambda_1^* + ... + a_{nj}\lambda_n^* + l_j \quad (j \leqslant n) \tag{4}$$

after the change. Dividing both sides of (4) by those of (3), we get

$$\frac{\lambda_j^*}{\lambda_j} = \frac{a_{1j}\lambda_1^* + ... + a_{nj}\lambda_n^* + l_j}{a_{1j}\lambda_1 + ... + a_{nj}\lambda_n + l_j} \quad (j \leqslant n). \tag{5}$$

The right-hand side of this expression equals the average of $\lambda_1^*/\lambda_1, ..., \lambda_n^*/\lambda_n$ and 1 with weights $a_{1j}\lambda_1, ..., a_{nj}\lambda_n$ and l_j respectively. $\lambda_1^*/\lambda_1, ..., \lambda_n^*/\lambda_n$ are all less than 1, since a decrease in l_i gives rise to a decrease in the value of each commodity. Because the weight l_j of 1 on the right-hand side of (5) is positive, it is at once seen that the average (hence, λ_j^*/λ_j on on the left-hand side of (5)) must be greater than the smallest of $\lambda_1^*/\lambda_1, ..., \lambda_n^*/\lambda_n$. This is a contradiction, therefore the value of any capital good other than commodity i cannot decrease at the fastest rate.

Next we consider a wage or luxury good j. We have the same equations (3) and (4) before and after the change respectively, and hence equation (5). The only amendment we have to make is that j is now greater than n, so that in these equations we have $j > n$ in place of $j \leqslant n$. But this change does not at all affect the argument that derives the conclusion

$$1 > \lambda_j^*/\lambda_j > \lambda_i^*/\lambda_i$$

from (5).

Thus when an increase in the productivity of labour (implied by a decrease in the labour-input coefficient l_i) occurs in a capital-good industry i it diminishes the values of all commodities, not only capital goods but also wage and luxury goods, in such a way that the relative value of the commodity i in terms of any other commodity is decreased. On the other hand, when a wage or luxury-good industry i makes an improvement in the technical method of production so as to reduce the labour-input coefficient, then there is no change in the value-determination equations for capital-good industries

$$\Lambda_\mathrm{I} = \Lambda_\mathrm{I} A_\mathrm{I} + L_\mathrm{I},$$

so that the values of capital goods are constant. As the labour-time congealed in the capital goods utilized is not affected in the value determination equation of each wage or luxury good, the value of the wage or luxury good remains unaltered, unless there is a change in the corresponding labour-input coefficient. Therefore the only good whose value diminishes is commodity i, whose labour-input coefficient is reduced. Thus as far as the determination of value is concerned, a technological change in a wage or luxury-good industry has no repercussions on any other industry, its effect being confined to its own industry; in this case Marx's comparative statics rule (a) is applicable and the relative value of commodity i in terms of any other is reduced.

When a technological improvement is made in an industry so as to save on the amount of capital good j required to produce a unit of commodity i, it is seen that the relative value of i in terms of the standard commodity 1 is diminished, and there is no commodity whose relative value is decreased at a greater rate than that of commodity i. In the case where the commodity i whose capital-input coefficient is saved is a capital good, this is shown in the following way. Differentiating the value-determination equations for capital goods with respect to a_{ji}, we have

$$\left.\begin{aligned}\frac{\partial \lambda_1}{\partial a_{ji}} &= a_{11}\frac{\partial \lambda_1}{\partial a_{ji}} + \ldots + a_{n1}\frac{\partial \lambda_n}{\partial a_{ji}} + 0, \\ &\vdots \\ \frac{\partial \lambda_i}{\partial a_{ji}} &= a_{1i}\frac{\partial \lambda_1}{\partial a_{ji}} + \ldots + a_{ni}\frac{\partial \lambda_n}{\partial a_{ji}} + \lambda_j, \\ &\vdots \\ \frac{\partial \lambda_n}{\partial a_{ji}} &= a_{1n}\frac{\partial \lambda_1}{\partial a_{ji}} + \ldots + a_{nn}\frac{\partial \lambda_n}{\partial a_{ji}} + 0, \end{aligned}\right\} \quad (6)$$

or, in the matrix form,

$$\frac{\partial \Lambda_{\mathrm{I}}}{\partial a_{ji}} = \frac{\partial \Lambda_{\mathrm{I}}}{\partial a_{ji}} A_{\mathrm{I}} + \lambda_j k_\delta, \tag{6}$$

where k_δ denotes, as before, the row vector of the Kronecker deltas $(\delta_{1i}, \delta_{2i}, \ldots, \delta_{ni})$. Comparing (6) with (1), we can easily see that

$$\frac{\partial \lambda_1}{\partial a_{ji}}, \ldots, \frac{\partial \lambda_n}{\partial a_{ji}} \text{ are proportional to } \frac{\partial \lambda_1}{\partial l_i}, \ldots, \frac{\partial \lambda_n}{\partial l_i};$$

that is to say,

$$\lambda_j \frac{\partial \Lambda_{\mathrm{I}}}{\partial l_i} = \frac{\partial \Lambda_{\mathrm{I}}}{\partial a_{ji}}.$$

Hence, the above proposition concerning the effects of an autonomous change in the capital-input coefficient a_{ji}, which we now want to establish, is a mere corollary from the previous proposition about the effects of a change in the labour-input coefficient l_i.

Similarly, in the case where commodity i is a wage or luxury good, it is obvious that a decrease in a_{ji} has no effect on the values of capital goods, so that only the value of commodity i diminishes.

These results are summarized as follows: Given a decrease in a technological coefficient, l_i or a_{ji}, then (i) the 'absolute value' λ_i of the output directly produced must decrease, (ii) the absolute value of any other commodity will decrease if it changes at all, and (iii) there is no commodity whose absolute value diminishes proportionately more than that of commodity i, so that the 'relative value' of i in terms of any other commodity must diminish. These three laws are formally identical with the laws Hicks obtained for equilibrium prices with respect to an autonomous shift in tastes, which I have called the three Hicksian laws.[2] We have seen above that Marx's rule (a) is applicable only in the case of a technological improvement occurring in a wage or luxury-good industry. Thus, the 'three Hicksian laws' are extensions of the Marxian rule. This offers an example of the possibilities for enriching Marx's economics by taking into account the analytical development of our science since his death.

We are now able to discuss Marx's famous idea of the 'organic composition of capital'. He distinguished the value-composition of capital from its technical composition, as follows: 'The composition of capital is to be understood in a two-fold sense. On the side of value, it is determined by the proportion in which it is divided into constant capital or value of the means of production, and variable capital or value of labour-power, the sum total of wages. On the side of material, as it functions in the process of production, all capital is divided into means of production and living labour-power. This latter composition is determined by the relation between the mass of the means of production employed, on the one hand, and the mass of labour necessary for their employment on the other. I call the former the *value-composition*, the latter the *technical composition* of capital. Between the two there is a strict correlation. To express this, I call the value-composition of capital, *in so far as it is determined by its technical composition and mirrors the changes of the latter*, the *organic composition* of capital.' (I, p.612, my italics.)

Let $b_{n+1}{}^*, \ldots, b_m{}^*$ be the amounts of wage goods, $n+1, \ldots, m$, which are necessary for the production of a unit of labour-power. (For luxury goods we set the amounts at zero.) Then the value-composition of capital of industry i may be written as

$$k_i = \frac{\sum\limits_{j=1}^{n} a_{ji}\lambda_j}{\left(\sum\limits_{j=n+1}^{m} b_j{}^*\lambda_j\right) l_i} \quad (i = 1, \ldots, m). \tag{7}$$

On the other hand, the technical composition of industry i

[2] J. R. Hicks, *Value and Capital* (Oxford University Press, 1939). See also my *Equilibrium, Stability and Growth* (Oxford University Press, 1964) pp. 6–11.

represents the relation between the mass of the means of production employed $(a_{1i}, a_{2i}, ..., a_{ni})$ and the mass of labour employed, l_i. A change in a physical-input coefficient a_{ji} or the labour-input coefficient l_i due to a technological improvement causes a change in the technical composition of capital. But it brings about changes in the values $\lambda_1, ..., \lambda_m$ as well, as we have seen above; so the value-composition of capital reflects not only the change in technical composition but also the induced change in the value structure. There are, however, cases in which we may ignore the latter and where the value-composition 'mirrors the changes in the technical composition'. For instance, a proportional decrease in the labour-input coefficients of all industries, i.e. all wage and luxury-good industries as well as capital-good industries, gives rise to a proportional decrease in the absolute values of all commodities; in this case Marx's rule (c) is applicable and the effects of the changes in absolute values are offset in the formula for the value-composition of capital (7). Another example is obtained when a decrease in the labour input is made possible by increasing some capital coefficient, say a_{ji}, such that $\Delta l_i = -\lambda_j \Delta a_{ji}$; in this case there is no change in the absolute values at all, for the change in the value-composition of capital reflects only the change in technical composition. When Marx discussed the effects and consequences of technical improvements by using the concept of the 'organic composition of capital', he assumed them to be neutral, in the sense that they had no effects on relative values (or absolute values). This is a neat assumption, simplifying the matter; nevertheless it does not satisfy us, as a change in the technical composition of capital usually disturbs the relative value structure. However, as may obviously be expected, 'biased' technological improvements are very difficult to deal with.

CHAPTER 4

Value, use-value and exchange-value

It was one of Marx's intentions to show by his theory of value 'that it is not the exchange of commodities which regulates the magnitude of their value; but, on the contrary, that it is the magnitude of their value which controls their exchange proportions.' (I, p. 63.) But at the same time he knew that the exchange-values of commodities could equal their relative values only in special cases, that is, either in the purely abstract society of 'simple commodity production' or in the special capitalist society which satisfies the very restrictive condition that each industry has the same value-composition of capital. Marx wrote: 'The exchange of commodities at their values, or approximately at their values, thus requires a much lower stage than their exchange at their prices of production, which requires a definite level of capitalist development.' (III, p. 177.) 'The price of production of the commodities would then equal [be proportional to] their value only in spheres, in which the composition [the value-composition of capital] would happen to be [the same].' (III, p. 163.)

These two special cases are important in different senses, i.e. in the normative sense and as a first approximation to reality. First, the society of simple commodity production is an imaginary society, where 'the labourers themselves are in possession of their respective means of production and exchange their commodities with one another.' (III, p. 175.) 'This is the condition of the land-owing farmer living off his own labour and the craftsman, in the ancient as well as in the modern world' (III, p. 177), so that no exploitation is possible. Marx showed that in such a society the prices of commodities were governed by the law of value, and that hence prices were proportional to values. Therefore, 'if the labour-time required for their production happens to shrink, prices fall; if it increases, prices rise, provided other conditions remain the same.' (III, p. 177.) By comparing capitalist society, where the exchange-values (or the relative prices) can deviate from the relative values, with this ideal society, we can see how capitalists' exploitation affects trade, the distribution of income, and so on. Such studies are

VALUE, USE-VALUE AND EXCHANGE-VALUE 37

similar, in their logical nature, to the welfare economics now popular among us, which compares the actual state with the ideal state of affairs where welfare is maximized and examines, say, the influences of monopoly on trade, the distribution of income and other questions.

On the other hand, in the second case of equal value-composition of capital, capitalist society, rather than the society of simple commodity production, is taken up as the object of study and differences in the value-composition of capital among industries are ignored, as a first approximation to reality. This neglect results in a great simplification in analysis, as will be seen in chapter 8 below. We have the grand rule of aggregation that all those industries which have the same value-composition of capital can be treated as if they are a single industry. By virtue of this rule, Marx constructed a one-department model in volume I, part VII, of *Capital*. The results of the analysis there are valid under the assumption of identical value-composition, but many of them cease to hold if this assumption is abandoned.

The one-department model was extended later, in volumes II and III, into a two-department analysis, by allowing the value-composition of capital of the capital-good industries to differ from that of the wage and luxury-good industries. It is a great development in Marx's economics, because the assumption of equal value-composition is an unsatisfactory assumption, under which exploitation has no effect on relative prices and, as far as the valuation of commodities is concerned, it is impossible to distinguish capitalist society from the society of simple commodity production. Marx wrote: 'In Books I and II we dealt only with the *value* of commodities. On the one hand, the *cost-price* has now been singled out as a part of this value, and, on the other, the *price of production* of commodities has been developed as its converted form.' (III, p. 163.) 'The value of the commodities produced by capital II would, therefore, be smaller than their price of production, the price of production of the commodities of III smaller than their value, and only in the case of capital I in branches of production in which the composition happens to coincide with the social average, would value and price of production be equal.' (III, p. 164.) '...the price of production may differ from the value of a commodity' (III,

p. 164.) '...the deviations from the value which are embodied in the prices of production compensate one another. Under capitalist production, the general law acts as the prevailing tendency only in a very complicated and approximate manner, as a never ascertainable average of ceaseless fluctuations.' (III, p. 161.) 'The annual product of society consists of two departments: one of them comprises the means of production, the other the articles of consumption. Each must be treated separately.' (II, p. 372.) 'So long as we looked upon the production of value and the value of the product of capital individually, the bodily form of the commodities produced was wholly immaterial for the analysis, whether it was machines, for instance, corn, or looking glasses. It was always but a matter of illustration, and any branch of production could have served that purpose equally well... This merely formal manner of presentation is no longer adequate in the study of the total social capital and of the value of its products. The reconversion of one portion of the value of the product into capital and the passing of another portion into the individual consumption of the capitalists as well as the working-class form a movement within the value of the product itself in which the result of the aggregate capital finds expression; and this movement is not only a replacement of value, but also a replacement in material and is therefore as much bound up with the relative proportions of the value-components of the total social product as with their use-value, their material shape.' (II, p. 398.) These passages outline the metastasis in Marx.

On the assumption that all capital-good industries form a group of industries which are identical in the value-composition of capital and that all wage and luxury-good industries form another such group, it can be shown on the one hand that we have a proportionality between the prices and values of all capital goods and a different proportionality between the prices and values of all wage and luxury goods, and on the other that all capital-good industries and all wage and luxury-good industries can be aggregated into two departments, a department producing means of production and a department producing articles of consumption respectively, without causing any aggregation bias. In volume II Marx developed the two-department analysis of simple and extended reproduction, the dual to which was discussed in volume III as the problem of the transformation of values into prices.

It is now evident that the aim of Marx was not to establish the proportionality of prices and values in a capitalist economy, but, on the contrary, to explain why they may differ from each other when the workers cease to possess the means of production, so that they have to sell their labour-power in the market. We should not regard volume III as a return to conventional economic theory, as critics of Marxian economics have often done. At the same time we should not regard volume I, based on the proportionality between all prices and values, as the essence of Marxian economics, as many Marxists have claimed. Thus between volumes I and III there is no contradiction but a development, from the one- to the two-department analysis.[3]

Our study proceeds as follows. In this chapter, we confine ourselves to establishing the general equilibrium of production in the society with simple commodity production, under the assumption that people do not save. In the next two chapters, 5 and 6, we are concerned with the general relationship between prices and values in capitalist society and show that exploitation is the source of profits. Then in chapter 7 we derive the implications of the assumption of identical value-composition of capital for the whole or a part of the economy, and chapter 8 is devoted to a discussion of aggregation.

It is obvious that the theory of value cannot by itself explain the consumer's demands and that no general equilibrium is possible without some theory of consumer's demand. It is true that Marx assumed very restrictive demand functions for wage and luxury goods, of the form:

$$x_i = \frac{wTb_i}{p_{n+1}b_{n+1} + \ldots + p_m b_m} \quad (i = n+1, \ldots, m),$$

where w represents the wage rate, p_is prices, T the daily labour hours per man, and b_is non-negative consumption coefficients, which are constant. (These equations follow from (1) below.)

[3] This view contrasts with Samuelson's, expressed in his 'Wages and Interest: A Modern Dissection of Marxian Economic Models', *American Economic Review*, vol. XLVII, December 1957, and his recent article, 'Understanding the Marxian Notion of Exploitation: A Summary of the So-Called Transformation Problem between Marxian Values and Competitive Prices', *Journal of Economic Literature*, June 1971.

It is the generally accepted view that it is impossible to find a germ of marginalism in *Capital*, although Marx knew differential and integral calculus.[4] But it is also true, on the other hand, that Marx began his theory of value by characterizing commodities as 'something two-fold, both objects of utility and, at the same time, depositories of value' (1, p. 47). On the basis of the following evidence I believe that Marx would have accepted the marginal utility theory of consumer's demands if it had become known to him.[5]

'A commodity is, in the first place, an object outside us, a thing that by its properties satisfies human wants of some sort or another. The nature of such wants, whether, for instance, they spring from the stomach or from fancy, makes no difference.' (1, p. 35.)

'The utility of a thing makes it a use-value... This property of a commodity is independent of the amount of labour required to appropriate its useful qualities... The use-values of commodities furnish the material for a special study, that of the commercial knowledge of commodities.' (1, p. 36.)

'In order to produce the latter [commodities], he must not only produce use-values, but use-values for others, social use-values... Lastly nothing can have value, without being an object of utility.' (1, p. 41.)

'His commodity possesses for himself [the owner of the commodity] no immediate use-value. Otherwise, he would not bring it to the market. It has use-value for others; but for himself its only direct use-value is that of being a depository of exchange-value, and, consequently, a means of exchange. Therefore, he makes up his mind to part with it for commodities whose value in use is of service to him. All commodities are non-use-values for their owners, and use-values for their non-owners. Consequently, they must all change hands.' (1, p. 85.)

'...an object of utility...forms a non-use-value for its owner ...when it forms a superfluous portion of some article required for his immediate wants.' (1, p. 87.)

The first quotation, especially its second sentence, suggests

---

[4] See K. Marx, *Matiematitzieske Rukopisi* (Moscow, 1968), Institute of Markisma–Leninisma at Central Committee of the Communist Party of the Soviet Union.
[5] His technical preparations were sufficient. *Matiematitzieske Rukopisi* shows that he studied the problem of maxima and minima.

VALUE, USE-VALUE AND EXCHANGE-VALUE 41

that the utility of a thing may differ among individuals, depending on their subjective tastes. In the last sentence of the second quotation, we may replace 'the study of the commercial knowledge of commodities' by 'the theory of consumer's behaviour'. The second quotation also states that demand theory can (and should) be developed independently of the theory of value, whilst the third quotation further implies that it is meaningless to apply the labour theory of value to the singular case of the marginal utility of a commodity being zero, since such a commodity is a free good.

Let us consider an individual who wants to convert the stocks of commodities $(\bar{x}_1, ..., \bar{x}_m)$ he owns initially into the optimal stocks $(x_1, ..., x_m)$ by exchange. Let u_i represent the use-value (the marginal utility) of commodity i, $i = 1, ..., m$, obtained by differentiating the utility function $u(x_1, ..., x_m)$ partially with respect to x_i. Let v_i be the non-use-value of commodity i for the owner as a depository of exchange value, which a superfluous unit of good i brings forth so that the total non-use-value amounts to $\Sigma v_i(\bar{x}_i - x_i)$. Evidently, v_is are proportional to the exchange-values, so that we may write $v_i = v p_i$, $i = 1, ..., m$, where p_i is the exchange-value of commodity i. The sum of the total use-value and the total non-use-value for the individual is given as

$$u(x_1, ..., x_m) + \sum_{i=1}^{m} v p_i (\bar{x}_i - x_i),$$

which is nothing else but the Lagrangian function, now familiar among us. Thus, Marx's idea of the commodities' non-use-value as the means of exchange and the use-value of their direct use, expressed in the fourth and fifth quotations above, naturally leads to the Walras–Hicks–Kuhn–Tucker formulation of demand theory. Maximizing the above Lagrangian with respect to x_i, we obtain

$$\frac{u_1}{p_1} = \frac{u_2}{p_2} = ... = \frac{u_m}{p_m} = v,$$

provided that all p_is are constant. These equations are equivalent to Marx's equations for the direct barter of products. He wrote: 'The direct barter of products attains the elementary form of the relative expression of value in one respect, but not in another. That form is x Commodity $A = y$ Commodity B.

The form of direct barter is x use-value $A = y$ use-value B.' (1, p. 87.) The first equation implies that x units of commodity A are worth (or are exchanged for) y units of commodity B, so that it may be written as

$$xp_A = yp_B.$$

On the other hand, the second equation is written in our notation as

$$xu_A = yu_B.$$

Hence, these two equations together imply

$$\frac{u_A}{p_A} = \frac{u_B}{p_B}.$$

This provides us with a basis for believing that if Marx had had a chance to read Walras' *Eléments d'économie politique pure* (1874), he would have integrated the subjective theory of demand into his model, or at least that the main part of Marx's economics is not incompatible with present-day demand theory. Nevertheless it is true that Marx, like von Neumann, did not allow substitution between goods in response to price changes. In the following, we study how the ideal society of simple commodity production works, first under the assumption of rigid consumption quotas and then under a more general assumption, that each individual maximizes his own utility subject to his budget constraint, to see how the results remain unaffected.

Let the consumption of the labourer at subsistence level be denoted by $b_{n+1}, b_{n+2}, ..., b_m$; these are given quantities of wage and luxury goods. Let $p_1, ..., p_m$ be the prices of commodities, $1, ..., m$. Let w be income per man-hour. Labourers are freely movable among jobs and are provided with the means of production necessary for their jobs, so that income per man is equalized throughout society. When the prices of commodities and income are given, the individual can determine his level of consumption β so as to satisfy the budget equation:

$$p_{n+1}\beta b_{n+1} + ... + p_m \beta b_m = wT, \tag{1}$$

where each individual is assumed to work T hours a day.[6] The

---

[6] Each $\beta b_i / T$ equals the corresponding b_i^*, defined at the end of the last chapter, if β is determined such that it results in the prevailing rate of exploitation (β takes on unity in the case of workers being paid wages at the subsistence level), whereas

VALUE, USE-VALUE AND EXCHANGE-VALUE 43

total demands for wage goods and luxury goods are given by the vectors

$$D = N\beta \begin{bmatrix} b_{n+1} \\ \vdots \\ b_m \end{bmatrix}, \tag{2}$$

where N is the number of labourers in the society. Then we have the demand–supply equilibrium conditions for wage and luxury goods, which are

$$x_{II} = D. \tag{3}$$

The production of wage and luxury goods in the amounts x_{II} induces the production of capital goods, and

$$x_I = A_I x_I + A_{II} x_{II} \tag{4}$$

gives the demand–supply equilibrium for capital goods.[7] Finally the demand for labour has to be equated to its supply in labour-time; hence

$$L_I x_I + L_{II} x_{II} = TN. \tag{5}$$

Since in our hypothetical society labourers possess all the means of production they require, there are as yet no capitalists to exploit them. The labourers will be fully paid, so that we must have

$$\left. \begin{array}{l} p_I = p_I A_I + w L_I \quad \text{for capital goods,} \\ p_{II} = p_I A_{II} + w L_{II} \quad \text{for wage and luxury goods,} \end{array} \right\} \tag{6}$$

where p_I and p_{II} are row vectors of the prices of capital and of wage and luxury goods respectively.

Equations (1)–(6) give the simplest system of general equilibrium of production (for a hypothetical economy of simple commodity production, but not for the capitalist economy). (2) gives the demand functions which satisfy Walras' law (1). Equations (3), (4), (5) are demand–supply equations, whilst (6) gives valuation equations. Comparing (6) with the value-determining equations (1) and (2) in chapter I, we at once find that prices are proportional to values, so that the price of each commodity i in terms of commodity 1, the numeraire, equals the relative value λ_i/λ_1; when the price of commodity 1 is set at 1

---

in the society with simple commodity production it is fixed at a level at which no exploitation is brought forth.

[7] The time lag between inputs and outputs may be ignored in the society with simple commodity production, because stationary equilibrium is established.

the rate of income w is determined as $1/\lambda_1$. Or alternatively, if we take labour power as the numeraire, then prices are equal to the corresponding values.

Once prices, the wage rate and labour hours per day are given, (1) determines the level of consumption β. Then the demands for consumption goods are determined by (2), which in turn determines supplies of capital goods as well as supplies of consumption goods, by (3) and (4). Therefore the demand for labour, i.e. the left-hand side of (5), is given, but it is written, in view of (2), (3), (4), as

$$[L_\mathrm{I}(I-A_\mathrm{I})^{-1}A_\mathrm{II}+L_\mathrm{II}]\,N\beta B, \tag{7}$$

where B represents the column vector having $b_{n+1}, ..., b_m$ as its components. Since the part of (7) in square brackets gives the values of wage and luxury goods, which in the society with simple commodity production equal their prices in terms of labour, we can rewrite (7) in the form,

$$N\left(\frac{p_{n+1}}{w}\beta b_{n+1}+...+\frac{p_m}{w}\beta b_m\right),$$

which is equal to TN because of (1). Hence (5) is established; that is to say, values are the general equilibrium prices in the society with simple commodity production.

Let us now proceed to show the compatibility of the last proposition with the subjective theory of demand. Let q_{ij} be the demand for good i of individual j and $u^j = u^j(q_{n+1,j}, ..., q_{mj})$ be his utility function. Maximizing the utility u^j subject to the budget equation of the individual j,

$$p_{n+1}q_{n+1,j}+...+p_m q_{mj} = wT,$$

we obtain the demand function

$$q_{ij} = q_{ij}\left(\frac{p_{n+1}}{w}, ..., \frac{p_m}{w}\right) \quad (i=n+1, ..., m).$$

Summing the budget equations and the demand functions over all individuals, we have

$$\frac{p_{n+1}}{w}q_{n+1}+...+\frac{p_m}{w}q_m = TN, \tag{1'}$$

and
$$D = \begin{bmatrix} q_{n+1}\left(\dfrac{p_{n+1}}{w}, \ldots, \dfrac{p_m}{w}\right) \\ \vdots \\ q_m\left(\dfrac{p_{n+1}}{w}, \ldots, \dfrac{p_m}{w}\right) \end{bmatrix}, \qquad (2')$$

where q_i denotes the total demand for good i.

Replacing (1) and (2) by (1') and (2'), we have a new model of general equilibrium of production, appropriate for the society with simple commodity production and flexible demands. As before, by the value-determining equations and (6), the price in terms of labour, p_i/w, of commodity i equals its value λ_i, $i = 1, \ldots, m$. Corresponding to the prices thus determined, the demands are determined by (2'), and supplies therefore by (3) and (4). Substituting for x_I and x_II from (3) and (4), and viewing the equality between values and prices in terms of labour, the left-hand side of (5) can be written

$$\dfrac{p_{n+1}}{w} q_{n+1}\left(\dfrac{p_{n+1}}{w}, \ldots, \dfrac{p_m}{w}\right) + \ldots + \dfrac{p_m}{w} q_m\left(\dfrac{p_{n+1}}{w}, \ldots, \dfrac{p_m}{w}\right),$$

which equals TN, because of Walras' law (1'); hence (5) is obtained. It is thus shown that the values are the equilibrium prices prevailing in the society with simple commodity production where people behave in the Walrasian manner.

It has so far been seen that with no exploitation, consumption has to be determined at some particular level. When there is exploitation, consumption is set at a different level, corresponding to the rate of exploitation; or conversely, the rate of exploitation cannot be determined unless the level of consumption (or the rate of real wages) is specified. On the other hand, as has recently been recognized and as will be seen below, the rate of real wages determines the equilibrium rate of profits. Thus to the rate of real wages there corresponds a rate of exploitation on the one hand, and a rate of profits on the other, so that the rate of profits may be considered as a function of the rate of exploitation. All those we have obtained in this chapter apply only to the singular point of the function at which the rate of exploitation vanishes in the ideal and imaginary society of simple commodity production. In the following chapters the argument is extended to the entire function, so that capitalists are allowed to exploit workers at some positive rate.

PART II
The Theory of Exploitation

CHAPTER 5
Surplus value and exploitation

In a capitalist economy, where workers do not own the means of production and cannot therefore produce commodities by themselves, they are forced to sell their labour-power to capitalists. Workers are in a weaker position with respect to wage determination, and so can easily be exploited by capitalists. Marx considered exploitation as necessary for the maintenance of capitalist society. In fact, capitalists exploit workers by making them work longer than the hours required to produce the amounts of wage goods which they can buy with the wages they receive; thus surplus outputs are produced, which are the source of profits. As capitalists would not be interested in their enterprises if they did not bring forth positive profits, they have a fundamental tendency towards exploitation. In this chapter we shall first explain what exploitation is, and then establish its inevitability in capitalist society.

In the capitalist economy (unlike the society with simple commodity production) values and prices, in general, no longer coincide; they should be distinct. For this reason Marxian economics, unlike orthodox economics, has dual accounting systems: one system in terms of value and the other in terms of price. But many people from both camps (such as Sweezy, Joan Robinson and Samuelson) have confused the two, since Marx himself sometimes confused them. For example, Marx wrote:

'If this surplus-value is related to the total capital instead of the variable capital, it is called profit, p, and the ratio of the surplus-value s to the total capital C, or s/C, is called the rate of profit, p'. Accordingly, $p' = s/C = s/(c+v)$. Now substituting for s its equivalent $s'v$, we find $p' = s'v/C = s'v/(c+v)$, which equation may be expressed by the proportion $p':s' = v:C$; the rate of profit is related to the rate of surplus-value as the variable capital is to the total capital.' (III, pp. 49–50.) '...the commodity-value = cost-price + surplus-value'.

Sweezy wrote: 'To the capitalist the crucial ratio is the rate of profit, in other words, the ratio of surplus value to total capital outlay. If we designate this by p, we have

$$s/(c+v) = p = \text{the rate of profit.}'[1]$$

Joan Robinson wrote: 'Marx's law of the falling tendency of profits then consists simply in the tautology: When the rate of exploitation is constant, the rate of profit falls as capital per man increases. Assuming constant periods of turnover, so that $c+v$ measures the stock of capital: when s/v is constant and c/v rising, $s/(c+v)$ is falling.'[2]

Samuelson also wrote: 'Volume I's first approximation of equal positive rates of surplus value, S_i/V_i, is not a simplifying assumption but rather – to the extent it contradicts equal profits rates $S_i/(V_i+C)$ – a complicating detour.'[3]

However, the rate of surplus value belongs to the value accounting system, whereas the rate of profits belongs to the price accounting system. It is not tautological to find that a proposition holds between them. As will be seen in chapter 7, there is no contradiction between the law of equal rates of surplus value and the law of equal profits rates.

In *Capital* there may be found three alternative definitions of the rate of surplus value or the rate of exploitation. They are all equivalent with each other. The first definition is given as follows. Let

$$B = \begin{bmatrix} b_{n+1} \\ \vdots \\ b_m \end{bmatrix}$$

denote the daily means of subsistence of a labourer, and let $\overline{T}$ and T be the maximum and the prevailing length of the working day respectively. The daily means of subsistence is evaluated, in terms of labour-time, at $\Lambda_{\text{II}} B$, which is assumed to satisfy the following inequality:

$$\overline{T} > \Lambda_{\text{II}} B. \tag{1}$$

This means that the labourer can work longer hours every day

[1] P. M. Sweezy, *The Theory of Capitalist Development* (London: Dennis Dobson Limited, 1942), p. 67.
[2] J. Robinson, *An Essay on Marxian Economics* (London: Macmillan, 1949), p. 36.
[3] P. A. Samuelson, 'Wages and Interest: A Modern Dissection of Marxian Economic Models', *American Economic Review*, vol. XLVII, December 1957, p. 892.

than he needs to in order to produce his necessities of life. This assumption is indispensable for a meaningful theory of exploitation, because otherwise a labourer can only produce, at best, the necessaries that he requires daily for his subsistence. In Marx's words: 'On the basis of capitalist production, ...this necessary labour [$\Lambda_{II}B$] can form a part only of the working-day [T]; the working-day itself can never be reduced to this minimum. On the other hand, the working-day has a maximum limit [$\overline{T}$]. It cannot be prolonged beyond a certain point.' (I, p. 232.) Thus Marx made the basic assumption of the theory of exploitation: $\overline{T} \geqslant T > \Lambda_{II}B$.

In a capitalist economy, where the labourer possesses no means of production but can freely sell his labour-power, the minimum supply price of labour-power per day will be set so as to enable the labourer to buy commodities B per day, i.e. at a level of $\Lambda_{II}B$ in terms of value, and the labourer will have to work T hours a day. Let $\omega = 1/T$; then the labourer will receive ω units of the daily means of subsistence per hour by offering one unit of labour-power for one hour. The payment ωB is equivalent to $\omega \Lambda_{II}B$ hours of labour, so that $\omega \Lambda_{II}B$ represents the paid part of labour and $1 - \omega \Lambda_{II}B$ the unpaid part. Thus in the capitalist economy the capitalist does not pay fully for labour but merely for labour-power, at a wage rate which equals the daily value of labour-power (i.e. the cost of production of the labour-power). The rate of exploitation, denoted by e, is then defined as the ratio of unpaid labour to paid labour (I, p. 534), which is

$$e = \frac{\text{Unpaid labour}}{\text{Paid labour}} = \frac{1 - \omega \Lambda_{II} B}{\omega \Lambda_{II} B}. \qquad (2)$$

Paid labour and unpaid labour per working-day, i.e. $\Lambda_{II}B$ and $T - \Lambda_{II}B$, were also alternatively called by Marx necessary labour and surplus labour respectively;[4] the former represents the labour expended during that portion of the working-day in

---

[4] 'In this work, we have, up to now, employed the term necessary labour-time, to designate the time necessary under given social conditions for the production of any commodity. Henceforward we use it to designate also the time necessary for the production of the particular commodity, labour-power. The use of one and the same technical term in different senses is inconvenient, but in no science can it be altogether avoided. Compare, for instance, the higher with the lower branches of mathematics.' (I, p. 217.)

which the workman produces the value of his labour-power, that is, the value of his means of subsistence. 'Now since his work forms part of a system, based on the social division of labour, he does not directly produce the actual necessaries which he himself consumes; he produces instead a particular commodity, yarn for example.' (I, p. 216.) But this labour is necessary in the sense that it is needed in order to produce the labourer's means of subsistence, that is 'necessary, as regards the labourer, because independent of the particular social form of his labour; necessary, as regards capital, and the world of capitalists, because on the continued existence of the labourer depends their existence also.' (I, p. 217.) On the other hand, during the second portion of the labour-process the workman labours but produces no value for himself. 'He creates surplus-value which, for the capitalist, has all the charms of a creation out of nothing.' (I, p. 217.) Thus we have an alternative expression of (2):

$$e = \frac{\text{Surplus labour}}{\text{Necessary labour}}. \tag{2'}$$

A further definition of the rate of exploitation can be given in terms of the distribution of labour among industries. Let there be $\bar{N}$ labourers, who work T hours a day, in society. In order to maintain them at the subsistence level, they must produce $B\bar{N}$ amounts of wage goods per day, for the production of which $A_{\text{II}} B \bar{N}$ amounts of capital goods are required. These demands for capital goods from wage-good industries have repercussions on the capital-good industries. After having taken all-round multiplier effects into account, capital goods of the amounts $\bar{x}_{\text{I}}$ have to be produced:

$$\bar{x}_{\text{I}} = A_{\text{I}} \bar{x}_{\text{I}} + A_{\text{II}} B \bar{N}. \tag{3}$$

Therefore the total amount of labour time directly or indirectly required for the production of the wage goods is given by

$$TN = L_{\text{I}} \bar{x}_{\text{I}} + L_{\text{II}} B \bar{N}, \tag{4}$$

where N is the number of necessary labourers. The rest of the labourers, $\bar{N} - N$, are unnecessary and can work either in the capital-goods industry for investment purposes, or in the luxury-goods industry for the benefit of the capitalists. The ratio of the total or social surplus labour to the socially necessary labour,

$(T\bar{N} - TN)/TN$, is shown, in view of (3) and (4), to equal the exploitation rate (2) or (2′) by Marx's original definition, since[5]

$$\frac{T\bar{N} - TN}{TN} = \frac{T\bar{N} - [L_{\mathrm{I}}(\mathrm{I} - A_{\mathrm{I}})^{-1}A_{\mathrm{II}} + L_{\mathrm{II}}]B\bar{N}}{[L_{\mathrm{I}}(\mathrm{I} - A_{\mathrm{I}})^{-1}A_{\mathrm{II}} + L_{\mathrm{II}}]B\bar{N}} = \frac{\mathrm{I} - \omega\Lambda_{\mathrm{II}}B}{\omega\Lambda_{\mathrm{II}}B}.$$

Hence, $\quad e = \dfrac{\text{Total surplus labour}}{\text{Socially necessary labour}} = \dfrac{T\bar{N} - TN}{TN}.$ (5)

The final definition of the rate of exploitation is given in terms of the total surplus value produced and the total value of labour-power. Let x_{I} and x_{II} be the output vectors of the capital-good industries and the wage and luxury-good industries. Then total employment (in terms of labour time) is given by

$$T\bar{N} = L_{\mathrm{I}}x_{\mathrm{I}} + L_{\mathrm{II}}x_{\mathrm{II}}. \tag{6}$$

In order to provide the $\bar{N}$ workers with the necessary means of subsistence, the wage-good industries must produce outputs of the amounts $B\bar{N}$, and for the production of the outputs x_{I} and x_{II} of the capital-good and the wage and luxury-good industries, capital goods have to be produced in the amounts

$$x_{\mathrm{I}}^{*} = A_{\mathrm{I}}x_{\mathrm{I}} + A_{\mathrm{II}}x_{\mathrm{II}}. \tag{7}$$

The surplus products of capital goods are given by $x_{\mathrm{I}} - x_{\mathrm{I}}^{*}$ and those of the wage and luxury-good industries by $x_{\mathrm{II}} - B\bar{N}$. It is clear that the total surplus value produced amounts to $\Lambda_{\mathrm{I}}(x_{\mathrm{I}} - x_{\mathrm{I}}^{*}) + \Lambda_{\mathrm{II}}(x_{\mathrm{II}} - B\bar{N})$, whilst the total value of labour-power amounts to $\Lambda_{\mathrm{II}}B\bar{N}$. The rate of surplus value, s' in Marx's notation, is defined as the ratio of the total surplus value produced to the total value of labour-power, that is

$$s' = \frac{\text{Total surplus value}}{\text{Total value of labour-power}} = \frac{\Lambda_{\mathrm{I}}(x_{\mathrm{I}} - x_{\mathrm{I}}^{*}) + \Lambda_{\mathrm{II}}(x_{\mathrm{II}} - B\bar{N})}{\Lambda_{\mathrm{II}}B\bar{N}}.$$
(8)

The equivalence of the rate of surplus value, s', thus defined with the rate of exploitation, e, of (2) or (5) is established in the

[5] We have $\bar{x}_{\mathrm{I}} = (\mathrm{I} - A_{\mathrm{I}})^{-1}A_{\mathrm{II}}B\bar{N}$ from (3), so that

$$TN = [L_{\mathrm{I}}(\mathrm{I} - A_{\mathrm{I}})^{-1}A_{\mathrm{II}} + L_{\mathrm{II}}]B\bar{N}$$

from (4). As has been seen in chapter 1, $\Lambda_{\mathrm{II}} = L_{\mathrm{I}}(\mathrm{I} - A_{\mathrm{I}})^{-1}A_{\mathrm{II}} + L_{\mathrm{II}}$, and, by definition, $\omega = \mathrm{I}/T$.

following way. First, it is clear from (6) that the total value of labour-power may be written as

$$\Lambda_{II} B \bar{N} = \omega \Lambda_{II} B(L_I x_I + L_{II} x_{II}) \qquad (9)$$

because $\omega = 1/T$. Also, eliminating $x_I{}^*$ and $\bar{N}$ by the use of (6) and (7), we may write the total value of surplus products as

$$\Lambda_I(x_I - x_I{}^*) + \Lambda_{II}(x_{II} - B\bar{N}) = (\Lambda_I - \Lambda_I A_I - \omega \Lambda_{II} BL_I) x_I$$
$$+ (\Lambda_{II} - \Lambda_I A_{II} - \omega \Lambda_{II} BL_{II}) x_{II}. \qquad (10)$$

Secondly, we have from (2)

$$(1+e)\omega \Lambda_{II} B = 1. \qquad (11)$$

Therefore, the value-determination equations, $\Lambda_I = \Lambda_I A_I + L_I$ and $\Lambda_{II} = \Lambda_I A_{II} + L_{II}$, can be put in the form

$$\Lambda_I = \Lambda_I A_I + \omega \Lambda_{II} BL_I + e\omega \Lambda_{II} BL_I, \qquad (12)$$

$$\Lambda_{II} = \Lambda_I A_{II} + \omega \Lambda_{II} BL_{II} + e\omega \Lambda_{II} BL_{II}. \qquad (13)$$

Because of these relations, the parts in parentheses on the right-hand side of (10) equal $e\omega \Lambda_{II} BL_I$ and $e\omega \Lambda_{II} BL_{II}$ respectively. Hence,

$$\Lambda_I(x_I - x_I{}^*) + \Lambda_{II}(x_{II} - B\bar{N}) = e\omega \Lambda_{II} B(L_I x_I + L_{II} x_{II}).$$

Dividing this by (9) we obtain the rate of exploitation, s', which is obviously equal to e. Thus the general formula is established:[6]

$$\frac{\text{Surplus value}}{\text{Value of labour power}} = \frac{\text{Surplus labour}}{\text{Necessary labour}} = \frac{\text{Unpaid labour}}{\text{Paid labour}}.$$

On the right-hand side of each equation of (12) and (13), say the ith equation, the first part, representing the value of the capital goods utilized by industry i, is called the constant capital of i; the second part, which represents the value of the labour-power employed by i, is called the variable capital of i; and the last part, which represents the surplus labour-time produced by i, is the surplus value of i. They are denoted by C_i, V_i, S_i, respectively; so we have

$$\Lambda_i = C_i + V_i + S_i \quad (i = 1, \ldots, m).$$

The rate of surplus value of industry i is defined as S_i/V_i, which equals e for all i, because of equations (12) and (13); that is to

[6] See *Capital*, vol. 1, p. 534.

say, the rate of exploitation is equalized throughout the economy. Clearly this follows if the length of the working-day is equalized throughout the economy, as is implicitly assumed in the definition of e above. In fact if it is different from industry to industry, then the rates of exploitation of industries i and j will be

$$e_i = \frac{T_i - \Lambda_{II} B}{\Lambda_{II} B} \quad \text{and} \quad e_j = \frac{T_j - \Lambda_{II} B}{\Lambda_{II} B};$$

and e_i is not equal to e_j because $T_i \neq T_j$. However, if $T_i > T_j$ industry j is preferable to i from the labourer's point of view, so that there has to be a migration of labourers from i to j, and we have $T_i = T_j$ in equilibrium. In Marx's words: 'This [the equalization of the rate of exploitation] would assume competition among labourers and equalization through their continual migration from one sphere of production to another.' (III, p. 175.)

We now examine Marx's proposition that surplus value is the source of profits. Let p_i be the price of commodity i, and write the price vectors of capital goods, and wage and luxury goods, as

$$p_I = (p_1, \ldots, p_n), \quad p_{II} = (p_{n+1}, \ldots, p_m),$$

respectively. The wage rate w is at least as high as the subsistence level, so that the labourer can buy ωB amounts of wage goods by spending his hourly wages; we therefore have

$$w \geq p_{II} \omega B. \tag{14}$$

This inequality is derived on the basis of the following bibliographical evidence: 'The sum of money which the labourer receives for his daily or weekly labour [$p_{II} B$], forms the amount of his nominal wages, ...But it is clear that according to the length of the working-day, that is, according to the amount of actual labour daily supplied [T], the same daily or weekly wage may represent very different prices of labour, i.e. very different sums of money for the same quantity of labour. We must, therefore, in considering time-wages, again distinguish between the sum total of the daily or weekly wages, etc., and the price of labour. How then to find this price, i.e. the money value of a given quantity of labour?' (I, pp. 543–4.) 'The value of labour-power is determined by the value of necessaries of life habitually required by the average labourer $[\Lambda_{II} B]$]...I assume (1) that commodities are sold at their value; (2) that the price of labour-power rises occasionally above its value, but never sinks below it.' (I, p. 519.) It is obvious that under Marx's assumption (1) prices may be normalized so that $\Lambda_{II} = p_{II}$, to the effect that $\Lambda_{II} B = p_{II} B$. Therefore, his assumption (2) implies that $W \geq p_{II} B$, where W stands for the price of labour-power, i.e. the sum total of the daily wages. Dividing both sides of this inequality by T, and denoting the rate of time-wages W/T by w, we finally obtain (14).

When every industry earns positive profits, we have inequalities

$$p_I > p_I A_I + w L_I, \qquad (15)$$

$$p_{II} > p_I A_{II} + w L_{II}. \qquad (16)$$

Then we may ask what conditions are necessary and sufficient for the existence of a set of non-negative prices and a wage rate yielding positive profits in every industry. This problem was first discussed by N. Okishio, in a satisfactory way creating no confusion between values and prices.[7] It is found that there exists a set of prices and a wage rate fulfilling (15) and (16) if and only if the 'real-wage rate' ω is given such that the rate of exploitation e is positive.[8] This result, whose necessity is due to Okishio, while its sufficiency, though not discussed by him, is also easily proved, may be claimed as the Fundamental Marxian Theorem, because it asserts that the exploitation of labourers by capitalists is necessary and sufficient for the existence of a price–wage set yielding positive profits or, in other words, for the possibility of conserving the capitalist economy.

Let us first show that exploitation is the source of profits, in the sense that it is impossible for each and every industry to earn positive profits simultaneously unless $e > 0$. Suppose now (15) and (16) hold. Substituting for w from (14), we have

$$p_I > p_I A_I + p_{II} \omega B L_I, \qquad (15')$$

$$p_{II} > p_I A_{II} + p_{II} \omega B L_{II}, \qquad (16')$$

[7] N. Okishio, 'A Mathematical Note on Marxian Theorems', *Weltwirtshaftliches Archiv*, 1963, pp. 287–99.
[8] The reciprocal of the daily working hours may be taken as an index of the level of the real-wage payment since the daily wages are fixed at the subsistence level.

from which we find that the matrix of capital coefficients and labour-feeding input coefficients,

$$\begin{bmatrix} A_{\mathrm{I}} & A_{\mathrm{II}} \\ \omega BL_{\mathrm{I}} & \omega BL_{\mathrm{II}} \end{bmatrix}$$

is 'productive', because p_{I} and p_{II} are positive. Therefore there are positive output vectors x_{I} and x_{II} such that

$$\begin{bmatrix} x_{\mathrm{I}} \\ x_{\mathrm{II}} \end{bmatrix} > \begin{bmatrix} A_{\mathrm{I}} & A_{\mathrm{II}} \\ \omega BL_{\mathrm{I}} & \omega BL_{\mathrm{II}} \end{bmatrix} \begin{bmatrix} x_{\mathrm{I}} \\ x_{\mathrm{II}} \end{bmatrix}. \tag{17}$$

(See chapter 2.) Now, premultiply (17) by the positive vector $(\Lambda_{\mathrm{I}}, \Lambda_{\mathrm{II}})$ and take (12) and (13) into account. We then obtain

$$(\Lambda_{\mathrm{I}} x_{\mathrm{I}} + \Lambda_{\mathrm{II}} x_{\mathrm{II}}) - \Lambda_{\mathrm{I}}(A_{\mathrm{I}} x_{\mathrm{I}} + A_{\mathrm{II}} x_{\mathrm{II}}) - \Lambda_{\mathrm{II}}(\omega BL_{\mathrm{I}} x_{\mathrm{I}} + \omega BL_{\mathrm{II}} x_{\mathrm{II}})$$
$$= e(\omega \Lambda_{\mathrm{II}} BL_{\mathrm{I}} x_{\mathrm{I}} + \omega \Lambda_{\mathrm{II}} BL_{\mathrm{II}} x_{\mathrm{II}}) > 0$$

from which e is found to be positive.

Next we show the converse; that is to say, when there is exploitation it is possible for all industries to earn positive profits. As $e > 0$, we have from (12) and (13)

$$\Lambda_{\mathrm{I}} > \Lambda_{\mathrm{I}} A_{\mathrm{I}} + \Lambda_{\mathrm{II}} \omega BL_{\mathrm{I}}, \quad \Lambda_{\mathrm{II}} > \Lambda_{\mathrm{I}} A_{\mathrm{II}} + \Lambda_{\mathrm{II}} \omega BL_{\mathrm{II}}.$$

Now put $p_{\mathrm{I}} = \alpha \Lambda_{\mathrm{I}}$, $p_{\mathrm{II}} = \alpha \Lambda_{\mathrm{II}}$ and $w = \alpha \Lambda_{\mathrm{II}} \omega B$, where α is any positive number. It is at once seen that they are all positive and satisfy the conditions for positive profits, (15) and (16).

In Marx's economics this Fundamental Theorem plays the role of the bridge connecting the value system (12), (13) and the price system (15), (16). It justifies the Marxian proposition that ω is set in the capitalist economy at such a level that[9] $\omega < 1/(\Lambda_{\mathrm{II}} B)$ even if we do not know the value of ω, Λ_{II} and B, if it is observed (as it is) that industries in the economy earn positive profits. That is to say, positive profits are observed in the actual economy, which implies that e is positive by the Fundamental Theorem, so that $\omega < 1/(\Lambda_{\mathrm{II}} B)$, i.e. the workers are not paid the full value of their product.

It is not difficult now for us to list the necessary and sufficient conditions for positive exploitation. First of all, the technology has already been developed to such a level that capital goods or means of production are 'productive'; otherwise we would have negative values (see chapter 2). Secondly, the techniques adopted by industries are so productive that the values of wage

[9] $1/\Lambda_{\mathrm{II}} B$ represents the real wage rate that would prevail if there were no exploitation.

SURPLUS VALUE AND EXPLOITATION

goods Λ_{II} are low enough to make the total value of the means of subsistence $\Lambda_{II} B$ less than the maximum length of the working-day $\overline{T}$ (see inequality (1) of this chapter). Thirdly, the actual working-day T is longer than the necessary labour-time $\Lambda_{II} B$; or in other words, the 'real-wage rate' ω is less than the maximum rate, $1/(\Lambda_{II} B)$. Under these conditions the formula (2) enables us to draw the exploitation-rate curve in the (e, ω)

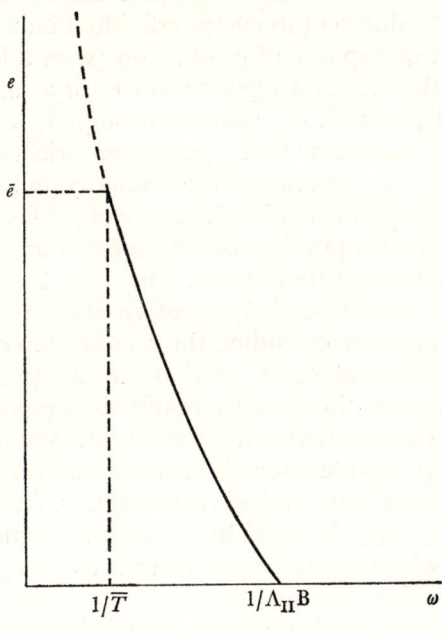

Fig. 1

plane. It traces out a downward sloping curve, starting from $\omega = 1/\overline{T}$ and ending at $\omega = 1/(\Lambda_{II} B)$. (See fig. 1.) 'The working day [hence, the reciprocal of the working day, ω] is thus not a constant, but a variable quantity.' (I, p. 232.) So the problem of determining the rate of exploitation is reduced to the problem of determining the length of the working day. When the worker's position is very weak, the working day will be prolonged as much as possible and the rate of exploitation will be maximized at $\bar{e}$, the rate corresponding to $\omega = 1/\overline{T}$.

CHAPTER 6

The rate of profit

In the previous chapter we have shown that if and only if surplus value is positive, there is a set of prices and a wage rate at which every industry is able to earn positive profits. These profits, however, are *not* necessarily equilibrium profits; the rate of profits may be different in every individual industry. Capital will move from one sphere of production (with a lower rate of profits) to another (with a higher rate) until a uniform, equilibrium rate of profits is established throughout the economy. In this chapter, we assume that equilibrium prices and an equilibrium rate of profits prevail in the economy and examine the relationship between the equilibrium rate of profits and the rate of surplus value. This problem of 'the conversion of the rate of surplus-value into the rate of profit' (III, part I), which is one of the problems of the so-called 'transformation problem', is no more than the problem of finding the relationship of the rate of profit π to the 'rate of real wages' ω (i.e. the problem of the factor–price frontier discussed by many contemporary growth economists[1]), because, as we have seen in the previous chapter, the rate of surplus value (or the rate of exploitation) e is a decreasing function of the rate of real wages, ω. In fact once the relationship, $\pi = \pi(e)$, is found by the transformation problem, it is combined with the exploitation curve, $e = e(\omega)$, to give the factor–price frontier, $\pi = g(\omega)$.

In his pioneering work on this very modern subject, Marx was unfortunately often confused between values and prices, so that he has been criticized not only by his opponents but also even by Marxian economists, although he gave almost correct solutions. He knew that equilibrium prices deviate from values in a capitalist economy unless some restrictive conditions are satisfied.[2] Accordingly, he was concerned first with the simple

---

[1] See P. A. Samuelson, 'Parable and Realism in Capital Theory: The Surrogate Production Function', *Review of Economic Studies*, 1962; and my *Theory of Economic Growth* (Oxford University Press, 1969), ch. 2.

[2] Marx wrote: 'We have seen how a deviation in prices of production from values arises from:

(1) addding the average profit instead of the surplus-value contained in a commodity to its cost-price;

THE RATE OF PROFIT 57

(but restrictive) case of no distortion of equilibrium prices from values and then with the general case of transformation of values into prices. He wrote: 'In this part [part I of volume III], the rate of profit is numerically different from the rate of surplus-value; while profit and surplus-value are treated as having the same numerical magnitude but only a different form. In the next part we shall see how the alienation goes further, and how profit represents a magnitude differing also numerically from surplus-value.' (III, p. 48.) But in spite of such carefulness, it is true that he failed to state the assumptions for his conclusions exactly and to explain his reasoning correctly. However, it is also true that his intuition was strong; his conjectures are found to be valid. His reasoning can be clarified or corrected, as we shall see below, so that the fundamental results which he obtained are established without any significant changes, and they can also be further generalized.

Marx's view of profit may be summarized briefly in the following way: 'As already shown in the first book, it is precisely the fact that non-workers own the means of production which turns labourers into wage-workers and non-workers into capitalists.' (III, p. 41.) 'The capitalist does not produce a commodity for its own sake, nor for the sake of its use-value, or his personal consumption' but is interested in 'excess value of the product over the value of the capital consumed by it.' (III, loc. cit.) The surplus value is a surplus over the advanced total capital. 'The proportion of this surplus to the total capital is therefore expressed by the fraction s/C, in which C stands for total capital. We thus obtain the *rate of profit* $s/C = s/(c+v)$, as distinct from the rate of surplus value s/v.' (III, p. 42.) On the other hand, 'The ratio of this surplus-value to the advanced variable capital, or s/v, is called the rate of surplus-value and designated s'. Therefore $s/v = s'$, and consequently $s = s'v$.' (III, p. 49.) 'Now, substituting for s its equivalent $s'v$, we find $p' = s'v/C = s'v/(c+v)$, which equation may also be expressed by the proportion, $p' : s' = v : C$ (III, p. 50), where p' represents

(2) the price of production, which so deviates from the value of a commodity, entering into the cost-price of other commodities as one of its elements, so that the cost-price of a commodity may already contain a deviation from value in those means of production consumed by it, quite aside from a deviation of its own which may arise through a difference between the average profit and the surplus-value.' (III, pp. 206–7.)

the rate of profit. 'It follows from this proposition that the rate of profit, p', is always smaller than s', the rate of surplus-value, because v, the variable capital, is always smaller than C, the sum of $v+c$, or the variable plus the constant capital.' (III, *loc. cit.*)

Then Marx went on 'to apply the above-mentioned equation of the rate of profit, $p' = s'v/C$, to the various possible cases' (III, p. 53). He separated the product on the right-hand side into its two factors s' and v/C and, treating one of them as constant, analysed the effect of the possible variations of the other. He obtained results such as (i) 'The rates of profit of two different capitals, or of one and the same capital in two successive different conditions, *are equal*, (1) if the per cent composition of the capitals is the same and their rates of surplus-value are equal; (2)....' (III, p. 69). (ii) 'They are *unequal*...if the rates of surplus-value are the same and the per cent composition is unequal.' (III, *loc. cit.*) (iii) The rate of profit falls 'if the constant capital is augmented to such an extent that the total capital grows at a faster rate than the variable capital' (III, p. 61).

However, these quotations from part I of volume III of *Capital* show that Marx had not fully realized the implications of his theory of value. First of all, these formulas and results were obtained under the assumption that the profits (in terms of money or some other numeraire) and surplus values (in terms of labour-time) of individual industries are proportional to each other, so that profits may be normalized at a level such that they are numerically equal to the corresponding surplus value. Let Π_i and S_i stand for the profits and the surplus value of industry i;[3] and let C_i^p and V_i^p be constant and variable capitals in terms of prices. If we assume $\Pi_i = S_i$ for each industry i (as Marx did in part I of volume III), then we have $C_i^p + V_i^p = C_i + V_i$ for each i (see p. 75 below for a proof). Hence

$$\pi_i = s_i' \frac{V_i}{C_i + V_i} \quad (i = 1, ..., m), \tag{1}$$

[3] The C_i, V_i, S_i in this chapter differ from those in chapters 5 and 7 in standing for the constant capital, the variable capital and the surplus value utilized or produced by industry i, but *not* constant and variable capitals and surplus value per unit of commodity i. Therefore in this chapter ΣC_i, for example, represents the total constant capital consumed in the economy, while in the other chapters C_is must be summed after being multiplied by the output of industry i, to give the total constant capital of the society. The same comment applies to C_i^p, V_i^p, and Π_i.

where π_i and s_i' are the rate of profit and the rate of surplus value respectively. We may then ask under what conditions we have $\Pi_i = S_i$ and $C_i{}^p + V_i{}^p = C_i + V_i$ for all i, and we shall find that we may equate profits and surplus value, and prices and values, if and only if all industries have the same value-composition of capital. (This conclusion will be established mathematically in the next chapter.) Therefore the equations (1) imply that

$$\frac{C_1}{V_1} = \frac{C_2}{V_2} = \ldots = \frac{C_m}{V_m}, \qquad (2)$$

so that it follows from (1) that $\pi_1 = \ldots = \pi_m$ if $s_1' = \ldots = s_m'$. Hence we cannot derive Marx's proposition (ii) quoted above from the formula (1), whilst in his proposition (i) the condition that 'the per cent composition of the capitals is the same' is redundant.

On the basis of the same formula (1), Samuelson criticized Marx as follows: 'Volume I's first approximation of equal positive rates of surplus value, S_i/V_i, is not a simplifying assumption, but rather – *to the extent it contradicts equal profits rates $S_i/(V_i + C_i)$* – a complicating detour.'[4] (My italics.) Thus he too failed to realize that the identity of the rate of profit with $S_i/(V_i + C_i)$ assumes equal value-compositions of capital, so that there is no contradiction between equal profits rates and equal rates of surplus values, once the identity of π_i with $S_i/(V_i + C_i)$ is assumed.

In part II of volume III Marx was concerned with the general case of profits of industries being not necessarily proportional to their surplus values. He assumed there that the value-composition of capital might differ from industry to industry and that the rate of exploitation was equalized throughout the economy. It is then seen that, with such techniques of production, the equilibrium prices deviate from the values of commodities and the profits of the industries at the equilibrium rate are not proportional to their surplus values. Even in such cases it is true that prices can be normalized so that the total profits are numerically equal to the sum of the surplus values. Marx had an equation, $\Sigma\Pi_i = \Sigma S_i$, and took $\pi = \Sigma S_i / \Sigma(C_i + V_i)$ as an approximation to the equilibrium rate of profits. He then

---

[4] Samuelson, 'Wages and Interest', p. 892.

calculated profits of individual industries as $\pi(C_i+V_i), i = 1,...,m$, and prices as $(1+\pi)(C_i+V_i)$.

However, it is evident that, except in the special case which is discussed in detail in the next chapter, profits and prices thus calculated are no more than first approximations to the true equilibrium profits and prices. Obviously, C_i and V_i are calculated in terms of value. They are the value of the raw materials and services of capital goods consumed in the process of producing commodity i and the value of wage goods consumed by the workers engaged in the production of i, respectively. When prices do not coincide with values, C_i and V_i no longer represent the costs of production in terms of money, on the basis of which production prices and the rate of profits are calculated. Marx wrote: 'Since the price of production may differ from the value of a commodity, it follows that the cost-price of a commodity containing this price of production of another commodity may also stand above or below that portion of its total value derived from the value of the means of production consumed by it. It is necessary to remember this modified significance of the cost-price, and to bear in mind that there is always the possibility of an error if the cost-price of a commodity in any particular sphere is identified with the value of the means of production consumed by it.' (III, pp. 164–5.) Therefore the costs of production have to be recalculated in terms of the prices $(1+\pi)(C_i+V_i)$ which Marx obtained as first approximations, and new prices as well as a new rate of profits are calculated on the basis of the revised costs of production. This process of recalculation has to be repeated until the correct equilibrium prices and rate of profit are obtained. However Marx completely avoided this iteration procedure and was reconciled to an approximate solution to the problem.

Samuelson has pointed out that there is a singular case in which Marx's approximation becomes exact. In this case, which he calls the case of 'equal internal compositions of capital', the following two conditions are satisfied: (1) 'every one of the departments happens to use the various raw materials and machine services [or more correctly, all kinds of commodities] in the same proportions that society produces them in toto', and (2) 'the minimum-subsistence budget is a market basket of goods that comes in those same relative proportions as the goods are used as inputs in production.'[5] In fact, under these assumptions, it is seen that the ratio, $\pi = \Sigma S_i/\Sigma(C_i+V_i)$, calculated from the value-determination equations, gives the equilibrium rate of profits and that the capital costs and the wage costs of m industries are proportional to their constant and variable capitals, C_i and V_i, $i = 1,...,m$, so that the relative prices may be calculated at $(1+\pi)(C_i+V_i)$, $i = 1,...,m$. Thus Samuelson is logically correct in concluding that Marx's algorithm is valid (i.e. his approximation is accurate) under the above mentioned conditions. But it must also be noticed that Marx's system never satisfies these conditions, because in his system wage goods are distinguished from capital goods, so that capital goods do not appear in the worker's market basket of goods (therefore condition (2) above is not applicable to his system), whilst wage goods cannot be direct inputs of the production of commodities (this contradicts condition (1)).

In any case, in deriving the equation, $p' = s'v/C$, Marx did not fully recognize that prices and the rate of profits are variables in the price system, while values and the rate of exploitation are variables in the value system. If this fact had been fully admitted, he could not have obtained the equation so simply as he actually derived it. We must therefore ask how we can establish his fundamental equation and whether his main conclusion, that the rate of profit is always smaller than the rate of exploitation, can remain valid if the problem is correctly dealt with. Furthermore, we may ask under what conditions the confusion Marx made between prices and values can be justified. In this section we confine ourselves to discussing the first two problems and postpone our examination of the last to the next chapter.

As we have so far implicitly assumed in the value-determining equations, 'we shall assume, for the sake of simplicity, that the constant capital is everywhere uniformly and entirely transferred to the annual product of the capitals' (III, p. 154). At prices taken arbitrarily, 'the rates of profit prevailing in the various branches of production are originally very different. These different rates of profit are equalised by competition to

---

[5] Samuelson, 'Understanding the Marxian Notion of Exploitation: A Summary of the So-Called Transformation Problem between Marxian Values and Competitive Prices', *Journal of Economic Literature*, June 1971.

a single general rate of profit.' (III, p. 158.) Let π be the equilibrium rate of profit, p_i the price of commodity i, and w the wage rate per labour-time. p_I and p_II are price vectors of capital goods and wage and luxury goods respectively. Then at the long-run equilibrium where the rates of profit are equalized we have[6]

$$p_\mathrm{I} = (1+\pi)(p_\mathrm{I} A_\mathrm{I} + w L_\mathrm{I}), \qquad (3)$$

$$p_\mathrm{II} = (1+\pi)(p_\mathrm{I} A_\mathrm{II} + w L_\mathrm{II}), \qquad (4)$$

or, in terms of labour,

$$p_{\mathrm{I},w} = (1+\pi)(p_{\mathrm{I},w} A_\mathrm{I} + L_\mathrm{I}), \qquad (3')$$

$$p_{\mathrm{II},w} = (1+\pi)(p_{\mathrm{I},w} A_\mathrm{II} + L_\mathrm{II}), \qquad (4')$$

where $p_{\mathrm{I},w}$ is the vector of prices of capital goods in terms of labour, i.e.
$$p_{\mathrm{I},w} = (p_1/w, p_2/w, \ldots, p_n/w);$$
similarly, $\quad p_{\mathrm{II},w} = (p_{n+1}/w, \ldots, p_m/w).$

Next it is assumed that wages are fixed at a level at which workers can only purchase the daily means of subsistence B. It is further assumed that workers must work T hours a day and are incapable of choosing goods. Then the wage rate per labour-time w is given as

$$w = p_\mathrm{II} \omega B, \qquad (5)$$

where $\omega = 1/T$ may be considered as the index of the real wage rate. From (5) we have

$$1 = p_{\mathrm{II},w} \omega B. \qquad (5')$$

If π is given, then (3') and (4') determine prices in terms of labour, $p_{\mathrm{I},w}$, $p_{\mathrm{II},w}$, and (5') therefore determines the real wage rate ω. Or conversely if ω is given, then the whole system of equations (3')–(5') determines prices and the rate of profit. As an increase in π gives rise to an increase in $p_{\mathrm{I},w}$ determined by (3') and hence to an increase in $p_{\mathrm{II},w}$ by (4'), the real wage rate obtained from (4') must be diminished. The downward

---

[6] Marx explained equations (3) and (4) as follows: 'under capitalist production the elements of productive capital are, as a rule, bought on the market, and...for this reason their prices include profit which has already been realised, hence, include the price of production of the respective branch of industry together with the profit contained in it, so that the profit of one branch of industry goes into the cost price of another.' (III, p. 160.)

sloping curve, $\omega = f(\pi)$ or $\pi = g(\omega)$, is called the factor–price frontier or the wage–profit frontier by recent writers,[7] and in addition to the slope property, it has the following two properties: (i) When the rate of profit is set at zero, prices in terms of labour equal the respective values, so that (5′) is reduced to $\omega = 1/(\Lambda_{II}B)$; that is to say, the wage rate is fixed at its maximum, or the entire net outputs are paid to the workers as we have observed with simple commodity production. (ii) When the real wage rate tends to zero, the rate of profits approaches a *positive* value π fulfilling[8]

$$p_{I,w} = (1+\pi)p_{I,w}A_I, \qquad (6)$$

with a row vector $p_{I,w}$, whose components are all positive. In view of these properties we may depict the wage–profit frontier as in figure 2.

Let us now establish Marx's main result, that the rate of profit is always less than the rate of exploitation (or the rate of surplus value), i.e. $\pi < e$ (or $p' < s'$ in Marx's notation). This was first proved by Seton and myself and also by Okishio.[9] As the rate of exploitation is defined as the ratio of unpaid labour $T - \Lambda_{II}B$ to paid labour $\Lambda_{II}B$, we have

$$(1+e)\Lambda_{II}B = T \quad \text{or} \quad (1+e)\Lambda_{II}\omega B = 1, \qquad (7)$$

where $\omega = 1/T$. e is positive since the value of the subsistence basket of goods $\Lambda_{II}B$ is less than the daily working hours T. The value-determining equations can be written

$$\Lambda_I = \Lambda_I A_I + L_I = \Lambda_I A_I + [(1+e)\Lambda_{II}\omega B]L_I, \qquad (8)$$

$$\Lambda_{II} = \Lambda_I A_{II} + L_{II} = \Lambda_I A_{II} + [(1+e)\Lambda_{II}\omega B]L_{II}, \qquad (9)$$

since the parts in square brackets are unity, because of (7). Let

---

[7] See, for example, my *Theory of Economic Growth*, p. 22.
[8] It is at once seen from (3′) that we have (6) when $\omega = 0$. (6) implies that $p_{I,w}$ is the eigenvector of A_I, while $1+\pi$ is the reciprocal of its eigenvalue. By the Frobenius theorem the non-negative matrix A_I, which is assumed to be indecomposable, has one and only one positive eigenvalue ν^*, which is associated with a non-negative eigenvector p^*. Moreover, p^* is found to be positive because of the indecomposability of A_I. As A_I is also assumed to be 'productive', there is a positive vector x such that $x > Ax$. Premultiply this inequality by p^* and postmultiply $\nu^* p^* = p^* A_I$ by such an x; we then have $p^* x > \nu^* p^* x = p^* A_I x$; so $1 > \nu^* > 0$. Putting $1+\pi = 1/\nu^*$ and $p_{I,w} = p^*$, we find $\pi > 0$ and $p_{I,w} > 0$.
[9] M. Morishima and F. Seton, 'Aggregation'; N. Okishio, 'Marxian Theorems'.

us now add $e\Lambda_I A_I$ and $e\Lambda_I A_{II}$ to the right-hand sides of (8) and (9) respectively. Then

$$\Lambda_I < (1+e)[\Lambda_I A_I + \Lambda_{II}\omega B L_I] \qquad (10)$$
$$\Lambda_{II} < (1+e)[\Lambda_I A_{II} + \Lambda_{II}\omega B L_{II}]. \qquad (11)$$

In (10), strict inequality must hold for each capital good because $e > 0$, $\Lambda_I > 0$ and each column of A_I has at least one positive element, as it is indecomposable, so that $e\Lambda_I A_I > 0$.

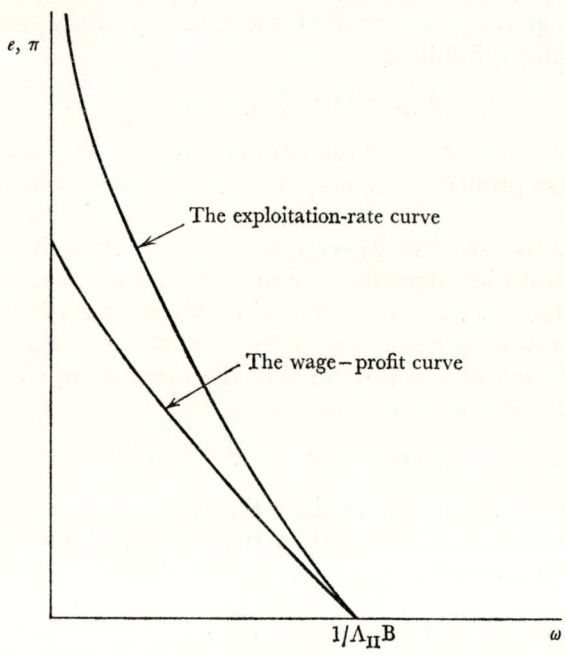

Fig. 2

Strict inequality (11) is obtained by strengthening assumption (ii) of chapter 2 into assumption (ii'), that each column of A_{II} has at least one positive element (that is, each wage or luxury good uses at least one capital good.[10] (10) and (11) can be written as
$$\Lambda < (1+e)\Lambda M, \qquad (12)$$
where $\Lambda = (\Lambda_I, \Lambda_{II})$ and $M = \begin{bmatrix} A_I & A_{II} \\ \omega B L_I & \omega B L_{II} \end{bmatrix}$.

[10] This modification of the assumption is necessary for Marx's conclusion $\pi < e$. Otherwise we cannot rule out the case of $\pi = e$, which is obtained when only those wage and luxury goods which do not use capital goods at all are produced.

We can then see that there is no non-negative, non-zero column vector x such that

$$x = (1+f) Mx, \quad \text{for some } f \geqslant e, \tag{13}$$

because if there were a non-negative, non-zero x, then it would follow from (12) and (13) that

$$\Lambda x < (1+e) \Lambda Mx \leqslant (1+f) \Lambda Mx = \Lambda x,$$

as self-contradiction.

On the other hand, substituting the wage equation (5) into the price-determining equations, we have

$$p_\text{I} = (1+\pi)[p_\text{I} A_\text{I} + p_\text{II} \omega B L_\text{I}],$$
$$p_\text{II} = (1+\pi)[p_\text{I} A_\text{II} + p_\text{II} \omega B L_\text{II}],$$

or, in a more concise form,

$$p = (1+\pi) pM, \tag{14}$$

where $p = (p_\text{I}, p_\text{II}) > 0$. Now suppose the contrary of Marx's result, that is $\pi \geqslant e$. Let x be a vector satisfying

$$x = (1+\pi) Mx. \tag{15}$$

As has been seen above, there is no non-negative, non-zero vector x because $\pi \geqslant e$, so that x contains some negative components. Let the vector obtained by replacing these components by 0 be denoted as x^*, then obviously $Mx \leqslant Mx^* \geqslant 0$. Therefore, from (15)[11]

$$x^* \leqslant (\neq)(1+\pi) Mx^*. \tag{16}$$

This contradicts (14), because we have $px^* = (1+\pi) pMx^*$ from it, whereas $px^* < (1+\pi) pMx^*$ from (16). This means that the contrary of Marx's result cannot be valid; that is to say, the equilibrium rate of profits cannot be as great as the rate of exploitation. In other words, in the state of equilibrium, where every industry yields profits at an equal positive rate, workers are inevitably exploited by capitalists at a greater positive rate.

The rest of this chapter is devoted to an extension of the above Morishima–Seton–Okishio theorem to the case where workers can choose goods. We assume that all workers are homogeneous

---

[11] (16) must hold with strict inequality for at least one commodity i; otherwise there is a non-negative, non-zero x fulfilling (15), a contradiction.

in tastes. Let F be the vector of the amounts of wage goods which a worker consumes by spending the whole of his daily wages. As he works T hours a day at the wage rate per hour w, we have

$$wT = p_{\mathrm{II}}F. \qquad (17)$$

When the worker can choose goods, each element of F, determined by maximizing his utility subject to the budget constraint (17), is homogeneous of degree zero in prices p_{II} and wages wT; that is to say, $F(\lambda p_{\mathrm{II}}, \lambda wT)$ remains unchanged for all positive λ. By taking $\lambda = 1/w$, we get

$$F = F(p_{\mathrm{II},w}, T)$$

since $p_{i,w} = p_i/w$. Therefore we have from (17)

$$T = p_{\mathrm{II},w} F(p_{\mathrm{II},w}, T) \quad \text{or} \quad 1 = p_{\mathrm{II},w} D \qquad (17')$$

where $\qquad D = (1/T) F(p_{\mathrm{II},w}, T).$

The rate of exploitation (or the rate of surplus value) is now defined as

$$e = \frac{T - \Lambda_{\mathrm{II}} F(p_{\mathrm{II},w}, T)}{\Lambda_{\mathrm{II}} F(p_{\mathrm{II},w}, T)} = \frac{1 - \Lambda_{\mathrm{II}} D}{\Lambda_{\mathrm{II}} D}; \qquad (18)$$

or in other words, by defining the 'necessary working-time' as the labour required for the production of the wage goods actually consumed each day by the average worker, and the 'surplus working-time' as the excess of the daily working-time over the 'necessary working-time', we extend the concept of the rate of exploitation so that it means the ratio of the 'surplus working-time' to the 'necessary working-time', thus defined. It is noted that the rate of exploitation thus redefined depends not only on T but also on $p_{\mathrm{II},w}$.

In order to define the real wage rate per labour-time, let us reintroduce the daily means of subsistence B as the reference consumption vector. The real-wage rate ω is then defined as the number of reference consumption baskets which a worker can purchase by his hourly wages

$$\omega = \frac{w}{p_{\mathrm{II}}B} = \frac{1}{p_{\mathrm{II},w}B}. \qquad (19)$$

As is easily seen from (17), ω equals $1/T$ as before when $F(p_{\mathrm{II},w}, T)$ is fixed at B; but now ω may differ from $1/T$, since

THE RATE OF PROFIT

the worker does not always choose the reference consumption basket B.

We can now draw a downward-sloping wage–profit frontier in exactly the same way as before. An increase in π yields an increase in $p_{I,w}$ by (3'), which in turn yields an increase in $p_{II,w}$ by (4'); finally it brings about a decrease in the real wage rate ω, because of (19). As for the slope of the exploitation-rate curve, however, we cannot say whether it is decreasing or increasing, because we do not know how

$$\Lambda_{II} D \quad \text{or} \quad \Lambda_{II}(1/T) F(p_{II,w}, T)$$

reacts to a change in the real wage rate.

It is rather surprising that, in spite of such poor information about the exploitation-rate curve, the Morishima–Seton–Okishio Theorem still remains valid. This is seen in the following way.[12] First (17') enables us to write the price-determining equations (3') and (4') as

$$p_I = (1+\pi)(p_I A_I + p_{II} DL_I),$$
$$p_{II} = (1+\pi)(p_I A_{II} + p_{II} DL_{II}),$$

or, in matrix form $\quad p = (1+\pi) pN, \quad (20)$

where $\quad p = (p_I, p_{II}) \quad$ and $\quad N = \begin{bmatrix} A_I & A_{II} \\ DL_I & DL_{II} \end{bmatrix}.$

As $p > 0$, $1+\pi > 0$, and N is a non-negative square matrix, we can show that there is a non-negative vector y such that[13]

$$y = (1+\pi) Ny. \quad (21)$$

---

[12] We could prove the extended theorem in exactly the same way as we have just proved the original theorem, but we choose a slightly different way (that is the way in which Morishima and Seton proved the latter) because equation (24) below, explicitly relating π to e (or *vice versa*), is very important.

[13] This is easily shown by using an argument which is already familiar. Suppose y contains some negative components; then we have

$$y^* \leq (\neq)(1+\pi) Ny^*,$$

where y^* is a non-negative vector obtained by replacing negative components of y by 0. Postmultiply (20) be y^* and premultiply the above inequality by p; we then have
$$py^* < (1+\pi) pNy^* = py^*$$
as $p > 0$ and $y^* \geq (\neq) 0$. This is a contradiction; hence $y \geq 0$.

Next, in view of (18), we can write the value-determining equations (8) and (9) as

$$\Lambda_I = \Lambda_I A_I + (1+e)\Lambda_{II} DL_I, \qquad (22)$$

$$\Lambda_{II} = \Lambda_I A_{II} + (1+e)\Lambda_{II} DL_{II}. \qquad (23)$$

Let y_I be the subvector of y consisting of the first n components and let y_{II} be the subvector consisting of the remaining $m-n$ components of y. Postmultiply (22) and (23) by y_I and y_{II} respectively, and then add them up. The result is then compared with (21) premultiplied by Λ. We obtain the Morishima–Seton equation

$$\pi = e\frac{V}{C+V}, \qquad (24)$$

where
$$V = \Lambda_{II} DL_I y_I + \Lambda_{II} DL_{II} y_{II},$$
$$C = \Lambda_I A_I y_I + \Lambda_I A_{II} y_{II}.$$

As will be seen later, y_I and y_{II} are the proportions of outputs along the balanced equilibrium growth path which is called the 'golden age' path by modern economists, and which could be established if capitalists did not consume and workers did not save. C/V gives the value-composition of capital of the whole economy along the 'golden age' equilibrium path. In the revised Marx formula (24), the total constant capital C and the total variable capital V are measured in terms of value. They are both positive, because (i) the values, Λ_I, Λ_{II}, are positive, (ii) the output vector y_I is strictly positive and y_{II} non-negative, non-zero, (iii) the capital-input coefficient matrix of the capital-good industries is non-negative and indecomposable, (iv) the worker's demands and the labour-input coefficient vector, D and L_I, are non-negative and non-zero, and (v) the capital-input and labour-input coefficients of the wage-good industries, A_{II} and L_{II}, are non-negative.[14] Hence it is evident that the rate of profits is lower than the rate of exploitation, unless the latter is zero. This revised and extended Marx result again confirms the necessity of 'exploitation' for positive profits in a capitalist economy.

Finally we compare the various conditions so far discussed, under which Marx's identification of the profit rate π with the

---

[14] Result (ii) is based *inter alia* on the assumption that each column of A_{II} has at least one positive entry. Otherwise it is possible that $y_I = 0$, $y_{II} \geq 0$, $\neq 0$, and $A_{II} y_{II} = 0$; therefore $C = 0$, so that $\pi = e$.

ratio of the surplus value to total capital $S/(C+V)$ has been shown to be admissible. Four cases deserve our attention, the first of which is the case of no exploitation and no profit satisfying $\pi = S/(C+V)$ at $0 = 0$ trivially. Such a state of affairs is no more than an imaginary state, conceivable only under simply commodity production, and can hardly happen in an actual capitalist economy.

Secondly, if all industries have the same value composition of capital, then prices are proportional to values (see chapter 7 below), so that
$$p_\mathrm{I} = \alpha \Lambda_\mathrm{I}, \quad p_\mathrm{II} = \alpha \Lambda_\mathrm{II} \qquad (25)$$
for some common α. Let x_I, x_II be the output vectors of the capital-good and wage and luxury-good industries respectively. Let C and V be the aggregate constant and variable capitals used, and S the aggregate surplus value produced in the economy. By definition we have
$$C = \Lambda_\mathrm{I}(A_\mathrm{I} x_\mathrm{I} + A_\mathrm{II} x_\mathrm{II}),$$
$$V = (\omega \Lambda_\mathrm{II} B)(L_\mathrm{I} x_\mathrm{I} + L_\mathrm{II} x_\mathrm{II}),$$
$$S = \Lambda_\mathrm{I} x_\mathrm{I} + \Lambda_\mathrm{II} x_\mathrm{II} - C - V.$$

Bearing (25) and the budget equation (5) in mind, we obtain
$$\alpha C = p_\mathrm{I}(A_\mathrm{I} x_\mathrm{I} + A_\mathrm{II} x_\mathrm{II}),$$
$$\alpha V = w(L_\mathrm{I} x_\mathrm{I} + L_\mathrm{II} x_\mathrm{II}),$$
$$\alpha S = p_\mathrm{I} x_\mathrm{I} + p_\mathrm{II} x_\mathrm{II} - \alpha C - \alpha V.$$

That is to say, $\alpha C + \alpha V$ equals the aggregate total capital in terms of money and αS gives the aggregate profit. Therefore $\pi = S/(C+V)$.

This view, too, is incompatible with Marx's other intention. In volume I he developed a one-sector analysis, but in volume III he wanted to construct a two- or three-departmental macroeconomic model, by aggregating all capital-good industries into one capital-good department, all wage-good industries into one wage-good department and all luxury-good industries into one luxury-good department. Disaggregation into wage and luxury-good departments is not essential, but Marx considered that the capital good department had to be distinguished from the wage-good department. This means that the aggregation condition is not satisfied between capital and wage-good industries.

As will be shown in chapter 8 below, the aggregation condition of Marx's model may be given in terms of the value composition of capital: If two industries have the same value composition of capital they can safely be aggregated into a larger sector. This implies that in constructing his two- or three-departmental model Marx tacitly assumed that all capital-good industries had the same value composition of capital, which was different from that of wage-good industries, which were also identical with each other in their value composition. Under this assumption p_I is proportional to Λ_I and p_{II} to Λ_{II} with different proportionality factors; accordingly it contradicts (25). Hence Marx would not accept the second escape route we have offered, although it is applicable to his analysis in volume I, where it is assumed that *all* industries are homogeneous in value structure.

The third justification for Marx's result has been proposed by Samuelson. He justifies Marx's formula of conversion of the rate of exploitation into the rate of profits by restricting the production processes and the market basket of goods so as to satisfy Samuelson's condition of equal internal compositions of capital. But this is an extremely special (and even odd) case which does not usually happen in the actual world, and moreover the condition is never satisfied in Marx's system, where wage goods are not directly used in the production of commodities and capital goods are not directly consumed by workers. Therefore Samuelson's proposal should also be rejected.

The resolution which I recommend here does not impose any stringent restriction on technology and worker's consumption. It only proposes to weight the constant and variable capitals of individual industries by the characteristic vectors y_I, y_{II}, instead of weighting the constant and variable industrial capitals by actual outputs. However, as long as we confine ourselves to the analysis of static equilibrium, there is no reason why commodities should be produced in the same proportion as y_I and y_{II}. Thus we are inclined to conclude at the outset that Marx would reject this resolution too; but it will later be seen that by reinterpreting y as the 'golden age' or von Neumann output vector, (24) is accepted as the relationship to be realized along the 'golden' equilibrium growth path. This means that the problem of justifying Marx's formula, $\pi = S/(C+V)$, can be solved only by coupling the system of value and price determination with the dynamic system of output determination. It may thus be worth emphasizing that the resolution of the problem requires a full recognition of the von Neumann duality between production and valuation. In view of the fact that since the von Neumann revolution the 'golden age' equilibrium prices and output proportions have often been used as the reference prices and output proportions,[15] it is not particularly surprising that Marx's formula can be fully rehabilitated in this way. Finally, it is added that irrespective of whether the 'golden age' is realized or not, (24) is always valid as a relationship for a hypothetical hybrid (or standardized) industry which produces all commodities in the von Neumann proportions.

The final paragraph is devoted to showing that wage-prices are greater than the corresponding values if all industries earn positive profits. It is easy to prove this. As every industry earns profits, we have

$$p_{\text{I},w} > p_{\text{I},w} A_{\text{I}} + L_{\text{I}},$$

so that

$$p_{\text{I},w} > L_{\text{I}}(I - A_{\text{I}})^{-1} = \Lambda_{\text{I}}$$

for capital-good industries because $(I - A_{\text{I}})^{-1} > 0$. Hence we have

$$p_{\text{II},w} > p_{\text{I},w} A_{\text{II}} + L_{\text{II}} > \Lambda_{\text{I}} A_{\text{II}} + L_{\text{II}} = \Lambda_{\text{II}}$$

for wage and luxury-good industries. It is noted that these inequalities hold even if rates of profit are not equalized since the equal rate of profit plays no part in the proof.

[15] See, for example, my *Theory of Economic Growth*. It is noted that Marx's production prices are no more than the 'golden age' equilibrium prices.

PART III

The Transformation Problem

CHAPTER 7

The static transformation problem

Marx's transformation problem consists of two subproblems: one is the problem of converting the rate of surplus value into the rate of profit, and the other the problem of converting the values of commodities into their production prices. The former was discussed in the last chapter, where it was seen that Marx's rather confusing formula – that the equilibrium rate of profit equals the surplus value divided by the value of constant and variable capitals – is always valid, with no restrictive assumptions, provided that the surplus value and the value of constant and variable capitals are evaluated in the equilibrium state of balanced growth. However, in this chapter, which is devoted to an examination of the second subproblem, we arrive at a completely different conclusion. We do not obtain the results which Marx derived by his peculiar algorithm of calculating production prices from values, even if we assume equilibrium balanced growth, unless an extra condition is satisfied. Although this additional condition required for the validity of Marx's algorithm is weaker than the traditional condition of equal value-compositions of capital and the condition of 'equal internal compositions of capital' newly proposed by Samuelson, it is still very restrictive, since it implies that industries are 'linearly dependent' (in the sense defined later) on each other. Therefore we must conclude that Marx's algorithm does not generally convert values into production prices correctly.

Before proceeding to a detailed examination of the transformation problem, let us first summarize Marx's conclusions. The following five conclusions are particularly important:

(i) 'the sum of the prices of production of all commodities produced in society – the totality of all branches of production – is equal to the sum of their values.' (III, pp. 159–60.)

(ii) 'It remains true, nevertheless, that the cost-price of a commodity is always smaller than its value.' (III, p. 165.)

THE STATIC TRANSFORMATION PROBLEM

(iii) 'Surplus-value and profit are identical from the standpoint of their mass.' (III. p. 167.)

(iv) 'Aside from possible differences in the periods of turnover, the price of production of the commodities would then equal their value only in spheres, in which the composition [of capital] would happen to be [the same].' (III, p. 163.)

(v) 'The value of the commodities produced by capital [of higher value composition] would, therefore, be smaller than their price of production, the price of production of the commodities [produced by capital of lower composition] smaller than their value.' (III, p. 164.)

From these, particularly from (iv) and (v), it is evident that Marx was aware that under a capitalist system of production the 'law of value' was not in force in its pure and simple form and that prices of commodities would deviate from their values. On the other hand, it is also clear from (i), (ii) and (iii) that he often confused an account in terms of values with the corresponding account in terms of price, in spite of the obvious fact that price and value are dimensionally different; the former is measured in terms of money or some other commodity taken as numeraire, the latter in terms of labour-time. Therefore a rigorous treatment of the transformation problem is possible only by normalizing prices so that they are dimensionally identical with values.

The problem of normalization is not difficult at all. If prices are measured in terms of labour they can be compared with values. The price of commodity i in terms of labour, denoted by $p_{i,w} = p_i/w$, expresses the amount of labour which can be obtained by offering a unit of commodity i, or the amount of labour which commodity i can command in exchange. Then the price $p_{i,w}$ and the value λ_i are both measured in terms of labour, so that propositions concerning their equality or inequality become meaningful. As has been seen in chapter 6, the price $p_{i,w}$ is greater than the value λ_i for any commodity i when all industries earn positive profits. It follows, therefore, that $p_{i,w} = \lambda_i, i = 1, ..., h$, if and only if the uniform rate of profit π is zero. On the other hand, it was also seen in chapter 6 that the uniform rate of profits π is zero if and only if the uniform rate of exploitation e is zero.

From these one might be inclined to conclude that the labour theory of value is only true in the trivial case of $e = \pi = 0$. In fact

Samuelson writes: 'I have not the space to deal with the defensive argument that volume I's labour theory is a (needed or unneeded?) simplifying first approximation... to my mind, the only legitimate first approximation would be that of Smith and Ricardo in which the labour theory is first introduced with zero surplus value or profits... but is then to be dropped as unrealistic. Volume I's first approximation of equal positive rates of surplus values, S_i/V_i, is not a simplifying assumption but rather – to the extent it contradicts equal profits rates $S_i/(V_i+C_i)$ – a complicating detour.'[1] However, this view of Samuelson's ignores Marx's intention of generalizing the classical labour theory of value. As will be made clearer at the end of this chapter, Marx extended it not primarily in order to verify the (exact or approximate) equality between prices and values, but to show how and why prices deviate from values under capitalist production; Marx was motivated by a desire to reveal the deceptiveness of capitalist accounting in terms of prices.

Thus the production prices of commodities in terms of labour are greater than the corresponding values, as long as the equilibrium rate of profit is positive. It is therefore impossible to have Marx's conclusions (i) and (iii), except in the trivial case where the rate of exploitation and the rate of profit are zero. They are meaningless unless we interpret them as asserting that the total outputs in terms of prices and the total profits are proportional to the total 'value' of outputs and the total surplus value. Similarly part I of volume III of *Capital*, where Marx was concerned with the case of profit and surplus value having the same numerical magnitude, should be interpreted as treating the case where the profits of all individual sectors are proportional to their surplus values.

Let us now show that profits and surplus values are proportional throughout the economy, if and only if all industries have the same value-composition of capital. Let C_i and V_i be the value of constant capital and the value of variable capital required for

---

[1] Samuelson, 'Wages and Interest', pp. 891–2. It must be pointed out again that Samuelson erroneously defines constant capital C_i, variable capital V_i and surplus value S_i in terms of prices, so that the uniform rate of profits contradicts the uniform rate of exploitation, unless very restricted conditions are satisfied. If he had defined C_i, V_i, S_i correctly in terms of values and had calculated the rate of profit from the price-determining equations, then equal exploitation rates would not contradict equal profit rates, as we have seen in chapter 6.

THE STATIC TRANSFORMATION PROBLEM 75

producing one unit of output of industry i, $i = 1, ..., m$, whilst the corresponding accounts in terms of prices are denoted by C_i^p and V_i^p. Evidently,

$$C_i = \sum_{j=1}^{n} \lambda_j a_{ji}, \quad V_i = \omega\left(\sum_{j=n+1}^{m} \lambda_j b_j\right) l_i, \\ C_i^p = \sum_{j=1}^{n} p_j a_{ji}, \quad V_i^p = \omega\left(\sum_{j=n+1}^{m} p_j b_j\right) l_i, \quad (1)$$

where a_{ji} and l_i represent material and labour-input coefficients, b_j the quantity of wage good j consumed by a worker per day, and ω the reciprocal of the working hours per day; it is noted that labour inputs are measured in terms of man-hours. Also, let S_i and Π_i be the surplus value and the profit per unit of output i respectively. Then the proposition we are now tackling may be stated as follows: $\Pi_1, ..., \Pi_m$ are proportional to $S_1, ..., S_m$, if and only if

$$\frac{C_1}{V_1} = \frac{C_2}{V_2} = ... = \frac{C_m}{V_m}. \quad (2)$$

First we show the necessity. We have

$$\lambda_i - (C_i + V_i) = S_i \quad (i = 1, ..., m), \quad (3)$$

$$p_i - (C_i^p + V_i^p) = \Pi_i \quad (i = 1, ..., m). \quad (4)$$

Since $S_i = \alpha \Pi_i$ (where α stands for the proportionality factor), we obtain, in view of the definitions of C_i, V_i, C_i^p and V_i^p,

$$(\Lambda - \alpha p)(I - M) = S - \alpha \Pi = 0, \quad (5)$$

where[2]

$$M = \begin{bmatrix} A_I & A_{II} \\ \omega B L_I & \omega B L_{II} \end{bmatrix}. \quad (6)$$

We can show that $I - M$ is not singular, because A_I is productive and exploitation is positive. Therefore (5) implies $\Lambda = \alpha p$; in other words prices are proportional to values. Then we obtain $C_i = \alpha C_i^p$ and $V_i = \alpha V_i^p$, $i = 1, ..., m$. We now have

$$\frac{\Pi_i}{C_i^p + V_i^p} = \frac{S_i}{C_i + V_i} = e\frac{V_i}{C_i + V_i} \quad (i = 1, ..., m), \quad (7)$$

---

[2] In the following, S, C, V denote m-dimensional vectors and should not be confused with the same symbols in the last chapter.

where e represents the rate of exploitation. As the rate of profit is equalized throughout the economy, the m ratios given by (7) are equal to each other, so that we obtain (2); that is to say, every industry must have an identical value composition of capital.

Next let us deal with the sufficiency. The equal value composition of capital (2) implies

$$e\frac{V_1}{C_1+V_1} = e\frac{V_2}{C_2+V_2} = \ldots = e\frac{V_m}{C_m+V_m}. \qquad (2')$$

Write this common ratio as π; then the value equation (3) can be written as

$$(1+\pi)(C_i+V_i) = \lambda_i \quad (i = 1,\ldots,m). \qquad (8)$$

As $C_i = \alpha C_i^p$ and $V_i = \alpha V_i^p$, $i = 1,\ldots,m$, for p fulfilling $\lambda = \alpha p$, (8) implies that the law of equal rates of profit holds at those prices which are taken so as to be proportional to values:

$$(1+\pi)(C_i^p+V_i^p) = p_i \quad (i = 1,\ldots,m); \qquad (9)$$

and we can prove the uniqueness of the equilibrium prices. Since $S_i = \pi(C_i+V_i)$ from (8) and $\Pi_i = \pi(C_i^p+V_i^p)$ from (9), we obtain $S_i = \alpha\Pi_i$, $i = 1,\ldots,m$, in view of $C_i = \alpha C_i^p$ and $V_i = \alpha V_i^p$; that is, profits are proportional to surplus values.

Now we turn to Marx's discussion in part II of volume III. He was concerned there with the transformation of values into prices under the assumption that the profits determined by the equilibrium price–cost equations are not proportional to the surplus values, so that the equations of the value-compositions of capital (2) are not assumed. In this case, as was seen in the last chapter, the prices are calculated by the following corrected Marxian algorithm: first outputs y_i, $i = 1,\ldots,m$, in the equilibrium state of balanced growth are calculated; then the total surplus value acquired in the equilibrium state, $\sum_{j=1}^{m} S_j y_j$, is divided by the corresponding total value of constant and variable capitals, $\sum_{j=1}^{m} (C_j+V_j) y_j$, to obtain the equilibrium rate of profit π; and finally the production prices are calculated by the formula:

$$q_i = (1+\pi)(C_i+V_i) \quad (i = 1,\ldots,m). \qquad (10)$$

These Marxian prices $q_1,\ldots,q_m$, however, may still deviate from the true equilibrium prices, $p_1,\ldots,p_m$, which are determined

THE STATIC TRANSFORMATION PROBLEM 77

by (9). In fact although the rate of profit in (10), which is given as $\pi = \Sigma S_j y_j / \Sigma (C_j + V_j) y_j$, equals the equilibrium rate of profit in (9) as we saw in the last chapter, $(C_i^p + V_i^p)$'s are not equal or proportional to $(C_i + V_i)$'s unless some additional conditions are satisfied, so that q_is are not equal or proportional to p_is. As was pointed out in the previous chapter, Marx knew this, so that he himself regarded his algorithm as the formula for obtaining first approximations to the true equilibrium production prices.[3] However there are some special cases where the first approximations give the true prices precisely.

It is clear from (8) and (10) that the Marxian prices equal values if all industries are identical in the value-composition of capital. In this case, they are also equal to the true equilibrium prices, since $q = \Lambda = (1 + \pi) \Lambda M$, because $C + V = \Lambda M$. Thus the equations (2) are sufficient (but not necessary) for the correctness of the Marxian algorithm. As the equations (2) are equivalent with[4]

$$\frac{C_i + V_i}{\Sigma(C_j + V_j) y_j} = \frac{S_i}{\Sigma S_j y_j} \quad (i = 1, ..., m), \quad (11)$$

the condition of identical value-composition of capital may be weakened into

$$\pi (C + V) M = SM \quad \text{or} \quad (\pi(C + V) - S) M = 0, \quad (12)$$

in view of $\pi = \Sigma S_j y_j / \Sigma (C_j + V_j) y_j$. (12) implies the singularity of M, i.e. $|M| = 0$,[5] but not vice versa.

Column i of the matrix M has capital-input coefficients $a_{1i}, ..., a_{ni}$ and labour-feeding input coefficients $\omega b_{n+1} l_i, ..., \omega b_m l_i$, of industry i as its components. The condition, $|M| = 0$, implies that one of the columns of M can be expressed as a linear

[3] It is noted that the matrix $(1 + \pi) M$ is a Markov matrix. The true production prices are ergodic solutions to the Markov-chain problem

$$p_t = p_{t-1}(1 + \pi) M.$$

Marx started the iteration process with the initial position $p_0 = \lambda$ and obtained the the first-round solution, $p_1 = q$. He stated that the iteration should be continued.

[4] Equations (11) at once follow from (2'), as $S_i = eV_i$.

[5] If $\pi(C + V) - S \neq 0$, then $|M| = 0$. If $\pi(C + V) - S = 0$, the value composition of capital is equated throughout the economy, so that $C = kV$, where k is a scalar. As $C = (\Lambda_I A_I, \Lambda_I A_{II})$ and $V = (\omega \Lambda_{II} B L_I, \omega \Lambda_{II} B L_{II})$, we have

$$C - kV = (\Lambda_I, -k\Lambda_{II}) M = 0;$$

hence $|M| = 0$, because $\Lambda_I \neq 0$ and $\Lambda_{II} \neq 0$. In any case we thus have $|M| = 0$ if (12) holds.

combination of the other columns. In spite of the fact that the singularity of M does not imply (12), the latter is, for the sake of convenience, referred to as the assumption of linearly dependent industries. It is seen that in the case of the economy having only two industries, the condition of linearly dependent industries is reduced to the traditional condition of the identical value composition of capital, while if the number of industries is greater than two, the former is weaker than the latter. It is also seen that Samuelson's singular case of equal internal compositions of capital which he proposed in order to justify Marx's algorithm (like the traditional case of identical value-composition of capital) is no more than a special case of the case of industries being linearly dependent. That is to say, if all industries have equal internal compositions of capital in Samuelson's sense, so that every column of M is proportional to every other, then industries are 'linearly independent';[6] but on the contrary, the linear independency (12) does not require Samuelson's condition. Thus the linear dependence of industries is weaker than Samuelson's condition of equal internal composition of capital, and we can show that though the condition (12) is still

---

[6] Samuelson, 'Understanding the Marxian Notion of Exploitation', p. 415. Whereas Marx assumed that capital goods and wage goods were distinct, Samuelson assumes that every good may be consumed by industries as well as workers. Samuelson then defines the case of equal internal compositions of capital as the case of $(a_{1i}, a_{2i}, \ldots, a_{mi})$, $i = 1, \ldots, m$, and $(b_1, b_2, \ldots, b_m)$ being proportional to the equilibrium balanced growth outputs $(y_1, y_2, \ldots, y_m)$, so that the matrix M (modified by Samuelson) can be written as $M = y(\alpha+\beta)$, where y is the column vector with elements y_i and α and β are m-dimensional non-negative row vectors. As π equals the equilibrium rate of balanced growth (by the von Neumann theorem), we have
$$y = (1+\pi)My = (1+\pi)y(\alpha+\beta)y,$$
so that $(\alpha+\beta)y = 1/(1+\pi)$. On the other hand, the value-determining equations may be written as
$$\Lambda = \Lambda M + S = \Lambda y(\alpha+\beta)+S.$$
Therefore, $\quad \Lambda M = \Lambda y(\alpha+\beta)y(\alpha+\beta)+SM = \dfrac{1}{1+\pi}\Lambda M+SM.$

Hence $\quad SM = \dfrac{\pi}{1+\pi}\Lambda M.$

Also we have
$$\pi(C+V)M = \pi\Lambda MM = \pi(\Lambda-S)M = \pi\left(\Lambda M - \dfrac{\pi}{1+\pi}\Lambda M\right) = \dfrac{\pi}{1+\pi}\Lambda M.$$
Therefore $\quad SM = \pi(C+V)M;$

that is to say, industries are linearly dependent.

restrictive, it is necessary and sufficient for the correctness of Marx's algorithm.[7]

We are now in a position to be able to examine Marx's main results, (i)–(v), concerning the conversion of accounts in terms of value into accounts in terms of prices. If labour is taken as numeraire (prices in terms of labour are the only prices which can be numerically compared with values), it is found that the first three conclusions of Marx are all wrong. First, as the price of commodity i in terms of labour, $p_{i,w}$, is greater than its value, λ_i, for all i, it is at once seen that the sum of the prices of production of all commodities is greater than the sum of their values. Secondly, the cost-price of commodity i, $\sum_{j=1}^{n} p_{j,w} a_{ji} + l_i$, is *greater* than its value $\lambda_i = \sum_{j=1}^{n} \lambda_j a_{ji} + l_i$ for the same reason; and similarly, the total profit that is the total price of the surplus outputs in terms of labour, is greater than their total value, i.e. the total surplus value. Unfortunately, it is evident that these three results all destroy the validity of Marx's (i), (ii) and (iii), stated earlier in this chapter.

This implies that Marx did not measure prices in terms of labour so as to compare them with values. Instead he normalized prices so that the costs of production could remain unaffected by the conversion of values into prices. Such a procedure is possible only under the assumption of linear dependence of industries (12). Then, as has been seen above, the equilibrium prices $p_1, \ldots, p_m$ are proportional to the $q_1, \ldots, q_m$ determined by Marx's algorithm, i.e. $p = \alpha q$. Therefore the cost-prices evaluated at p, $C^p + V^p$, are proportional to the cost-prices at q, $C^q + V^q$, so that $C^p + V^p = \alpha(C^q + V^q)$. Hence the equilibrium conditions (9) yield

$$q_i = (1+\pi)(C_i^q + V_i^q) \quad (i = 1, \ldots, m), \tag{13}$$

---

[7] *Necessity*. Substituting $q = (1+\pi)\Lambda M$ into $q = (1+\pi)qM$ and dividing by $(1+\pi)$, we obtain $\Lambda M = (1+\pi)\Lambda MM$. Hence

$$(C+V+S)M = (1+\pi)(C+V)M$$

because $\Lambda = C+V+S$ and $\Lambda M = C+V$. Therefore $SM = \pi(C+V)M$.

Sufficiency. From the last equation we obtain

$$\Lambda M = (1+\pi)\Lambda MM,$$

which may be written as $q = (1+\pi)qM$, where $q = (1+\pi)\Lambda M$.

and therefore we have

$$C_i^q + V_i^q = C_i + V_i \quad (i = 1, ..., m), \tag{14}$$

from (10). Thus we find that if the linear dependence of industries is assumed in order to normalize the equilibrium prices, so that they equal the prices calculated according to Marx's algorithm, q, then the cost of production of each commodity remains unchanged in spite of the transformation of values Λ into prices q.

Because
$$\pi = \sum_{j=1}^{m} S_j y_j \Big/ \sum_{j=1}^{m} (C_j + V_j) y_j,$$

we now have from (13) and (14)

$$\sum_{i=1}^{m} q_i y_i = \sum_{i=1}^{m} (C_i + V_i + S_i) y_i = \sum_{i=1}^{m} \lambda_i y_i, \tag{15}$$

which leads to a revised version of Marx's result (i); that is, the sum of the prices of outputs, *in terms of the Marxian prices q, in the equilibrium state of balanced growth* is equal to the sum of their values. Secondly, as $\lambda_i > C_i + V_i$, it immediately follows from (14) that the cost-price of a commodity *in terms of q* is always smaller than its value – this is no more than a revised version of Marx's (ii). Finally, from (14) and (15), we have at once

$$\sum_{i=1}^{m} \Pi_i^q y_i = \sum_{i=1}^{m} (q_i - C_i^q - V_i^q) y_i = \sum_{i=1}^{m} S_i y_i.$$

Therefore we obtain a revised version of (iii); that is, the total surplus equals the total profits *in terms of q, in the state of balanced growth*. Thus we find that Marx's results (i)–(iii), which are all negated when labour is taken as numeraire, are all rehabilitated, with some revisions, by taking q_i, $i = 1, ..., m$, as prices. However it must be remembered that this is possible only under the restrictive assumption that industries are 'linearly dependent'; otherwise the Marxian prices q would deviate from (i.e. would not be proportional to) the true equilibrium prices p and Marx's results would be nullified.

Next we examine Marx's results (iv) and (v). It can be shown that even if the assumption of linearly dependent industries is made, (iv) and (v) cannot be verified, so that some revisions of

THE STATIC TRANSFORMATION PROBLEM 81

them are inevitable. Assume that industries are linearly dependent. Let the average value composition of capital be defined as

$$\bar{k} = \sum_{i=1}^{m} C_i y_i \bigg/ \sum_{i=1}^{m} V_i y_i,$$

which is compared with the composition of capital of individual industry i, $k_i = C_i/V_i$. As

$$\pi = \frac{\Sigma S_i y_i}{\Sigma (C_i + V_i) y_i} = e \frac{\Sigma V_i y_i}{\Sigma (C_i + V_i) y_i} = e \frac{1}{\bar{k}+1},$$

we have from (10)

$$q_i = \left(1 + e \frac{1}{\bar{k}+1}\right)(C_i + V_i) = C_i + V_i + S_i \frac{k_i + 1}{\bar{k}+1}$$

because $S_i = eV_i$. Therefore we have revised Marxian rules:

(iv') The price of production of commodity i, q_i, equals its value, λ_i, only in the sphere in which the composition of capital happens to be equal to the average composition.

(v') The value of the commodities produced by capital of higher (or lower) value composition than the average is smaller (or larger) than their price of production.

These are not the only possible revisions of results (iv) and (v). They may alternatively be corrected, again under the assumption of linearly dependent industries, into other forms:

(iv") The prices of commodities are proportional to their values only in spheres in which the value composition of capital happens to be the same.

(v") The price of commodity i relative to that of commodity j, p_i/p_j ($= p_{i,w}/p_{j,w} = q_i/q_j$), is greater (or less) than the relative value of i to j, λ_i/λ_j, if commodity j is higher (or lower) than commodity i in the value-composition of capital.

In order to prove these propositions we divide equation (10) for industry i by the same equation for industry j. Considering the relationship $p_i = \beta q_i$ (where β stands for the proportionality factor) which we obtain under the assumption of linear dependence of industries, we get

$$\frac{p_i}{p_j} = \frac{q_i}{q_j} = \frac{C_i + V_i}{C_j + V_j} = \frac{(k_i + 1)V_i}{(k_j + 1)V_j}.$$

On the other hand, from the value-determining equation, $\lambda_i = C_i + V_i + S_i = (k_i + 1 + e) V_i$, $i = 1, \ldots, m$, we have

$$\frac{V_i}{V_j} = \frac{k_j + 1 + e}{k_i + 1 + e} \frac{\lambda_i}{\lambda_j}.$$

Hence,
$$\frac{p_i}{p_j} = \left[\frac{k_i + 1}{k_j + 1}\right] \left[\frac{k_j + 1 + e}{k_i + 1 + e}\right] \frac{\lambda_i}{\lambda_j}.$$

We can now see at once that $p_i/p_j = \lambda_i/\lambda_j$ if $k_i = k_j$. Bearing in mind that the rate of exploitation e is positive, we can also show that $p_i/p_j >$ (or $<$) λ_i/λ_j if $k_i >$ (or $<$) k_j. Therefore the revised Marxian results (iv″) and (v″) are established.

It has so far been seen, under the stringent assumption of linearly dependent industries, that Marx's algorithm for calculating equilibrium prices can be justified and that all of Marx's results (i)–(v) can be derived with some alterations. If this assumption is removed, then the Marxian prices $q_1, \ldots, q_m$ are no longer proportional to the true equilibrium prices, so that the results (i)–(v), or their revised versions, are not necessarily obtained. However, even though industries are *not* linearly dependent, the revised Marxian laws (iv″)–(v″) may still remain valid between the relative values and the true equilibrium relative prices of commodities.

This is seen as follows. Let us assume that any two industries classified as capital-good industries have the same value composition of capital, k_I, i.e.

$$\frac{C_1}{V_1} = \frac{C_2}{V_2} = \ldots = \frac{C_n}{V_n} = k_\mathrm{I}. \tag{16}$$

This condition will be seen in chapter 8 below to be a necessary and sufficient condition for aggregating n capital-good industries into one capital-good department. It is clear that it does not necessarily imply the linear dependence of industries if some of the wage-good industries are different from the capital-good industries in the value-composition of capital. We can establish (iv″) and (v″) on the assumption (16) in the following way.

Let us now put
$$p_{\mathrm{I},w} = \alpha_\mathrm{I} \Lambda_\mathrm{I}, \tag{17}$$
and consider whether (17) can be a solution to the price-determining equations of capital-good industries.

$$p_\mathrm{I} = (1 + \pi)(p_\mathrm{I} A_\mathrm{I} + w L_\mathrm{I}). \tag{18}$$

THE STATIC TRANSFORMATION PROBLEM   83

α_I is a scalar to be determined; if (17) is found to be a solution to (18), the equilibrium prices of capital goods in terms of labour are proportional to their values. Substituting for $p_{\mathrm{I},w}$ from (17), (18) may be written as

$$\alpha_\mathrm{I} \Lambda_\mathrm{I} = (1+\pi)(\alpha_\mathrm{I}\Lambda_\mathrm{I}A_\mathrm{I}+L_\mathrm{I}), \qquad (19)$$

which expresses n equations,

$$\alpha_\mathrm{I}\lambda_i = (1+\pi)(\alpha_\mathrm{I}C_i+l_i) \quad (i = 1, \ldots, n),$$

in matrix form. These n equations are, however, reduced to a single equation,

$$\alpha_\mathrm{I}\lambda_1 = (1+\pi)(\alpha_\mathrm{I}C_1+l_1), \qquad (20)$$

because[8]

$$\frac{\lambda_1}{l_1} = \frac{\lambda_2}{l_2} = \ldots = \frac{\lambda_n}{l_n} \quad \text{and} \quad \frac{C_1}{l_1} = \frac{C_2}{l_2} = \ldots = \frac{C_n}{l_n}, \qquad (21)$$

since the n capital-goods industries have the same value-composition of capital.

On the other hand, we have the value-determining equation

$$\lambda_1 = C_1+V_1+S_1, \qquad (22)$$

by which we can eliminate λ_1 from (20); we can write

$$\alpha_\mathrm{I} = \frac{1+\pi}{1-\pi C_1/l_1}, \qquad (23)$$

since $V_1+S_1 = l_1$. (20) and hence (19) hold for the α_I determined as (23); consequently (17) is a solution to the price-determining equations. We can show that $\pi C_1/l_1$ is less than one for all π not exceeding the maximum rate of profit $\bar{\pi}$ which is realized when the real wage rate is zero, and that α_I approaches one when π approaches zero. From (17) and (23) we find that the higher the rate of profit, the more the prices of capital goods will deviate from their values. We can also see that the relative prices of capital goods equal the corresponding relative values.

For non-capital (wage or luxury) good i, let $p_{i,w} = \alpha_i \lambda_i$; then its price-determining equation can be written as

$$\alpha_i \lambda_i = (1+\pi)(\alpha_\mathrm{I}C_i+l_i),$$

[8] Thus the equality of the value composition of capital throughout the capital good industries implies that these industries have the same productivity of labour λ_i/l_i and the same capital–labour ratio, C_i/l_i. The first set of equations of (21) follows from $\lambda_i = C_i+V_i+S_i$, $S_i/V_i = e$, $C_i/V_i = k_\mathrm{I}$, $V_i/l_i = \omega \Lambda_\mathrm{II} B$, $i = 1, \ldots, n$, whilst the second follows directly from $C_i/l_i = k_\mathrm{I}\omega\Lambda_\mathrm{II}B$.

from which we obtain, by taking its value-determining equation and (23) into account,

$$\alpha_i = \begin{cases} \dfrac{1+\pi}{\left(1+\dfrac{C_i}{l_i}\right)} + \dfrac{(1+\pi)^2 \dfrac{C_i}{l_i}}{\left(1-\pi\dfrac{C_1}{l_1}\right)\left(1+\dfrac{C_i}{l_i}\right)}, \\[2ex] \alpha_\mathrm{I} + \dfrac{\pi(1+\pi)\left(\dfrac{C_i}{l_i}-\dfrac{C_1}{l_1}\right)}{\left(1-\pi\dfrac{C_1}{l_1}\right)\left(1+\dfrac{C_i}{l_i}\right)}. \end{cases}$$

The first expression of α_i shows that α_i is an increasing function of π, to the effect that the deviation of the price of wage (or luxury) good i from its value becomes larger when the rate of profit rises. On the other hand, the second expression of α_i implies that $\alpha_i = \alpha_\mathrm{I}$ if and only if the value-composition of wage (or luxury) good i happens to coincide with that of the capital-good industries, i.e. $C_i/l_i = C_1/l_1$; while α_i is larger (or smaller) than α_I if i is higher (or lower) than the capital-good industries in the composition of capital. It can also be shown that we have

$$\alpha_i = \alpha_j + \dfrac{\pi(1+\pi)\left(1+\dfrac{C_1}{l_1}\right)\left(\dfrac{C_i}{l_i}-\dfrac{C_j}{l_j}\right)}{\left(1-\pi\dfrac{C_1}{l_1}\right)\left(1+\dfrac{C_i}{l_i}\right)\left(1+\dfrac{C_j}{l_j}\right)}$$

between two wage or luxury goods i and j; it follows that $\alpha_i \gtreqless \alpha_j$ according to $C_i/l_i \gtreqless C_j/l_j$. It is now clear that we have the revised Marxian rules of transformation (iv″) and (v″). These rules enable us to conclude that under capitalist production with $e > \pi > 0$, (*a*) it is impossible to obtain prices in terms of labour with no deviations from values and (*b*) it is nevertheless possible to obtain relative prices which are equal to relative values, if the commodities are produced by techniques or processes which are identical in the value-composition of capital.

We conclude our investigation of the transformation problem as follows. Many of Marx's propositions are found to be correct with some revisions and under some additional assumptions. But as these assumptions are rather restrictive, one might think that Marx was unsuccessful in solving the transformation problem. For example, Samuelson wrote: 'This mathematical fact [that prices of commodities will not be proportional to their values when there is exploitation] will not be of comfort to one looking for a labour theory of value as a base point for a theory of labour exploitation; the proportionality of market price to labour content applies validly only when surplus value is zero and not worth talking about!'[9] 'And even had Marx lived to write a fourth or fortieth volume of *Capital*, he could not have altered his arithmetic obstacle to the relevance of his labour theory of value.'[10] However, in the transformation problem Marx did not intend to establish a proportionality between values and prices but, on the contrary, to show that individual exploitation and individual profit are disproportional unless some restrictive conditions are imposed. We consider that Marx wanted to establish the following two positive and one negative propositions; the first is $e > \pi$, concerning the conversion of the rate of surplus value into the equilibrium rate of profit, the second $p_{i,w} > \lambda_i$, $i = 1, ..., m$, concerning the conversion of values into equilibrium prices in terms of labour, and the third $\Pi_i \neq \alpha S_i$, $i = 1, ..., m$, concerning the conversion of surplus values into profits. And we have seen in the previous chapter and in this chapter that the first two hold true without any reservation and any extra assumption, while the third is subject to only one exception, which is obtained when all industries are identical in the value-composition of capital.

Marx thought that he had successfully removed the mask of capitalism. He wrote: 'the rate of profit is from the very outset distinct from the rate of surplus value... But... this serves, also from the outset, to obscure and mystify the actual origin of surplus-value, since the rate of profit can rise or fall while the rate of surplus-value remains the same, and vice versa, and since the capitalist is in practice solely interested in the rate of profit.' (III, p. 167.) 'The transformation of values into [different] prices of production serves to obscure the basis for determining value itself.' (III, p. 168.) 'The individual capitalist (or all the capitalists in each individual sphere of production), whose outlook is limited, rightly believes that his profit is not derived solely from

---

[9] P. A. Samuelson, 'Wages and Interest: A Modern Dissection of Marxian Economic Models', *American Economic Review*, vol. XLVII, December 1957, p. 888.
[10] *Ibid.*, p. 888.

the labour employed by him, or in his line of production. This is quite true, as far as his average profit is concerned. To what extent this profit is due to the aggregate exploitation of labour on the part of the total social capital, i.e. by all his capitalist colleagues – this interrelation is a complete mystery to the individual capitalist; all the more so, since no bourgeois theorists, the political economists, have so far revealed it.' (III, p. 170.)

Thus it is clear that the transformation problem has the aim of showing how 'the aggregate exploitation of labour on the part of the total social capital' is, in a capitalist economy, obscured by the distortion of prices from values; the other aim is to show how living labour can be the sole source of profit. We may say that although Marx was often confused, he was very successful in the transformation problem, because his third conclusion, $\Pi_i \neq \alpha S_i$, which holds except in the trivial case of identical value composition of capital, implies a disproportionality between individual exploitation and individual profit, while the first, $e > \pi$, implies the necessity of aggregate exploitation of labour by capitalists for the existence of positive profit.

However it must be remembered that this victory of Marx was brought about by making the assumptions $(a)-(f)$, listed in chapter 1. It remains for us to remove these assumptions so as to examine whether Marx's conclusions are valid under more general conditions. We shall see in chapter 14 that some of the assumptions can safely be removed, while the removal of others is fatal.

CHAPTER 8

The aggregation problem

As we have seen, Marx was concerned with microeconomics when he discussed the problem of the determination of values and prices of commodities in volumes I and III of *Capital*. At the very beginning of volume I he wrote: 'The wealth of those societies in which the capitalist mode of production prevails, presents itself as "an immense accumulation of commodities", its unit being a single commodity. Our investigation must therefore begin with the analysis of a commodity.' (I, p. 35.)

On the other hand, in volume II, especially in part III where he was concerned with the problem of determination of outputs, a counterpart to the problem of determination of values or prices, he appeared as a macroeconomist and developed the famous two-sector model of 'reproduction and circulation of the aggregate social capital'. Marx began the description of his model by saying:

'The total product, and therefore the total production, of society may be divided into two major departments:

I. *Means of Production*, commodities having a form in which they must, or at least may, pass into productive consumption.

II. *Articles of Consumption*, commodities having a form in which they pass into the individual consumption of the capitalist and the working-class.

All the various branches of production pertaining to each of these two departments form one single great branch of production, that of the means of production in the one case, and that of articles of consumption in the other. The aggregate capital employed in each of these two branches of production constitutes a separate large department of the social capital.' (II, p. 399.)

However it is true that Marx did not discuss the problem of aggregating many primitive sectors (or 'branches of production' or industries) into two major departments, or the more general problem of reducing a microeconomic model consisting of many sectors to a quasi-macroeconomic model with a smaller number of sectors. There are basic questions concerning the relationships between disaggregated and aggregate systems. First, under what conditions do the results obtained from the disaggregated value-determining system coincide with the corresponding results from the aggregate value-determining system? (Or, if it is impossible to avoid errors due to aggregation, how can we minimize them?) Secondly, we may ask the same question concerning production prices and outputs; that is to say, under what conditions can an aggregation of the price-determining (or output-determining) system be correct, so that the prices (or outputs) determined by the aggregate system are not distorted from the true prices obtained from the disaggregated system? Thirdly, are the conditions for correct (or 'non-distorting') aggregation of values, production prices and outputs consistent or compatible with each other? Marx was concerned with none of these problems; in fact, he was not even aware of their existence. Nevertheless, it is clear that, in his analysis of the reproduction schemes, he aggregated the output-determining system in terms of values. It is also clear from the quotation below that Marx would not have supported Keynes in aggregating microeconomic variables, such as consumption of various commodities and industrial outputs in terms of wage-units, by using the ratios of their market prices to the wage rate as weights of aggregation. (However, it will be seen at the end of this chapter that there would be no significant differences between the Marxian and Keynesian methods of aggregation, if Keynes had taken the equilibrium production prices, instead of the market prices in terms of labour, as aggregators.) Marx wrote: 'Exchange-value... presents itself as... a relation constantly changing with time and place. Hence exchange-value appears to be something accidental and purely relative, and consequently an intrinsic value, i.e. an exchange-value that is inseparably connected with, inherent in commodities, seems a contradiction in terms.' (I, p. 36.) Thus Marx's view of aggregation is relatively clear, though not explicit.

Being distinguished from market prices in terms of labour, the values which Marx used as weights of aggregation remain unaltered, so that they are intrinsic to commodities as long as there are no changes in the methods of production adopted in society. In this chapter we examine Marxian aggregation in terms of values in relation to the problems stated above; that is to say, we clarify the conditions under which an aggregation of primitive sectors (industries) into hybrid sectors (departments) in terms of values does not give rise to any distortion; that is, the conditions under which the values, prices and outputs calculated from the aggregate value-determining, price-determining and output-determining equation systems coincide with the corresponding true ones, which are obtained by aggregating those determined by the original micro-systems. By doing so, we try to build a bridge between Marx's microscopic analysis of values and prices and his macroscopic analysis of the determination of outputs. We also compare Marx's aggregation with Keynes' in terms of wage-units, to see in what ways Marx's is more satisfactory than Keynes'. We shall see that Keynes' aggregate input coefficients will fluctuate when prices in terms of labour (or 'wage-prices') change, unless they are not mere market wage-prices but the equilibrium production prices, which are in a definite relationship to values; whereas Marx's aggregate input coefficients are not influenced by a change in prices and the wage-rate as long as it induces no change in the production techniques utilized and the Marxian conditions for non-distorting aggregation are satisfied. Thus values are more solid and firmly founded aggregators than market wage-prices; and this is the most important analytical rationale for the labour theory of value.

Let us begin by formulating (but not solving) the general problem of aggregating a model of many sectors into a model of fewer sectors. We consolidate m industries into r departments in the following way:

Industries		Department	
$1, 2, ..., n_1{}^*$	$\rightarrow$	1	
$n_2, n_2 + 1, ..., n_2{}^*$	$\rightarrow$	2	for capital goods,
$n_s, n_s + 1, ..., n$	$\rightarrow$	s	
$n+1, n+2, ..., n_{s+1}{}^*$	$\rightarrow$	$s+1$	
$n_{s+2}, n_{s+2} + 1, ..., n_{s+2}{}^*$	$\rightarrow$	$s+2$	for wage and luxury goods,
$n_r, n_r + 1, ..., m$	$\rightarrow$	r	

where $n_i{}^*$ is the numeral for the last industry of department i, which is less by one than n_{i+1}, the numeral for the first industry of department $i+1$. We have, at the level of the original m industries, the equations for value, price and output determination,

$$\left.\begin{array}{l}\Lambda_{\mathrm{I}} = \Lambda_{\mathrm{I}} A_{\mathrm{I}} + L_{\mathrm{I}}, \\ \Lambda_{\mathrm{II}} = \Lambda_{\mathrm{I}} A_{\mathrm{II}} + L_{\mathrm{II}}, \end{array}\right\} \quad (1)$$

$$\left.\begin{array}{l}p_{\mathrm{I}} = (1+\pi)(p_{\mathrm{I}} A_{\mathrm{I}} + wL_{\mathrm{I}}), \\ p_{\mathrm{II}} = (1+\pi)(p_{\mathrm{I}} A_{\mathrm{II}} + wL_{\mathrm{II}}), \end{array}\right\} \quad (2)$$

$$\bar{x}_{\mathrm{I}} = A_{\mathrm{I}} x_{\mathrm{I}} + A_{\mathrm{II}} x_{\mathrm{II}}, \quad (3)$$

respectively, where A_{I} is the $n \times n$ matrix of industrial capital-input coefficients of capital goods and L_{I} the n-dimensional row vector of industrial labour-input coefficients for capital goods; A_{II} and L_{II} are similarly defined as the $n \times (m-n)$ matrix of industrial capital-input coefficients and the $(m-n)$-dimensional row vector of industrial labour-input coefficients, both for wage and luxury goods, respectively; Λ_{I} and p_{I} are the vector of values and the vector of prices of capital goods respectively; Λ_{II} and p_{II} are the corresponding vectors of wage and luxury goods; π represents the rate of profit and w the wage rate per hour. Equation (3) expresses that the industrial demands for capital goods are equated with their supplies.[1] $\bar{x}_{\mathrm{I}}$ stands for the n-dimensional column vector of the industrial outputs of capital goods which have already been produced and are available in the economy; x_{I} is the n-dimensional column vector of the industrial outputs of capital goods which are going to be produced and x_{II} the $(m-n)$-dimensional column vector of the industrial outputs of wage and luxury goods to be produced. The industrial demands for capital goods by the capital-good industries amount to $A_{\mathrm{I}} x_{\mathrm{I}}$ and those of wage and luxury-good industries to $A_{\mathrm{II}} x_{\mathrm{II}}$. While we have already discussed the equations of value-determination (1) and the equations of price-determination (2) in the preceding chapters concerning Marx's labour theory of value, his theory of production prices and the transformation problem, the input–output equations (3) are the subject of Marx's theory of reproduction, which will be examined in chapter 9 below and subsequent chapters.

[1] It is noted that the demand–supply equations for wage and luxury goods are missing in (3). Aggregation of them will be discussed in the next chapter for the simplest case of aggregating $m-n$ wage and luxury goods into one commodity.

After the aggregation of m industries into r departments we also have three sets of equations for value, price and output determination, which are the departmental counterparts of equations (1), (2) and (3) respectively. Let H_I be the matrix of departmental capital-input coefficients for capital goods, that is, of s by s; H_II the matrix of departmental capital-input coefficients for wage and luxury goods, that is, of s by $r-s$; M_I the s-dimensional vector of departmental labour-input coefficients for capital goods, and M_II the $(r-s)$-dimensional vector of departmental labour-input coefficients for wage and luxury goods. We may then write the departmental equations as

$$\left.\begin{array}{l}\Phi_\mathrm{I} = \Phi_\mathrm{I} H_\mathrm{I} + M_\mathrm{I}, \\ \Phi_\mathrm{II} = \Phi_\mathrm{I} H_\mathrm{II} + M_\mathrm{II},\end{array}\right\} \quad (4)$$

$$\left.\begin{array}{l}q_\mathrm{I} = (1+\pi)(q_\mathrm{I} H_\mathrm{I} + w M_\mathrm{I}), \\ q_\mathrm{II} = (1+\pi)(q_\mathrm{I} H_\mathrm{II} + w M_\mathrm{II}),\end{array}\right\} \quad (5)$$

$$\bar{y}_\mathrm{I} = H_\mathrm{I} y_\mathrm{I} + H_\mathrm{II} y_\mathrm{II}. \quad (6)$$

The aggregate value-determining equations (4) determine the departmental value vectors, $\Phi_\mathrm{I} = (\phi_1, ..., \phi_s)$ of capital goods and $\Phi_\mathrm{II} = (\phi_{s+1}, ..., \phi_r)$ of wage and luxury goods; the aggregate price-determining equations (5) determine the departmental price vectors,

$$q_\mathrm{I} = (q_1, ..., q_s)$$

of capital goods and

$$q_\mathrm{II} = (q_{s+1}, ..., q_r)$$

of wage and luxury goods;[2] and finally the aggregate input–output equations (6) determine the departmental output vector y_I of capital goods, provided that the departmental availability of capital goods $\bar{y}_\mathrm{I}$ (an s-dimensional column vector) and the departmental outputs of wage and luxury goods y_II (an $(r-s)$-dimensional column vector) are given.

We may now state our problems precisely: (i) Under what conditions are the values of the departmental outputs calculated by means of the aggregate valuation system (4) equal to the true

---

[2] The prices q_t should not be confused with the prices q in the last chapter, which are the prices of the individual commodities calculated according to Marx's transformation algorithm.

values obtained by aggregating the values of elementary commodities, determined by (1), according to the composition of departmental outputs? (ii) Under what conditions does the departmental price system (5) give, *for all possible values of the rate of profit π specified*, the same prices q_I and q_II as the true prices of departmental outputs obtained by aggregating the prices of elementary commodities, determined by the disaggregated price system (2), into departmental prices according to the composition of departmental outputs? (iii) Under what conditions does the departmental input–output system (6) give, *for all possible availability vectors of capital goods $\bar{x}_\mathrm{I}$ and output vectors of wage and luxury goods x_II specified*, the correct departmental outputs obtained from the basic industrial input–output equations (3)? Finally, (iv) are the conditions for non-distorting aggregation which are found in regard to the above three questions consistent with each other?

In the aggregation, one unit of output of department i is so constituted that it contains δ_{n_i} units of output of industry n_i, δ_{n_i+1} units of output of industry $n_i + 1$, and so on up to $\delta_{n_i^*}$ units of output of industry n_i^*, for each $i = 1, ..., r$; values of commodities per unit of output are utilized as weights of aggregation. We then find, first of all, that with no special conditions on technological coefficients, $A_\mathrm{I}, A_\mathrm{II}, L_\mathrm{I}$ and L_II, and independently of the intradepartmental composition of industries, the values of departmental outputs Φ_I and Φ_II determined by the aggregate system are always equal to the true values of departmental outputs, which are given as

$$\lambda_{n_i}\delta_{n_i} + \lambda_{n_i+1}\delta_{n_i+1} + ... + \lambda_{n_i^*}\delta_{n_i^*} \quad (i = 1, ..., r),$$

so that no conditions are required for the non-distorting aggregation of the value equations. We also find that the prices of outputs of industries which belong to the same department are proportional to their values if those industries which are blockwise identical in the value composition of capital are aggregated into one department. It is, moreover, seen that aggregation according to the same criterion does not give rise to any distortion in the determination of departmental outputs; that is to say, the aggregate input–output system (6) with $\bar{y}_i = \lambda_{n_i}\bar{x}_{n_i} + ... + \lambda_{n_i^*}\bar{x}_{n_i^*}$ for all capital-good departments, $i = 1, ..., s$, and

$$y_j = \lambda_{n_j}x_{n_j} + ... + \lambda_{n_j^*}x_{n_j^*}$$

THE AGGREGATION PROBLEM 93

for all wage and luxury-good departments, $j = s+1, ..., n$ yields departmental outputs of capital goods which are exactly equal to the true values,

$$\lambda_{n_i} x_{n_i} + ... + \lambda_{n_i^*} x_{n_i^*} \quad (i = 1, ..., s),$$

where x_ks are the industrial outputs determined by the industrial input–output equations (3), provided that industries are classified into departments so that those in each department have the same value-composition of capital. It is therefore found that the blockwise (or department-wise) identity of the value-composition of capital is the common condition under which we have no distortion in the aggregation of values, prices and quantities of outputs.

Obviously Marx knew none of these conditions for non-distorting aggregation, but we may say that he was near to finding them. As evidence we may quote the following sentence from volume III again: 'Aside from possible differences in the periods of turnover, the price of production of the commodities would then [be proportional to] their value only in spheres, in which the composition [of capital] would have to be [the same].' (III, p. 163.) It is evident that if the prices of outputs of some industries are always proportional to their values, these industries can safely be aggregated into one department in terms of values, and that the prices of individual commodities are obtained by multiplying their values by the corresponding proportionality factors, which are determined, as prices of departmental outputs of unit values, by the aggregate price-determining equations.

The rest of this chapter is devoted to establishing these aggregation rules. We first concentrate our attention on the case Marx dealt with, i.e. the simplest case of aggregating all capital good industries into one department and all wage and luxury-good industries into another department. The resulting two-department equations, particularly those of output-determination, are the subject of volume II, part III, so that the following argument would build a bridge between the microeconomic analysis of values and prices in volumes I and III on the one hand, and the macroeconomics of reproduction and accumulation in volume II on the other.

Let us consider two kinds of composite commodities, which are referred to as commodities I and II; one unit of commodity I contains δ_1 units of capital good 1, δ_2 units of capital good 2, ..., and δ_n units of capital good n, while one unit of commodity II consists of δ_{n+1} units of wage or luxury good $n+1$, ..., and δ_m units of wage or luxury-good m. We define column vectors

$$\Delta_I = \begin{bmatrix} \delta_1 \\ \vdots \\ \delta_n \end{bmatrix} \quad \text{and} \quad \Delta_{II} = \begin{bmatrix} \delta_{n+1} \\ \vdots \\ \delta_m \end{bmatrix}.$$

Obviously, the true values of the composite commodities are calculated according to the formulas:

$$\lambda_I = \Lambda_I \Delta_{II} \quad \text{and} \quad \lambda_{II} = \Lambda_{II} \Delta_{II}. \tag{7}$$

The total value of capital goods required per unit of commodity I amounts to $\Lambda_I A_I \Delta_I$, which is equivalent to

$$h_I = \Lambda_I A_I \Delta_I / \Lambda_I \Delta_I \tag{8}$$

units of commodity I in value. Similarly, the capital goods required for producing one unit of commodity II are equivalent to

$$h_{II} = \Lambda_I A_{II} \Delta_{II} / \Lambda_I \Delta_I \tag{9}$$

units of commodity I in value. Production of commodities I and II requires, per unit of output, direct labour of the amounts

$$m_I = L_I \Delta_I \quad \text{and} \quad m_{II} = L_{II} \Delta_{II} \tag{10}$$

respectively.

As h_I and h_{II} may be considered as capital-input coefficients and m_I and m_{II} as labour-input coefficients with regard to composite commodities I and II, we may consider the following formal aggregate value-determining equations:

$$\left.\begin{aligned} \phi_I &= \phi_I h_I + m_I, \\ \phi_{II} &= \phi_I h_{II} + m_{II}, \end{aligned}\right\} \tag{11}$$

on the basis of which we may calculate the value of commodity I at ϕ_I and the value of commodity II at ϕ_{II}. The question (i) stated above asks under what condition ϕ_I and ϕ_{II} are equal to the true values, λ_I and λ_{II}, respectively.

It is easy to answer this question. From the microeconomic value-determining equations we have

$$\Lambda_I \Delta_I = \Lambda_I A_I \Delta_I + L_I \Delta_I,$$
$$\Lambda_{II} \Delta_{II} = \Lambda_I A_{II} \Delta_{II} + L_{II} \Delta_{II}.$$

Considering the definitions of the coefficients (8), (9), (10), these equations can be written

$$\begin{aligned}\Lambda_I \Delta_I &= \Lambda_I \Delta_I h_I + m_I, \\ \Lambda_{II} \Delta_{II} &= \Lambda_I \Delta_I h_{II} + m_{II}.\end{aligned} \quad (12)$$

Comparing these with (11), we at once find that $\phi_I = \Lambda_I \Delta_I$ and $\phi_{II} = \Lambda_{II} \Delta_{II}$; that is to say, without any additional condition, the aggregate value equations determine the values of composite commodities correctly.

Next we turn to question (ii), concerning the production prices of composite commodities. We confine ourselves here to showing that the aggregation into two departments I and II brings forth no distortion of the prices of composite commodities obtained from the aggregate price-determining equations from their true prices, if all capital-good industries form a group of industries, within which the value-composition of capital is equalized from industry to industry. The fact that this condition is also necessary for non-distorting aggregation into the two departments is not discussed here; it is merely noted that it is a corollary of the general necessary and sufficient conditions for non-distorting aggregation of m industries into r departments, which will be discussed later in this chapter.

Let us write constant capital and variable capital per unit of good j as

$$C_j = \sum_{i=1}^{n} \lambda_i a_{ij} \quad \text{and} \quad V_j = (\omega \Lambda_{II} B) l_j,$$

and assume that all capital-good industries have an identical value-composition of capital, k_I, which may be different from the value-compositions of capital of the wage or luxury-good industries. Note that at this stage of the discussion wage and luxury-good industries may be different from each other in the value-composition of capital, though it is shown later that their identity is required for the non-distorting aggregation of the input–output equations of wage and luxury-good industries into one departmental equation. Thus we have

$$\frac{C_1}{V_1} = \frac{C_2}{V_2} = \ldots = \frac{C_n}{V_n} = k_I. \quad (13)$$

Then, as was seen in the last chapter, values and prices are

proportional to each other within the capital-good department, that is
$$p_j = \alpha_{\mathrm{I}} \lambda_j \quad (j = 1, ..., n). \tag{14}$$
Therefore, we have, in view of definition (8),
$$p_{\mathrm{I}} A_{\mathrm{I}} \Delta_{\mathrm{I}} = \alpha_{\mathrm{I}} \Lambda_{\mathrm{I}} A_{\mathrm{I}} \Delta_{\mathrm{I}} = p_{\mathrm{I}} \Delta_{\mathrm{I}} h_{\mathrm{I}}. \tag{15}$$
Similarly, from (9)
$$p_{\mathrm{I}} A_{\mathrm{II}} \Delta_{\mathrm{II}} = p_{\mathrm{I}} \Delta_{\mathrm{I}} h_{\mathrm{II}}. \tag{16}$$
We now postmultiply the two sets of industrial price–cost equations (2) by Δ_{I} and Δ_{II} respectively; taking (15) and (16) into account, we then have
$$\left.\begin{aligned} p_{\mathrm{I}} \Delta_{\mathrm{I}} &= (1 + \pi)(p_{\mathrm{I}} A_{\mathrm{I}} \Delta_{\mathrm{I}} + w L_{\mathrm{I}} \Delta_{\mathrm{I}}) \\ &= (1 + \pi)(p_{\mathrm{I}} \Delta_{\mathrm{I}} h_{\mathrm{I}} + w m_{\mathrm{I}}), \\ p_{\mathrm{II}} \Delta_{\mathrm{II}} &= (1 + \pi)(p_{\mathrm{I}} A_{\mathrm{II}} \Delta_{\mathrm{II}} + w L_{\mathrm{II}} \Delta_{\mathrm{II}}) \\ &= (1 + \pi)(p_{\mathrm{I}} \Delta_{\mathrm{I}} h_{\mathrm{II}} + w m_{\mathrm{II}}), \end{aligned}\right\} \tag{17}$$
which are no more than the two-departmental price–cost equations. Thus, in the case where all capital-good industries are identical in the value-composition of capital, it is seen that $p_{\mathrm{I}} \Delta_{\mathrm{I}}$ and $p_{\mathrm{II}} \Delta_{\mathrm{II}}$ are the solutions, q_{I} and q_{II}, to the departmental price–cost equations.[3] That is to say, the aggregation into the two departments is accurate and the prices of the departmental outputs are correctly calculated on the basis of the aggregate equation system, with no distortions.

Concerning question (iii), let us introduce an additional assumption that wage and luxury-good industries form another group of industries, as they are identical with each other in the value-composition of capital, i.e.
$$\frac{C_{n+1}}{V_{n+1}} = \frac{C_{n+2}}{V_{n+2}} = \cdots = \frac{C_m}{V_m} = k_{\mathrm{II}}. \tag{13$'$}$$
As equations (21) in the last chapter show, values λ_j and constant capitals C_j are proportional to each other within each of the two groups of commodities, if all industries belonging to the same group are identical in the value-composition of capital; that is, assumptions (13) and (13$'$) imply
$$\left.\begin{aligned} C_j &= \beta_{\mathrm{I}} \lambda_j \quad (j = 1, ..., n), \\ C_j &= \beta_{\mathrm{II}} \lambda_j \quad (j = n+1, ..., m). \end{aligned}\right\} \tag{18}$$

[3] We may normalize the units of departmental outputs so that $\Lambda_{\mathrm{I}} \Delta_{\mathrm{I}} = 1$ and $\Lambda_{\mathrm{II}} \Delta_{\mathrm{II}} = 1$. Then $\alpha_{\mathrm{I}} = p_{\mathrm{I}} \Lambda_{\mathrm{I}} = q_{\mathrm{I}}$ and $\alpha_{\mathrm{II}} = p_{\mathrm{II}} \Lambda_{\mathrm{II}} = q_{\mathrm{II}}$.

It is then obvious that $\Lambda_I A_I x_I / \Lambda_I x_I$ and $\Lambda_I A_{II} x_{II} / \Lambda_{II} x_{II}$ are independent of x_I and x_{II} respectively, so that

$$\frac{\Lambda_I A_I x_I}{\Lambda_I x_I} = \frac{\Lambda_I A_I \Delta_I}{\Lambda_I \Delta_I} = \beta_I$$

and

$$\frac{\Lambda_I A_{II} x_{II}}{\Lambda_{II} x_{II}} = \frac{\Lambda_I A_{II} \Delta_{II}}{\Lambda_{II} \Delta_{II}} = \beta_{II}.$$

In view of the definition of (8) and (9) we at once find that $\beta_I = h_I$ and $\beta_{II} = h_{II} \Lambda_I \Delta_I / \Lambda_{II} \Delta_{II}$.[4]

Now, by aggregating the industrial input–output equations (3) in terms of value, we obtain

$$\Lambda_I \bar{x}_I = \Lambda_I A_I x_I + \Lambda_I A_{II} x_{II}$$

$$= \frac{\Lambda_I A_I x_I}{\Lambda_I x_I} \Lambda_I x_I + \frac{\Lambda_I A_{II} x_{II}}{\Lambda_{II} x_{II}} \Lambda_{II} x_{II}$$

$$= h_I \Lambda_I x_I + h_{II} \frac{\Lambda_I \Delta_I}{\Lambda_{II} \Delta_{II}} \Lambda_{II} x_{II}.$$

Hence

$$\frac{\Lambda_I \bar{x}_I}{\Lambda_I \Delta_I} = h_I \frac{\Lambda_I x_I}{\Lambda_I \Delta_I} + h_{II} \frac{\Lambda_{II} x_{II}}{\Lambda_{II} \Delta_{II}}, \qquad (19)$$

where $\Lambda_I x_I / \Lambda_I \Delta_I$ may be taken as the quantity index of output of department I, since its outputs are measured in terms of the composite commodity which consists of δ_1 units of commodity 1, ..., and δ_n units of commodity n, so that outputs x_I are equivalent in terms of value, to $\Lambda_I x_I / \Lambda_I \Delta_I$ units of the composite commodity. Comparing (19) with the aggregate input–output equations,

$$\bar{y}_I = h_I y_I + h_{II} y_{II}, \qquad (20)$$

we find that the aggregation gives rise to no error in calculating the output y_I of department I; that is y_I from (20) equals the true output $\Lambda_I x_I / \Lambda_I \Delta_I$, provided that

$$\bar{y}_I = \Lambda_I \bar{x}_I / \Lambda_I \Delta_I \quad \text{and} \quad y_{II} = \Lambda_{II} x_{II} / \Lambda_{II} \Delta_{II}.$$

The above investigation makes it clear that industries may be aggregated, as a first approximation, with respect to prices and outputs as well as values, into two major departments, if we may ignore the differences in the value composition of capital among

---

[4] If we set $\Lambda_I \Delta_I$ and $\Lambda_{II} \Delta_{II}$ at one, then $\beta_I = h_I$ and $\beta_{II} = h_{II}$. β_I and β_{II} are denoted as c_I and c_{II}, respectively, in chapter 9 and the subsequent.

capital-good industries and among wage and luxury-good industries. Marx did not known this rule of aggregation, but by virtue of it he could be considered a two-sector macroeconomist in his output theory as well as a microeconomist in his value theory. (As he observed in volumes II and III a difference in the value-composition of capital between the capital-good and the wage and luxury-good industries, he could not agree to one-sector economists aggregating all industries into one giant national firm, although he was concerned with a one-sector model in the later part of volume I.[5]) However, it is obvious that the conditions (13) and (13′) for the two departmental aggregation are very stringent; in the following, therefore, we are concerned with more general conditions for aggregating m industries into several, say r, departments, which are still given in terms of the Marxian concept of the value-composition of capital.

For the sake of simplicity, let us confine ourselves to the aggregation of capital-good industries; the same result *mutatis mutandis* is derived for wage and luxury-good industries as well. Let E be an $s \times n$ matrix whose ith row consists of $n_{i-1}{}^*$ zeros followed by $n_i{}^* - n_{i-1}{}^*$ unities and then $n - n_i{}^*$ zeros, where $n_i{}^*$ is the numeral for the last industry of department i; then

$$E = \begin{bmatrix} 1 & \ldots & 1 & 0 & \ldots & 0 & \ldots & 0 & \ldots & 0 \\ 0 & \ldots & 0 & 1 & \ldots & 1 & \ldots & 0 & \ldots & 0 \\ \vdots & & \vdots & \vdots & & \vdots & & \vdots & & \vdots \\ 0 & \ldots & 0 & 0 & \ldots & 0 & \ldots & 1 & \ldots & 1 \end{bmatrix}.$$

Let $\hat{\Lambda}_I$ denote the diagonal matrix whose diagonal elements are $\lambda_1, \lambda_2, \ldots, \lambda_n$, and U the r-dimensional row vector with elements which are all unities. We can then easily verify the following formulas:

$$E\hat{\Lambda}_I = \begin{bmatrix} \lambda_1 & \ldots & \lambda_{n_1{}^*} & 0 & \ldots & 0 & \ldots & 0 & \ldots & 0 \\ 0 & \ldots & 0 & \lambda_{n_2} & \ldots & \lambda_{n_2{}^*} & \ldots & 0 & \ldots & 0 \\ \vdots & & \vdots & \vdots & & \vdots & & \vdots & & \vdots \\ 0 & \ldots & 0 & 0 & \ldots & 0 & \ldots & \lambda_{n_s} & \ldots & \lambda_n \end{bmatrix}, \quad (21)$$

$$\Lambda_I = UE\hat{\Lambda}_I. \quad (22)$$

Next, we suppose that one unit of output of department f is so constituted that it contains δ_{n_f} units of the n_fth capital good,

[5] Marx's one-sector model has been developed, for example, by L. R. Klein, 'Theories of Effective Demand and Employment', *Journal of Political Economy*, April, 1947, pp. 108–31.

THE AGGREGATION PROBLEM

δ_{n_f+1} units of the (n_f+1)th capital good, ..., and $\delta_{n_f^*}$ units of the n_f^*th capital good; then the value of output of department f, per unit of output, amounts to

$$\theta_f = \lambda_{n_f}\delta_{n_f} + \ldots + \lambda_{n_f^*}\delta_{n_f^*} = \sum_{i \in f} \lambda_i \delta_i. \qquad (23)$$

By defining Δ' as

$$\Delta' = \begin{bmatrix} \delta_1 & \ldots & \delta_{n_1^*} & 0 & \ldots & 0 & \ldots & 0 & \ldots & 0 \\ 0 & \ldots & 0 & \delta_{n_2} & \ldots & \delta_{n_2^*} & \ldots & 0 & \ldots & 0 \\ \vdots & & \vdots & \vdots & & \vdots & & \vdots & & \vdots \\ 0 & \ldots & 0 & 0 & \ldots & 0 & \ldots & \delta_{n_s} & \ldots & \delta_n \end{bmatrix},$$

and the transposition of Δ' as Δ as usual, we obtain

$$E\hat{\Lambda}_I \Delta = \hat{\theta}_I \quad \text{or} \quad E\hat{\Lambda}_I \Delta \hat{\theta}_I^{-1} = I \quad \text{or} \quad \hat{\theta}_I^{-1} E\hat{\Lambda}_I \Delta = I, \quad (24)$$

where $\hat{\theta}_I$ is the diagonal matrix with $\theta_1, \theta_2, \ldots, \theta_s$ on the diagonal.

Let us first examine the aggregation concerning outputs. Premultiply the industrial input–output equations (3) by $E\hat{\Lambda}_I$; then

$$E\hat{\Lambda}_I \bar{x}_I = E\hat{\Lambda}_I A_I x_I + E\hat{\Lambda}_I A_{II} x_{II}, \qquad (25)$$

which is compared with the departmental input–output equation,

$$\bar{y}_I = H_I y_I + H_{II} y_{II}. \qquad (26)$$

As in the previous case of the aggregation into two departments, the aggregate output vectors, y_I and y_{II}, are measured in terms of the composite commodities, so that their elements are equal to

$$\sum_{i \in f} \lambda_i x_i / \sum_{i \in f} \lambda_i \delta_i \quad (f = 1, \ldots, s),$$

if there are no aggregation errors; similarly, the elements of $\bar{y}_I$ are the ratios of $\sum_{i \in f} \lambda_i \bar{x}_i$ to $\sum_{i \in f} \lambda_i \delta_i, f = 1, \ldots, s$. Therefore, in view of the definition of θ_f, (23), we find that $\hat{\theta}_I \bar{y}_I$ and $\hat{\theta}_I y_I$ are comparable with $E\hat{\Lambda}_I \bar{x}_I$ and $E\hat{\Lambda}_I x_I$ respectively. Similarly $\hat{\theta}_I H_{II} y_{II}$ is comparable with $E\hat{\Lambda}_I A_{II} x_{II}$.

We may now ask what are the necessary and sufficient conditions for $\hat{\theta}_I y_I$, calculated from the aggregate system (26), to be identical, for all possible $\bar{x}_I$ and x_{II} specified, with $E\hat{\Lambda}_I x_I$, obtained from the input–output system (3) at the industrial level, provided that there are no errors in aggregating $\bar{x}_I$ and $A_{II} x_{II}$, that is,

$$\hat{\theta}_I \bar{y}_I = E\hat{\Lambda}_I \bar{x}_I \quad \text{and} \quad \hat{\theta}_I \bar{H}_{II} y_{II} = E\hat{\Lambda}_I A_{II} x_{II}. \qquad (27)$$

As (27) is assumed, (25), together with (26) multiplied by $\hat{\theta}_I$, yields
$$\hat{\theta}_I H_I y_I = E\hat{\Lambda}_I A_I x_I,$$
so that
$$\hat{\theta}_I H_I \hat{\theta}_I^{-1} E\hat{\Lambda}_I x_I = E\hat{\Lambda}_I A_I x_I, \tag{28}$$
if the aggregation is accurate with respect to y_I. Equation (28) must hold for all $\bar{x}_I$ and x_{II} and hence for all x_I; so we obtain
$$\hat{\theta}_I H_I \hat{\theta}_I^{-1} E\hat{\Lambda}_I = E\hat{\Lambda}_I A_I \tag{29}$$
as the necessary condition which may be written as
$$H_I \hat{\theta}_I^{-1} E\hat{\Lambda}_I = \hat{\theta}_I^{-1} E\hat{\Lambda}_I A_I. \tag{30}$$

It is also easy to show that (29) is sufficient for accurate aggregation concerning y_I.

Next, we turn to the aggregation of the price-determining system. Let us define $M_I = L_I \Delta$. Then we can show that solutions q_I to
$$q_I = (1+\pi)(q_I H_I + w M_I) \tag{31}$$
satisfy
$$q_I = p_I \Delta \tag{32}$$
if the aggregation condition (29) for outputs is satisfied. To prove this, we first write the value-determining equations as
$$UE\hat{\Lambda}_I = UE\hat{\Lambda}_I A_I + L_I \tag{33}$$
since we have (22). This is further re-written as
$$UE\hat{\Lambda}_I = U\hat{\theta}_I H_I \hat{\theta}_I^{-1} E\hat{\Lambda}_I + L_I$$
from (29). Hence,
$$L_I = U(I - \hat{\theta}_I H_I \hat{\theta}_I^{-1}) E\hat{\Lambda}_I. \tag{34}$$
By definition,
$$M_I = L_I \Delta = U(\hat{\theta}_I - \hat{\theta}_I H_I)$$
from (24). Substituting this into (31), we have
$$q_I = (1+\pi)[q_I \hat{\theta}_I^{-1} \hat{\theta}_I H_I + wU(\hat{\theta}_I - \hat{\theta}_I H_I)].$$
Postmultiply this by $\hat{\theta}_I^{-1} E\hat{\Lambda}_I$ and considering (29) and (34) again, we finally obtain
$$q_I \hat{\theta}_I^{-1} E\hat{\Lambda}_I = (1+\pi)(q_I \hat{\theta}_I^{-1} E\hat{\Lambda}_I A_I + wL_I),$$
which is no more than the industrial price-determining equation for capital goods; therefore,
$$p_I = q_I \hat{\theta}_I^{-1} E\hat{\Lambda}_I. \tag{35}$$

Hence, $p_\text{I}\Delta = q_\text{I}$ because of (24). Thus, if the aggregation of the input–output system of capital goods is non-distorting, then so is the aggregation of the price-determining system. As for the value-determining system, as has been seen in the case of aggregation into two departments, aggregation is always non-distorting without any additional condition; so that we may now conclude that the condition (29) is necessary and sufficient for the entire system, consisting of value, price and output determining systems of n capital-good industries, to be aggregated accurately into a smaller system of s capital-good departments.

The above argument holds *mutatis mutandis* for wage and luxury goods. The necessary and sufficient condition for consistent, non-distorting aggregation of wage and luxury goods is found to be exactly parallel to (29). It is seen that these conditions are extensions of the Marxian condition for two-departmental aggregation in terms of the value-composition of capital. To show this, we partition the matrix of capital-input coefficients of the original, primitive industries into the $s \times s$ departmental blocks:

$$A_\text{I} = \begin{bmatrix} A_{11} & A_{12} & \cdots & A_{1s} \\ A_{21} & A_{22} & \cdots & A_{2s} \\ \vdots & \vdots & & \vdots \\ A_{s1} & A_{s2} & \cdots & A_{ss} \end{bmatrix}.$$

Bearing (21) in mind, we see that the (f, j) element of matrix $E\hat{\Lambda}_\text{I} A_\text{I}$ represents the total value of those capital goods classified as belonging to department f which are required per unit of primitive industry j. Dividing it by the labour-input coefficient of industry j, we obtain the capital–labour ratio of industry j (in terms of value) with respect to the capital goods produced by department f. This is further divided by $\omega\Lambda_\text{II} B$ to yield the coefficient k_{fj}, expressing the departmentwise value composition of capital of industry j; that is

$$k_{fj} = (\sum_{i \in f} a_{ij} \lambda_i)/\Omega l_j = C_{fj}/V_j$$

where Ω represents $\omega\Lambda_\text{II} B$, C_{fj} the value of the capital goods produced by department f which are used by industry j per unit of its output and V_j the variable capital of industry j. As C_{fj} is the (f, j) element of $E\hat{\Lambda}_\text{I} A_\text{I}$, the aggregation condition which is equivalent to (29) states that C_{fj}s are departmentwise proportional to the values of commodities, that is, for all $g = 1, ..., s$,

$$C_{fn_g} : C_{fn_g+1} : .... : C_{fn_g*} = \lambda_{n_g} : \lambda_{n_g+1} : .... : \lambda_{n_g*}$$
$$(f = 1, ..., s), \quad (36)$$

and *vice versa*. If (36) holds for all f and g, it follows from the value-determining equations that values λ_{n_i}s are departmentwise proportional to labour-input coefficients, so that we have

$$C_{fn_g} : C_{fn_g+1} : .... : C_{fn_g*} = V_{n_g} : V_{n_g+1} : .... : V_{n_g*}$$
$$\text{for all } f \text{ and } g, \quad (37)$$

which means that the industries classified in the same department g are departmentwise identical in the value composition of capital. Conversely, if industries are departmentwise identical in capital composition, it is seen that values of commodities are departmentwise proportional to their labour-input coefficients, so that we have, from (37), the condition (36), equivalent to (29) or (30). Thus the condition of non-distorting aggregation is reduced to the condition of the departmentwise identity of the composition of capital. It is important to see that the latter is evidently independent of the composition of outputs Δ within each department, as well as the rate of profit π and the real wage rate ω; it is given only in terms of values and technical production coefficients, which are intrinsic to the commodities.

Finally, the above Marxian aggregation in terms of values is compared with the Keynesian aggregation in terms of wage-units.[6] Keynes took the ratios of the market prices of the commodities to the wage rate as the aggregators. As was pointed out by Marx, relative market prices fluctuate with time, so that they affect the coefficients of the macroeconomic model in terms of wage-units, on the basis of which macro-analyses are made in order to explain market prices and other things that happen in the market. This obvious circularity is the Achilles heel of orthodox economics pointed out by Joan Robinson,[7] which Marx

---
[6] See J. M. Keynes, *The General Theory of Employment, Interest and Money* (London: Macmillan, 1936), pp. 37–45.
[7] Joan Robinson, 'The Production Function and the Theory of Capital', *Review of Economic Studies*, XXI (2), 1953–4, pp. 81–106.

could avoid because he was concerned with the transformation problem, a 'pointless' problem according to Samuelson, whereas Keynes and post-Keynesians could not because they were not. As Marx aggregated production coefficients in terms of values, he could determine the aggregate outputs and their prices by a system of equations with aggregate production coefficients which were independent of market prices. Thus, apart from ideological reasons, values are necessary in Marxian economics, not because they are first approximations of prices, but because they are more fundamental than prices and enable us to get rid of the circularity.

It must be noted that the value system is not the only system of weights according to which industries can be aggregated without causing the circularity. The equilibrium production prices, which are the 'transformed' values, can also play a role in the aggregation problem equivalent to that of values. If Keynes had been interested in the problem of production prices, he would have used production prices in terms of labour, p_i/w or $p_{i,w}$, instead of market prices in terms of labour, as the aggregators. He would then have obtained the departmentwise identity of the composition of capital in terms of production prices as a necessary and sufficient condition for consistent non-distorting aggregation of output and price determining systems; that is, for all departments g,

$$C_{fn_g}{}^p : C_{fn_g+1}{}^p : \ldots : C_{fn_g*}{}^p = l_{n_g} : l_{n_g+1} : \ldots : l_{n_g*}$$
$$(f = 1, \ldots, s), \quad (38)$$

where $C_{fj}{}^p = \sum_{i \in f} a_{ij} p_{i,w}$. He would also have obtained the departmental capital-input coefficients, $H_I{}^p$, fulfilling the conditions for non-distorting aggregation,

$$H_I{}^p \hat{Q}_I^{-1} E \hat{p}_{I,w} = \hat{Q}_I^{-1} E \hat{p}_{I,w} A_I, \quad (39)$$

where $\hat{p}_{I,w}$ is the $n \times n$ diagonal matrix with $p_{1,w}, \ldots, p_{n,w}$ on the diagonal and $\hat{Q}_I$ the $s \times s$ diagonal matrix with

$$\sum_{i \in f} p_{i,w} \delta_i \quad (f = 1, \ldots, s)$$

on the diagonal. He could have shown that the conditions (38)

imply a departmentwise proportionality between prices and values, so that
$$\hat{Q}_\mathrm{I}^{-1} E \hat{p}_{\mathrm{I},w} = \theta_\mathrm{I}^{-1} E \hat{\Lambda}_\mathrm{I}.$$

Therefore $H_\mathrm{I}^p = H_\mathrm{I}$, from (30) and (39); that is to say, Keynes could have agreed with Marx on the aggregation problem. He could have proceeded with his macroeconomic analysis on the basis of solid aggregate production coefficients. This shows the importance of production prices as well as values.

PART IV
The Reproduction Scheme

CHAPTER 9
Simple reproduction

The existence of Quesnay's *Tableau économique* gave French economists advantages in the search for a theory of general equilibrium. Having been profoundly influenced by Quesnay, Marx was among the vanguard in this greatest adventure in economics and formulated his models of general equilibrium as early as Walras. In fact the second volume of *Capital* in which the relevant discussion appears, though at first appeared in 1885 after Marx's death, was written almost at the same time as Walras' *Eléments d'économie politique pure* was published.[1] In spite of the disastrous hostilities between their followers, which continue nearly a century after the great master's death, Marx's models are very similar to Walras' in many aspects; Marx's scheme of simple reproduction, or reproduction on the same scale, corresponds to Walras' static general equilibrium system of production, and Marx's scheme of reproduction on an extended scale is a counterpart of Walras' dynamic general equilibrium system of capital formation and credit. It is of course true that there are some other aspects in which they are very different. For example, Marx's scope is broader than Walras', because in his theory of reproduction he was concerned not only with the usual problem of reproduction of commodities, but also with 'the reproduction (i.e. maintenance) of the capitalist-class and the working-class, and thus the reproduction of the capitalist character of the entire process of production.' (II, p. 396.) However, if a substantial identity is recognized, it must be admitted that the differences are not sufficiently important to justify a hundred years of cold war.

Marx's models have two unique characteristics which are related to each other. First, like every modern system of general equilibrium, his models consist of sub-systems which are 'duals' of each other; but unlike other systems, they have, in addition to

[1] See Engels' preface to *Capital*, vol. II, pp. 1–5.

a price-determining sub-system which is a dual of the output-determining sub-system, a value-determining sub-system which is also a dual of the output sub-system, so that they have *dual* dualities. Secondly, the duality between the value and output sub-systems enabled Marx to aggregate his models in terms of values into two departments by assuming, as a first approximation to reality, that the value structure of the industries is similar within each of the two major departments. Our attention will be focused on these peculiarities of Marx's system.

We are concerned in this section only with Marx's static model, postponing the examination of the more interesting dynamic model to the next section. Let x_I be the output vector of capital-goods and x_II that of the wage and luxury-good industries. They are n and $m-n$ dimensional column vectors. It is assumed in the simple reproduction model that workers spend their whole income on wage goods and capitalists also do not save, so that their income is entirely devoted to consumption of wage goods – to the extent that they are necessities of life – and luxury goods. Let d_i denote the consumption of wage good i of a worker per unit of labour-time, and f_i the total quantity of wage or luxury good i consumed by the capitalist-class. D and F represent column vectors:[2]

$$D = \begin{bmatrix} d_{n+1} \\ d_{n+2} \\ \vdots \\ d_m \end{bmatrix}, \quad F = \begin{bmatrix} f_{n+1} \\ f_{n+2} \\ \vdots \\ f_m \end{bmatrix}.$$

When industries produce outputs in the amounts x_I, x_II, they require capital goods of the amounts $A_\mathrm{I} x_\mathrm{I}$, $A_\mathrm{II} x_\mathrm{II}$ respectively. They employ workers amounting to $L_\mathrm{I} x_\mathrm{I} + L_\mathrm{II} x_\mathrm{II}$, measured in labour-time, so that their consumption of wage goods is given as

$$D \left(\sum_{i=\mathrm{I}}^{\mathrm{II}} L_i x_i \right).$$

The equations between demand and supply of commodities may now be written as

$$x_\mathrm{I} = A_\mathrm{I} x_\mathrm{I} + A_\mathrm{II} x_\mathrm{II} \quad \text{for capital goods,} \tag{1}$$

$$x_\mathrm{II} = D(L_\mathrm{I} x_\mathrm{I} + L_\mathrm{II} x_\mathrm{II}) + F \quad \text{for wage and luxury goods.} \tag{2}$$

[2] Note that $D = \omega B$ when workers may not choose between goods.

SIMPLE REPRODUCTION

On the other hand, we have two valuation sub-systems which are duals of the above output-determining sub-system: One of them is the price-determining sub-system:

$$p_\text{I} = (1+\pi)(p_\text{I} A_\text{I} + w L_\text{I}), \quad (3)$$

$$p_\text{II} = (1+\pi)(p_\text{I} A_\text{II} + w L_\text{II}), \quad (4)$$

while the other is the value-determining sub-system:

$$\Lambda_\text{I} = \Lambda_\text{I} A_\text{I} + L_\text{I}, \quad (5)$$

$$\Lambda_\text{II} = \Lambda_\text{I} A_\text{II} + L_\text{II}, \quad (6)$$

In addition to these, we have budget equations,[3]

$$w = p_\text{II} D \quad \text{for each worker}, \quad (7)$$

and $\quad \Pi = p_\text{II} F \quad$ for capitalists as a whole, $\quad (8)$

where Π represents the total amount of profit given as

$$\Pi = \pi \left[\sum_{i=\text{I}}^{\text{II}} (p_\text{I} A_\text{I} + w L_i) x_i \right]. \quad (9)$$

Also, premultiplying (1), (2) by Λ_I, Λ_II, and postmultiplying (5), (6) by x_I, x_II respectively, we get

$$\sum_{i=\text{I}}^{\text{II}} L_i x_i = \Lambda_\text{II} D \left(\sum_{i=\text{I}}^{\text{II}} L_i x_i \right) + \Lambda_\text{II} F. \quad (10)$$

Therefore by considering the definition of the rate of exploitation,[4]

$$e = (1 - \Lambda_\text{II} D)/\Lambda_\text{II} D, \quad (11)$$

we obtain $\quad e \Lambda_\text{II} D \left(\sum_{i=\text{I}}^{\text{II}} L_i x_i \right) = \Lambda_\text{II} F, \quad (12)$

which implies that the consumption of the capitalist-class, in terms of values, equals the total surplus value acquired by exploiting workers, while, as (8) shows, in terms of prices, it equals the total amount of profit earned.

---

[3] As is so in Walras' system, one of the equations in the system (1)–(4) and (7)–(9) follows from the rest.

[4] Note that D denotes a worker's consumption of wage goods per unit of labour-time, so that he consumes TD amounts of wage goods per day, where T represents working hours per day. The daily rate of exploitation is defined as

$$e = (T - \Lambda_\text{II} TD)/(\Lambda_\text{II} TD),$$

from which (11) follows.

These twelve equations complete Marx's static, general equilibrium model, whose first sub-system, consisting of (1) and (2), examines the process of reproduction from the point of view of the flow of commodities, while the second, of (3), (4) and (7)–(9), examines the same process from the point of view of the circulation of money, and the third, of (5), (6) and (10)–(12), examines it from the point of view of the replacement of value.

Marx wrote: 'The circular movement of capital takes place in three stages... *First stage*. The capitalist appears as a buyer on the commodity- and the labour-market; his money is transformed into commodities... *Second stage*. Productive consumption of the purchased commodities by the capitalist... *Third stage*. The capitalist returns to the market as a seller,...' (II, p. 25.) 'The wage-labourer lives only by the sale of his labour-power. Its preservation – his self-preservation – requires daily consumption. Hence payment for it must be continually repeated...' (II, p. 35.) '*a*) Articles of consumption, which enter into the consumption of the working-class, and to the extent that they are necessities of life – even if frequently different in quality and value from those of the labourers – also form a portion of the consumption of the capitalist class... *b*) Articles of *luxury*, which enter into the consumption of only the capitalist class and can therefore be exchanged only for spent surplus-value, which never falls to the share of the labourer.' (II, p. 407.) Obviously, these transactions are actually made *not* in terms of values but in terms of prices. Equations (3) and (4) describe accounts, per unit of each output, of industries, (7) describes the accounts of a worker per unit of labour-time, and (8) the family expenditures of the capitalist class.

He also wrote: 'For our present purpose this process of reproduction must be studied from the point of view of the replacement of the value as well as the substance of the individual component parts of [commodities].' (II, p. 397.) 'So long as we looked upon the production of value and the value of the product of capital individually, the bodily form of the commodities produced was wholly immaterial for the analysis, whether it was machines, for instance, corn, or looking glasses. It was always but a matter of illustration, and any branch of production could have served that purpose equally well... This merely formal manner of presentation is no longer adequate in the study of the total social capital and of the value of its products. The conversion of one portion of the value of the product into capital and the passing of another portion into the individual consumption of the capitalist as well as the working-class form a movement within the value of the product itself in which the result of the aggregate capital finds expression; and this movement is not only a replacement of value but also *a replacement in material* and is therefore as much bound up with the relative proportions of the value-components of the total social product as with *their use-value, their material shape.*' (II, p. 398, my italics.) Thus for the reproduction and circulation of the aggregate social capital, commodities have to be produced in definite proportions, which are determined by demand–supply equations (1) and (2). There is no commensurability between capital goods, since each capital good is materially different from the others; the demand for each capital good has to be equated with its supply. It is evident that the outputs of capital goods thus determined by n simultaneous equations (1) depend, as is seen in (2), on workers' and capitalists' demands, D and F, reflecting the use-values of the wage and luxury goods.

The replacement of value was studied by Marx in a two-department macroeconomic model. If it were the sole purpose of the construction of the model, aggregability would be an unnecessary specification. In fact Marx wrote: 'What is arbitrary here is the ratio of the variable to the constant capital of both I and II and so is the identity of this ratio for I and II and their sub-divisions.' (II, p. 411.) However the two-department model has another objective, for which the aggregability or constancy of the coefficients of the model is vital. That is to say, Marx had the intention of applying the model, as he did in the chapter succeeding that on simple reproduction, to the explanation of dynamic movement of the economy, by putting it in the form of a difference-equation system. It is true that there is no non-trivial movement in the state of simple reproduction, so that the model at this stage need not concern itself with the aggregation condition. However, Marx constructed the model of simple reproduction not for its own sake, but as an introduction to the dynamic model of 'reproduction in an extended scale', of which it is a special case, with the steady rate of growth being zero. Therefore I believe the theory of aggregation discussed in the last chapter should be applied to the model of simple reproduction too, to see how it can be reduced to a two-department model with constant structural coefficients.

Although we gave a full explanation of the aggregation of capital-good industries into one department in the previous chapter, we discuss it again here, together with the remaining problem of aggregating wage and luxury-good industries into the second department. As has already been seen, the condition for aggregating all capital-good industries into one sector (called department I) is that the ratio of the variable to the constant capital is identical throughout the industries producing capital goods and also throughout the industries producing wage and luxury goods. It will be seen below that the same condition implies that all wage and luxury-good industries may be aggregated into another sector (called department II) with no errors due to aggregation.

This aggregation condition implies that within each department there prevails the same proportion between the labour-input coefficient and the value of capital per output throughout its component industries; therefore labour-input coefficients and values of commodities are proportional within each of the two departments;[5] that is to say,

$$l_i/\lambda_i = \ldots = l_n/\lambda_n; \quad l_{n+1}/\lambda_{n+1} = \ldots = l_m/\lambda_m. \quad (13)$$

Multiply l_i/λ_i, $i = 1, \ldots, n$, by the value of labour-power, $\Lambda_{II} D$, and multiply the products thus obtained by the rate of exploitation e; then we get, by definition

$$\Lambda_{II} D \frac{l_i}{\lambda_i} = \frac{V_i}{\lambda_i} \quad \text{and} \quad e\Lambda_{II} D \frac{l_i}{\lambda_i} = \frac{S_i}{\lambda_i} \quad (i = 1, \ldots, n), \quad (14)$$

where V_i and S_i represent the variable capital and the surplus value per unit of commodity i. The ratio V_i/λ_i is further multiplied by the value composition of capital of department I, k_I; we get, again by definition,

$$k_I \frac{V_i}{\lambda_i} = \frac{C_i}{\lambda_i} \quad (i = 1, \ldots, n), \quad (15)$$

where C_i denotes the constant capital required for the production of a unit of commodity i. We have similar equations for the

[5] As we find from equations (13) and (18) in chapter 8.

industries in department II. As $\Lambda_{II} D$ and e are the same for all industries and k_I (or k_{II}) is common among the industries in department I (or II), (13) implies the following six sets of equations:

$$\left.\begin{array}{l} C_1/\lambda_1 = \ldots = C_n/\lambda_n, \\ V_1/\lambda_1 = \ldots = V_n/\lambda_n, \\ S_1/\lambda_1 = \ldots = S_n/\lambda_n; \end{array}\right\} \quad (16)$$

$$\left.\begin{array}{l} C_{n+1}/\lambda_{n+1} = \ldots = C_m/\lambda_m, \\ V_{n+1}/\lambda_{n+1} = \ldots = V_m/\lambda_m, \\ S_{n+1}/\lambda_{n+1} = \ldots = S_m/\lambda_m. \end{array}\right\} \quad (16')$$

Let the common ratios of (16) be denoted by c_I, v_I, s_I respectively, and those of (16') by c_{II}, v_{II}, s_{II}. Also, denote the two common ratios of (13) by l_I and l_{II}. Then, under the aggregation conditions, Marx's macro-reproduction model may be given in terms of these eight fundamental coefficients $l_i, c_i, v_i, s_i, i = $ I, II. First of all, we evidently have

$$\left.\begin{array}{l} c_I + l_I = c_I + v_I + s_I = 1, \\ c_{II} + l_{II} = c_{II} + v_{II} + s_{II} = 1, \end{array}\right\} \quad (17)$$

by definition. (17) means that departments I and II are so composed of their elementary industries that the value of the composite commodity produced by each department is unity per unit of its output; that is to say, in the notation of the last chapter, δ_is are taken such that

$$\sum_{i=1}^{n} \lambda_i \delta_i = 1 \quad \text{and} \quad \sum_{i=n+1}^{m} \lambda_i \delta_i = 1.$$

Second, outputs of industries are aggregated into departmental outputs in the following way. Premultiply (1) by the value vector Λ_I and consider proportionalities (13) and (16) derived from the aggregation condition; then we get

$$y_I = c_I y_I + c_{II} y_{II}, \quad (18)$$

where y_I denotes the value of outputs of department I and y_{II} the value of outputs of department II; i.e.[6]

$$y_I = \Lambda_I x_I \quad \text{and} \quad y_{II} = \Lambda_{II} x_{II}.$$

[6] These definitions of departmental outputs are the same as those given in chapter 8 above. $y_I = \Lambda_I x_I / \Lambda_I \Delta_I$ and $y_{II} = \Lambda_{II} x_{II} / \Lambda_{II} \Delta_{II}$ because $\Lambda_I \Delta_I = \Lambda_{II} \Delta_{II} = 1$. It is seen that c_I and c_{II} here are h_I and h_{II} there.

Similarly, by premultiplying (2) by Λ_{II} and taking (12) and (14) into account, we obtain[7]

$$y_{II} = (v_I + s_I) y_I + (v_{II} + s_{II}) y_{II}. \quad (19)$$

(18) and (19) constitute the output-determining sub-system of Marx's two-department model of simple reproduction, whose dual sub-system consists of equations,

$$y_I = c_I y_I + v_I y_I + s_I y_I, \quad (20)$$

$$y_{II} = c_{II} y_{II} + v_{II} y_{II} + s_{II} y_{II}, \quad (21)$$

which are equivalent to the value-determining equations (5) and (6), or (17).

Marx analysed the value of output into constant and variable capitals and surplus value, as (20) and (21) show, and then he argued that the equilibrium conditions (18) and (19) should be established in the following way.

'(1) The $500v$ [$v_{II} y_{II}$ in our notation], representing wages of the labourers, and $500s$ [i.e. $s_{II} y_{II}$], representing surplus-value of the capitalists, in department II, must be spent for articles of consumption. But their value exists in articles of consumption worth 1,000 [i.e. $(v_{II} + s_{II}) y_{II}$], held by the capitalists of department II, which replace the advanced $500v$ [i.e. $v_{II} y_{II}$] and represent the $500s$ [i.e. $s_{II} y_{II}$]. Consequently the wages and surplus-value of department II are exchanged within this department for products of this same department. Thereby articles of consumption to the amount of $(500v + 500s)$ II = 1,000 [i.e. $v_{II} y_{II} + s_{II} y_{II}$] drop out of the total product.

'(2) The $1,000v$ plus $1,000s$ [i.e. $v_I y_I$ plus $s_I y_I$] of department I must likewise be spent for articles of consumption; in other words, for products of department II. Hence they must be exchanged for the remainder of this product equal to the constant capital part, $2,000c$ [i.e. $c_{II} y_{II}$]. Department II receives in return an equal quantity of means of production, the product of I, in which the value of $1,000v + 1,000s$ [i.e. $v_I y_I + s_I y_I$] of I is incorporated. Thereby $2,000II_c$ and $(1,000v + 1,000s)$ I, [i.e. $c_{II} y_{II}$ and $v_I y_I + s_I y_I$] drop out of the calculation.

---

[7] It is of course true that (19) can alternatively be obtained directly from (18) in view of (17). But the problem here is not to establish (19) but to show that it is the aggregate version of the demand–supply equations of the wage and luxury goods (2).

SIMPLE REPRODUCTION   113

'(3) There still remain 4,000I_c [i.e. $c_I y_I$]. These consist of means of production which can be used only in department I to replace its consumed constant capital, and are therefore disposed of by mutual exchange between the individual capitalists of I, just as the (500v+500s) I [i.e. $v_{II} y_{II} + s_{II} y_{II}$] by an exchange between the labourers and capitalists, or between the individual capitalists of II.' (II, pp. 401–2.)

As Marx saw in (2) above, and as we can more directly confirm algebraically by using (18) and (20), 'on the basis of simple reproduction, the sum of the values of $v+s$ of the commodity-capital of I (and therefore a corresponding proportional part of the total commodity-product of I) must be equal to the constant capital II_c, which is likewise taken as a proportional part of the total commodity-product of department II; or $I_{(v+s)} = II_c$.' (II, p. 406.) The last equation is written in our notation as

$$(v_I + s_I) y_I = c_{II} y_{II},$$

which obviously determines the ratio of equilibrium outputs of both departments, or, more mathematically, the eigenvector associated with the largest characteristic root of the matrix of Marx's coefficients of simple reproduction,[8]

$$\begin{bmatrix} c_I & c_{II} \\ v_I + s_I & v_{II} + s_{II} \end{bmatrix}. \qquad (22)$$

We have so far followed Marx in measuring the total output of each department in terms of value by aggregating the elementary industries of the respective departments in terms of values. Under our aggregation conditions, however, the production prices relative to the wage rate, or the long-run equilibrium wage-prices, p_i/w or $p_{i,w}$, are proportional to values, λ_i, within each department, as was seen in the previous chapter, so that it is clear that we may alternatively aggregate industries into the same two departments in terms of equilibrium wage-prices (or production prices in terms of labour). In a way parallel with the above procedure, that is, by premultiplying (1) and (2) by $p_{I,w}$

[8] As the matrix is of the Markov type, the largest characteristic root is one. The other root is calculated at $c_I - c_{II}$, which is negative if and only if department II is more capital intensive than I, i.e. $c_I/v_I < c_{II}/v_{II}$. The eigenvectors associated with these roots are
$$\begin{bmatrix} c_{II} \\ v_I + s_I \end{bmatrix} \text{ and } \begin{bmatrix} 1 \\ -1 \end{bmatrix} \text{ respectively.}$$

and $p_{\text{II},w}$ respectively, and taking the proportionalities, $p_{\text{I},w} = \alpha_\text{I} \Lambda_\text{I}$ and $p_{\text{II},w} = \alpha_\text{II} \Lambda_\text{II}$ into account, we obtain, under the aggregation conditions, the two departmental equilibrium conditions,
$$y_\text{I} = c_\text{I} y_\text{I} + c_\text{II} y_\text{II}, \qquad (23)$$

$$y_\text{II} = \left[\frac{l_\text{I}}{\alpha_\text{II}} + \pi\left(\frac{\alpha_\text{I} c_\text{I}}{\alpha_\text{II}} + \frac{l_\text{I}}{\alpha_\text{II}}\right)\right] y_\text{I} + \left[\frac{l_\text{II}}{\alpha_\text{II}} + \pi\left(\frac{\alpha_\text{I} c_\text{II}}{\alpha_\text{II}} + \frac{l_\text{II}}{\alpha_\text{II}}\right)\right] y_\text{II}, \quad (24)$$

because of (7), (8), (9), where

$$y_\text{I} = p_{\text{I},w} x_\text{I} / p_{\text{I},w} \Delta_\text{I} = \Lambda_\text{I} x_\text{I} / \Lambda_\text{I} \Delta_\text{I},$$

$$y_\text{II} = p_{\text{II},w} x_\text{I} / p_{\text{II},w} \Delta_\text{II} = \Lambda_\text{II} x_\text{II} / \Lambda_\text{II} \Delta_\text{II},$$

which are identical in terms of value with the departmental outputs of the reproduction system, (20) and (21), because of $\Lambda_\text{I} \Delta_\text{I} = 1$ and $\Lambda_\text{II} \Delta_\text{II} = 1$. It is at once seen that equation (23) is exactly the same as the corresponding equation (20) of the value reproduction system, whereas equation (24) is *prima facie* different from (21). Since the price-determining equations (3) and (4) may be put, under the aggregation conditions, in the form,

$$\alpha_\text{I} = (1+\pi)(\alpha_\text{I} c_\text{I} + l_\text{I}) \quad \text{and} \quad \alpha_\text{II} = (1+\pi)(\alpha_\text{I} c_\text{II} + l_\text{II}),$$

we have
$$\frac{l_\text{I}}{\alpha_\text{II}} + \pi\left(\frac{\alpha_\text{I} c_\text{I}}{\alpha_\text{II}} + \frac{l_\text{I}}{\alpha_\text{II}}\right) = \frac{\alpha_\text{I}}{\alpha_\text{II}} - \frac{\alpha_\text{I} c_\text{I}}{\alpha_\text{II}},$$

$$\frac{l_\text{II}}{\alpha_\text{II}} + \pi\left(\frac{\alpha_\text{I} c_\text{II}}{\alpha_\text{II}} + \frac{l_\text{II}}{\alpha_\text{II}}\right) = 1 - \frac{\alpha_\text{I} c_\text{II}}{\alpha_\text{II}}.$$

These are equal to
$$1 - c_\text{I} = v_\text{I} + s_\text{I} \quad \text{and} \quad 1 - c_\text{II} = v_\text{II} + s_\text{II},$$

respectively, if $\alpha_\text{I} = \alpha_\text{II}$, that is, if all capital, wage and luxury good industries have the same value-composition of capital, so that the prices of all commodities are proportional to their values.[9] The other case in which the coefficients of (24) are identical with those of (19) is the trivial case of no exploitation. In this case we obtain $\pi = 0$ (because exploitation is necessary for positive profits), so that the coefficients of (24) are reduced to

---

[9] In this case, $c_\text{I} = c_\text{II}$, so that we have $v_\text{I} + s_\text{I} = v_\text{II} + s_\text{II}$ too. Therefore, matrix (22) is singular, and hence (23) and (24) leave y_I and y_II indeterminate. The system should be aggregated into a one-sector model.

SIMPLE REPRODUCTION   115

$l_{\mathrm{I}}/\alpha_{\mathrm{II}}$ and $l_{\mathrm{II}}/\alpha_{\mathrm{II}}$, while those of (19) reduce to v_{I} and v_{II}; and we have[10]

$$l_i/\alpha_{\mathrm{II}} = v_i \quad (i = \mathrm{I, II}). \tag{25}$$

Thus the coefficients of the second equation of the reproduction system aggregated in terms of the equilibrium wage-prices are different from those of the corresponding equation aggregated in terms of values, except in the two very special cases which had very little interest for Marx. However the equations are identical with each other, in spite of the different coefficients. This is easily seen from (8), (9) and (12). In fact, from (8) and (9) we get, under the aggregation conditions,

$$p_{\mathrm{II},w} F = \alpha_{\mathrm{II}} \Lambda_{\mathrm{II}} F = \pi[(\alpha_{\mathrm{I}} c_{\mathrm{I}} + l_{\mathrm{I}}) y_{\mathrm{I}} + (\alpha_{\mathrm{I}} c_{\mathrm{II}} + l_{\mathrm{II}}) y_{\mathrm{II}}],$$

while from (12) $\Lambda_{\mathrm{II}} F = s_{\mathrm{I}} y_{\mathrm{I}} + s_{\mathrm{II}} y_{\mathrm{II}}.$

Therefore,

$$\pi\left[\left(\frac{\alpha_{\mathrm{I}} c_{\mathrm{I}}}{\alpha_{\mathrm{II}}} + \frac{l_{\mathrm{I}}}{\alpha_{\mathrm{II}}}\right) y_{\mathrm{I}} + \left(\frac{\alpha_{\mathrm{I}} c_{\mathrm{II}}}{\alpha_{\mathrm{II}}} + \frac{l_{\mathrm{II}}}{\alpha_{\mathrm{II}}}\right) y_{\mathrm{II}}\right] = s_{\mathrm{I}} y_{\mathrm{I}} + s_{\mathrm{II}} y_{\mathrm{II}}. \tag{26}$$

This, together with (25), enables us to find that equation (24) is identical with (19), despite the differences in their corresponding coefficients.

The rest of this chapter is devoted to a comparison of Marx's view of simple reproduction with the view of some of the orthodox economists. We take Dorfman, Samuelson and Solow's as an authoritative view. They write:[11] 'In a long-run competitive equilibrium we may put prices equal to unit costs.' 'Relative prices of commodities will depend only on their direct and indirect labour content.' 'The total value of net output is just imputed as wages to the scarce factor labour.' These quotations imply that (i) the rate of profit is zero, i.e. $\pi = 0$; (ii) there is no deviation of prices from values, i.e. $p_{i,w} = \lambda_i$ for all i, and (iii) there is no share for capitalists in the net output; everything is eaten by workers so that there is no accumulation of capital stocks.

This view of Dorfman, Samuelson and Solow contrasts greatly

[10] As $p_{\mathrm{II},w} D = 1$, we have
$$l_i = (p_{\mathrm{II},w} D) l_i = \alpha_{\mathrm{II}} \Lambda_{\mathrm{II}} D l_i = \alpha_{\mathrm{II}} v_i \quad (i = \mathrm{I, II}).$$

[11] R. Dorfman, P. A. Samuelson and R. M. Solow, *Linear Programming and Economic Analysis* (New York: McGraw-Hill, 1958), pp. 224, 227 and 229.

with Marx's. According to him, only the abstract and imaginary society of simple commodity production can be characterized by these three features. Marx insisted on the prevalence of a *positive* rate of profit in the state of simple reproduction in a capitalist society, because if it were zero no capitalist would be interested in his enterprise, so that the capitalist character of the entire process of production would not be reproduced. In Marx's view, $\pi > 0$ and hence $p_{i,w} > \lambda_i$ for all i,[12] but the society is in a stationary state since capitalists do not save. Of course, as he recognized, 'Simple reproduction, reproduction on the same scale, appears as an abstraction, inasmuch as...the absence of all accumulation or reproduction on an extended scale is a strange assumption in capitalist conditions...' (II, pp. 398–9.) But he was interested in it as a convenient base for tackling the more realistic problem of extended or expanding reproduction; by removing the assumption of no capitalists' savings his model can easily be put into motion.

[12] See chapter 7 above.

CHAPTER 10

Extended reproduction

In order for a transition from simple to extended reproduction to take place, a positive portion of the surplus value must remain after capitalists' consumption, which may be spent on the acquisition of new constant and variable capitals. In fact, as Marx wrote, he 'assumed in the analysis of simple reproduction that the entire surplus-value of [departments] I and II is spent as revenue. As a matter of fact, however, one portion of the surplus-value is spent as revenue, and the other is converted into capital. Actual accumulation can take place only on this assumption.' (II, p. 507.) Consequently, reproduction on an extended scale is not possible in a society where it is technically and biologically infeasible to exploit workers so as to yield a total surplus value greater than the value of the necessities of life which the capitalists require.

There is another precondition. For an expansion of the economy to be possible, there must be a sufficient supply of labour-power from the working-class, which presupposes among other things, 'a development of all the circumstances which produces a relative surplus population among the working-class'. (II, p. 518.) Marx also wrote as follows: 'We have explained at great length in book I that labour-power is always available under the capitalist system of production, and that more labour can be rendered fluent, if necessary, without increasing the number of labourers or the quantity of labour-power employed. We therefore need not go into this any further, but shall rather assume that the portion of the newly created money-capital capable of being converted into variable capital will always find at hand the labour-power into which it is to transform itself.' (II, p. 505.) Thus he assumed, as von Neumann did,[1] that the labour force could be expanded at a rate which was higher than the maximum rate of growth of capital, or at least that the supply of labour could adjust itself quickly and smoothly to demand.

Under these fundamental assumptions, Marx's analysis proceeded in terms of numerical examples. He presented two main

[1] J. von Neumann, 'A Model of General Economic Equilibrium', *Review of Economic Studies*, XIII, 1945–6, pp. 1–9.

illustrations of the same kind, the first of which assumed the following structural coefficients:[2] The rate of exploitation is 1 for both departments I and II; the value-composition of capital is 4 for department I and 2 for department II. Let the ratios of the constant and variable capitals used by department i to the total value of its output be denoted by c_i and v_i, and the ratio of surplus value produced by i to the total value of output i by s_i. As $c_i + v_i + s_i = 1$ for $i =$ I, II, the rate of exploitation and the value-compositions of capital which Marx assumed for the purpose of illustration imply, in view of their definitions, the following values of the coefficients:

	c_i	v_i	s_i
Department I	$\frac{2}{3}$	$\frac{1}{6}$	$\frac{1}{6}$
Department II	$\frac{1}{2}$	$\frac{1}{4}$	$\frac{1}{4}$

The accumulation of capital may start from an arbitrary initial point which Marx took as $y_\text{I}(0) = 6{,}000$ and $y_\text{II}(0) = 3{,}000$, where $y_i(0)$ represents the value of output of department i in year 0. Then we have the following 'Initial Scheme for Reproduction on an Extended Scale

I $4{,}000c + 1{,}000v + 1{,}000s = 6{,}000$

II $1{,}500c + 750v + 750s = 3{,}000$

Total   9,000.'   (II, p. 514.)

Marx then introduced his very peculiar investment function, such that (i) capitalists of department I devoted a constant proportion of their surplus value to accumulation, (ii) it was reinvested in department I so that it was converted into constant and variable capitals in the proportion $k_\text{I} : 1$ and (iii) capitalists of department II adjusted their investment so as to maintain the balance between the supply and demand for capital goods. In his example, one half of surplus value I, i.e. 500, is assumed to be accumulated. Then 400 of the 500I_s are to be converted into

[2] In this chapter, for the sake of simplicity and also with the intention of later revising or generalizing Marx's analysis of the process of accumulation, in a way suggested by von Neumann, we deliberately confine ourselves to the simplest case of one period of turnover of constant and variable capitals, although Marx was concerned with a more general case. It is therefore assumed throughout the following discussion that 'the constant capital is everywhere uniformly and entirely transferred to the annual product of the capitals' (III, p. 154).

constant capital, and 100 into variable capital. This makes a total demand for capital goods of department I of the amount $4,000c + 400c$, which would imply an excess supply of the amount $100 = 6,000 - 4,400 - 1,500$ if there were no investment demand from department II. In his model, however, capitalists of department II have been assigned the role of adjuster, so that there must be an additional investment demand of $100c$ due from department II. This means that out of their surplus value $750s$ capitalists of department II accumulate $150 = 100c + 50v$, since the value-composition of capital II is assumed to be 2.

We now have a demand for wage and luxury goods from the workers recurrently and newly employed in department I of the amount $1,100 = 1,000v + 100v$, from the workers in department II of the amount $800 = 750v + 50v$ and from the capitalists of both departments demand of the amount $1,100 = 500s + 600s$, the amount remaining for their consumption after the surplus value of $500s + 150s$ has been spent for accumulation. The total demand for products of department II amounts to 3,000, which is equal to their supply. Since demand is equated with supply in each department, goods are distributed as they are demanded. Actual accumulation will take place exactly as it has been scheduled by capitalists. Capitals are augmented in the two departments in the following way:

I $4,000c \to 4,400c,\quad 1,000v \to 1,100v,$

II $1,500c \to 1,600c,\quad\ \ 750v \to\ \ 800v.$

If production goes on with these augmented capitals and capitalists maintain the same rate of exploitation as before, we shall obtain at the end of year 1:

I $4,400c + 1,100v + 1,100s = 6,600,$

II $1,600c +\ \ 800v +\ \ 800s = 3,200.$

In year 2, accumulation in department I continues at the same rate as in year 1, so that surplus value of the amount $550s$ is accumulated and the other $550s$ is spent for personal consumption. The accumulated part is invested for department I and divided into $440c$ and $110v$, according to the value-composition of capital of I. The total demand for capital goods of department I, which includes both replacement and net investment demands, amounts to 4,840c, which in turn, together with the replacement demand of department II, produces an aggregate demand of 6,440c, so that capital goods of 160c can be used for the expansion of department II. Capitalists of department II have to save 240s = 160s + 80v out of their surplus value 800s. The products of the wage and luxury goods industries, of the value 3,200, are all sold to workers and capitalists, because they demand these goods in the amounts 1,210v + 880v and 550s + 560s respectively. If reproduction is carried on at the same rate of exploitation as before without any structural change, we obtain at the end of year 2:

I   4,840c + 1,210v + 1,210s = 7,260,

II 1,760c +   880v +   880s = 3,520.

It is now seen that the rate of growth of output of department I is 10 per cent from year 0 to year 1 and from year 1 to year 2, while that of department II is 6.67 per cent from year 0 to year 1 and 10 per cent from year 1 to year 2. Therefore we have only one year of unbalanced growth before year 2, when both departments expand at the same rate, 10 per cent. Thus the figures at the end of year 2 are exactly the same as those at the end of year 1 multiplied by the common number 1.1. Year 3 is no more than a repetition of year 2 on an extended scale, and so forth for ever. It is thus seen that in Marx's economy there prevails a tendency towards balanced growth, which is much stronger than the convergence claimed by neoclassical economists such as Solow, Meade, and Uzawa,[3] because any state of unbalanced growth will disappear in Marx's economy in a single year.

It can easily be shown that such a strange conclusion is not specific to the numerical illustration used by Marx, but is a logical implication of his investment function. Let a_I and a_{II} be the rates at which the surplus values of departments I and II, respectively, are accumulated; a_I is kept constant while a_{II} is

[3] R. M. Solow, 'A Contribution to the Theory of Economic Growth', *Quarterly Journal of Economics*, LXX, 1956, pp. 65–94; J. E. Meade, *A Neoclassical Theory of Economic Growth* (London: George Allen and Unwin, Ltd, 1961); H. Uzawa, 'On a Two-Sector Model of Economic Growth', *Review of Economic Studies*, XXIX, 1961, pp. 40–7. R. Sato has shown that about one hundred years are required for a neoclassical economy to settle in a balanced growth state.

adjusted. The accumulated surplus value $a_I s_I y_I(0)$ is divided into

$$\frac{c_I}{c_I+v_I} a_I s_I y_I(0) \quad \text{and} \quad \frac{v_I}{c_I+v_I} a_I s_I y_I(0),$$

the former being added to the constant capital of department I in year 0, $c_I y_I(0)$, to make its constant capital in year 1. There will be an excess supply of capital goods of the amount

$$y_I(0) - \left[c_I + \frac{c_I}{c_I+v_I} a_I s_I\right] y_I(0) - c_{II} y_{II}(0)$$

if no net investment is made by the capitalists of department II. The adaptive rate of accumulation in year 1, $a_{II}(1)$, is determined such that

$$a_{II}(1) \left[\frac{c_{II}}{c_{II}+v_{II}} s_{II}\right] y_{II}(0)$$

$$= y_I(0) - \left[c_I + \frac{c_I}{c_I+v_I} a_I s_I\right] y_I(0) - c_{II} y_{II}(0). \quad (1)$$

From year 0 to year 1, the rate of growth of department I is given as

$$g_I(0) = \frac{a_I s_I}{c_I+v_I}, \quad (2)$$

and that of department II as

$$g_{II}(0) = \frac{a_{II}(1) s_{II}}{c_{II}+v_{II}} = \frac{1}{c_{II}} \left[1 - c_I - \frac{c_I}{c_I+v_I} a_I s_I\right] \frac{y_I(0)}{y_{II}(0)} - 1 \quad (3)$$

because of (1).

In exactly the same way, the rate of growth from year 1 to year 2 is given as

$$g_I(1) = \frac{a_I s_I}{c_I+v_I} \quad \text{for department I}, \quad (4)$$

and

$$g_{II}(1) = \frac{a_{II}(2) s_{II}}{c_{II}+v_{II}} = \frac{1}{c_{II}} \left[1 - c_I - \frac{c_I}{c_I+v_I} a_I s_I\right] \frac{y_I(1)}{y_{II}(1)} - 1 \quad (5)$$

for department II.

On the other hand, we have

$$y_I(1) = [1+g_I(0)] y_I(0), \quad y_{II}(1) = [1+g_{II}(0)] y_{II}(0),$$

and

$$1+g_{II}(0) = \frac{1}{c_{II}} \left[1 - c_I - \frac{c_I}{c_I+v_I} a_I s_I\right] \frac{y_I(0)}{y_{II}(0)} \quad \text{(from (3))}.$$

Substituting these into (5) we can easily verify $g_{II}(1) = g_I(0)$. As $g_I(0) = g_I(1)$ because of the constancy of a_I, we have $g_I(1) = g_{II}(1)$, so that the outputs of departments I and II grow in balance from year 1 to year 2 and thenceforth.

This strange conclusion has been derived from Marx's special investment function, which is not only unnatural but conflicts with his reasonings on the formation of the equilibrium rate of profit. He wrote as follows: 'the rates of profit prevailing in the various branches of production are originally very different. These different rates of profit are equalized by competition to a single general rate of profit.' (III, p. 158.) Therefore, as long as the rate of profit is equalized between departments I and II, capitalists of one department will be interested in investing their profits in the other department as well. Thus their investment activities will not be confined within their own department.

We now propose to replace Marx's assumptions concerning investment behaviour by the following more reasonable assumptions. We assume that (i) capitalists of departments I and II have the same propensity to save, a, and (ii) they are interested equally in investment opportunities in both departments, because the same equilibrium rate of profit prevails in both. Then $a[s_I y_I(t) + s_{II} y_{II}(t)]$ is devoted to accumulation, a part of which, $c_I \Delta y_I(t) + c_{II} \Delta y_{II}(t)$, is invested in capital goods by the capitalists of both departments, while the rest is spent on variable capital. Because the workers' propensity to save is assumed to be zero, the investment in variable capital (i.e. real wages spent for new employment) equals the consumption of wage goods by the newly employed workers. The demand–supply equations for outputs of the two departments may be written as

$$y_I(t) = c_I y_I(t) + c_{II} y_{II}(t) + c_I \Delta y_I(t) + c_{II} \Delta y_{II}(t), \qquad (6)$$

$$y_{II}(t) = v_I y_I(t) + v_{II} y_{II}(t) + v_I \Delta y_I(t)$$
$$+ v_{II} \Delta y_{II}(t) + b s_I y_I(t) + b s_{II} y_{II}(t), \qquad (7)$$

where $b = 1 - a$ stands for the capitalists' propensity to consume.

By definition,
$$\Delta y_I(t) = y_I(t+1) - y_I(t)$$

and
$$\Delta y_{II}(t) = y_{II}(t+1) - y_{II}(t);$$

therefore, (6) and (7) can be written more simply as
$$\begin{bmatrix} y_I(t) \\ y_{II}(t) \end{bmatrix} = \begin{bmatrix} c_I & c_{II} \\ v_I & v_{II} \end{bmatrix} \begin{bmatrix} y_I(t+1) \\ y_{II}(t+1) \end{bmatrix} + \begin{bmatrix} 0 & 0 \\ bs_I & bs_{II} \end{bmatrix} \begin{bmatrix} y_I(t) \\ y_{II}(t) \end{bmatrix}, \quad (8)$$
which in turn may be rewritten as
$$\begin{bmatrix} y_I(t) \\ y_{II}(t) \end{bmatrix} = \begin{bmatrix} M_{11} & M_{12} \\ M_{21} & M_{22} \end{bmatrix} \begin{bmatrix} y_I(t+1) \\ y_{II}(t+1) \end{bmatrix} \quad (9)$$
by putting
$$M_{1i} = c_i \quad \text{and} \quad M_{2i} = \frac{bs_I c_i + v_i}{1 - bs_{II}} \quad (i = I, II). \quad (10)$$
The simultaneous difference equations (9) may be described as the fundamental equations of the theory of reproduction, whose solutions may be written as
$$\left.\begin{aligned} y_I(t) &= \eta_1 m_{11}(1+g_1)^t + \eta_2 m_{21}(1+g_2)^t, \\ y_{II}(t) &= \eta_1 m_{12}(1+g_1)^t + \eta_2 m_{22}(1+g_2)^t, \end{aligned}\right\} \quad (11)$$
where η_1 and η_2 are constants determined by initial outputs, $y_I(0)$ and $y_{II}(0)$; $1+g_1$ and $1+g_2$ are the reciprocals of two latent roots, μ_1 and μ_2, of the characteristic equation,
$$\begin{vmatrix} M_{11} - \mu & M_{12} \\ M_{21} & M_{22} - \mu \end{vmatrix} = 0; \quad (12)$$
and the ms are obtained by solving the two sets of equations
$$\left.\begin{aligned} (M_{11} - \mu_i) m_{i1} + M_{12} m_{i2} &= 0 \\ M_{21} m_{i1} + (M_{22} - \mu_i) m_{i2} &= 0 \end{aligned}\right\} \quad (i = 1, 2). \quad (13)$$

The solutions (11) have the following properties. It is first noted that all M_{ij}s are positive, because both the capitalists' propensity to save, b, and the surplus value per unit of output of department II, s_{II}, are positive and less than one. The characteristic equation (12) has roots,

$$\begin{aligned} \mu_1 &= \frac{M_{11} + M_{22} + \sqrt{[(M_{11} - M_{22})^2 + 4M_{12}M_{21}]}}{2} \\ &= \frac{M_{11} + M_{22} + |M_{11} - M_{22}| + u}{2}, \\ \mu_2 &= \frac{M_{11} + M_{22} - \sqrt{[(M_{11} - M_{22})^2 + 4M_{12}M_{21}]}}{2} \\ &= \frac{M_{11} + M_{22} - |M_{11} - M_{22}| - u}{2}, \end{aligned}$$

where u is a positive number because $M_{12}M_{21} > 0$. It is seen that μ_1 is greater than either M_{11} or M_{22}, while μ_2 is smaller than either of them. Obviously μ_1 is positive but μ_2 may be negative. When it is positive, we have $\mu_1 > \mu_2$, of course. When it is negative, its absolute value is smaller than μ_1.[4] Thus, in any case, $\mu_1 > |\mu_2|$, so that
$$1+g_1 < |1+g_2|.$$

Next, as $M_{11} < \mu_1$, the first equation of (13), for $i = 1$, implies that m_{11}/m_{12} is positive; so both m_{11} and m_{12} may be taken as positive. On the other hand, as $M_{11} > \mu_2$, we find, by exactly the same method, that m_{21}/m_{22} is negative; so m_{21} may be taken as positive and m_{22} as negative. Moreover we can show that $\mu_1 < 1$, because adding the second equation of (13) for $i = 1$, multiplied by $1 - bs_{II}$ to the first for $i = 1$ and bearing definitions (10) and $c_i + v_i + s_i = 1$, $i = I, II$ in mind, we obtain

$$\mu_1[(1 - bs_I)m_{11} + (1 - bs_{II})m_{12}] = (c_I + v_I)m_{11} + (c_{II} + v_{II})m_{12}$$
$$= (1 - s_I)m_{11} + (1 - s_{II})m_{12},$$

which implies $\mu_1 < 1$, as $1 - bs_i > 1 - s_i > 0$, for $i = I, II$, $m_{11} > 0$, and $m_{12} > 0$. Finally, subtracting the second equation of (13) for $i = 2$, multiplied by $c_I(1 - bs_{II})$ from the first for $i = 2$ multiplied by v_I, we get

$$\mu_2[(v_I + bs_I c_I)m_{21} - c_I(1 - bs_{II})m_{22}] = (c_{II}v_I - v_{II}c_I)m_{22}.$$

On the left-hand side of this equation, the part in square brackets is positive because of the assumed signs of m_{21} and m_{22}. On the other hand, the right-hand side is negative if and only if $c_{II}/v_{II} > c_I/v_I$. Hence μ_2 is negative if and only if $c_{II}/v_{II} > c_I/v_I$.

As μ_1 is positive and less than one, g_1 is positive. If the initial position $(y_I(0), y_{II}(0))$ is given so as to make $\eta_2 = 0$, then $y_I(t)$ and $y_{II}(t)$ grow in balance at the common positive rate g_1. If the initial point is displaced from the balanced growth path, then η_2 cannot be zero. As $\mu_1 > |\mu_2|$ implies $1 + g_1 < |1 + g_2|$, the non-balanced growth parts $\eta_2 m_{2i}(1 + g_2)^t$, $i = 1, 2$, will become the dominant parts in the general solutions (11) for large t. Furthermore, if $\mu_2 < 0$ we have $1 + g_2 < 0$, which implies that the second

---

[4] *Proof:* Suppose the contrary, that is $\mu_2 < 0$ and $\mu_1 < |\mu_2| = -\mu_2$. Then
$$\frac{M_{11} + M_{22} + |M_{11} - M_{22}| + u}{2} < -\frac{M_{11} + M_{22} - |M_{11} - M_{22}| - u}{2}.$$
Therefore, $M_{11} + M_{22} < 0$, a contradiction.

terms of the solutions (11) change their sign every period. Therefore we may now conclude as follows: The balanced growth is unstable and an economy starting from an initial point away from the balanced growth path will diverge from it as time goes on. In more detail, we have explosive oscillations (of period 2) around the balanced growth path, if department II, producing wage and luxury goods, is higher in the value composition of capital (or more capital-intensive) than department I, producing capital goods, i.e. $k_{II} = c_{II}/v_{II} > k_I = c_I/v_I$. Otherwise we have monotonic divergence from the balanced growth path.[5]

Obviously this instability result is the very opposite of what Marx derived from the numerical analysis of his Scheme of Reproduction. But we can adduce evidence to show that the model Marx originally intended to examine does not differ very much from ours. In fact, he began the section on the 'Schematic Presentation of Accumulation' by studying reproduction of commodities under the assumption 'that *both* I and II accumulate one half of their surplus-value' (II, p. 511, my italics), and later changed this reasonable assumption into the unnatural one which we have already discussed, because he was unsuccessful, in spite of every effort,[6] in solving simultaneous difference equations as simple as (9) under the original assumption. The unnatural adjustment of the rate of accumulation by capitalists of department II to the exogenously determined rate of accumulation in department I was invented by Marx merely as a *deus ex machina*. However we should not be too surprised that Marx performed so poorly in this case. Even Walras could not properly solve the simultaneous differential (or difference) equations describing the process of *tâtonnement*. Remembering that Marx

---

[5] It is interesting to compare these results with those which are popular among contemporary economists. Formulating the process of reproduction in terms of differential equations:
$$Y(t) = PY(t) + Q\,dY/dt,$$
where $P = \begin{bmatrix} c_I & c_{II} \\ v_I + bs_I & v_{II} + bs_{II} \end{bmatrix}$ and $Q = \begin{bmatrix} c_I & c_{II} \\ v_I & v_{II} \end{bmatrix}$,

Shinkai, for example, has found that the balanced-growth path is stable if and only if department II is more capital-intensive than I. I prefer our formulation in the text to Shinkai's because, as we shall observe in a later section, our model can more easily be merged into von Neumann's, so that it can be extended to a more generalized system where capital goods may be used for a number of periods and the production period is different from commodity to commodity.

[6] See K. Marx, *Matiematitzieskie Rukopisi*, Moscow, 1968.

had begun his academic career as a philosophical student and learned mathematical economics by himself, we should be greatly impressed by his model, which may be taken as the prototype of the present-day Leontief–von Neumann models. In mathematical economics, like other sciences, the most important thing is to pose fundamental problems. Once models have been formulated, their solution may be relegated to assistants or even to computers.

Marx was unable by the use of his model of reproduction to explain the 'course characteristic of modern industry, viz., a decennial cycle (interrupted by smaller oscillations), of periods of average activity, production at high pressure, crisis and stagnation.' (I, pp. 632–3.) However, it is not very difficult to graft the modern theory of the trade cycle onto his model (8) or (9). In fact, by premultiplying (8) by $(v_\mathrm{I}, -c_\mathrm{I})$, we can eliminate $y_\mathrm{I}(t+1)$:

$$(v_\mathrm{I} + bs_\mathrm{I} c_\mathrm{I}) y_\mathrm{I}(t) = c_\mathrm{I}(1 - bs_\mathrm{II}) y_\mathrm{II}(t) + (c_\mathrm{II} v_\mathrm{I} - v_\mathrm{II} c_\mathrm{I}) y_\mathrm{II}(t+1),$$

which enables us to eliminate $y_\mathrm{I}(t)$ and $y_\mathrm{I}(t+1)$ from the first equation of (8). The result is:

$$a_0 y_\mathrm{II}(t+2) + a_1 y_\mathrm{II}(t+1) + a_2 y_\mathrm{II}(t) = 0, \quad (14)$$

where

$$a_0 = c_\mathrm{II} v_\mathrm{I} - v_\mathrm{II} c_\mathrm{I}, \quad a_1 = c_\mathrm{I}(1 - bs_\mathrm{II}) + v_\mathrm{II} + bs_\mathrm{I} c_\mathrm{II},$$

$$a_2 = -(1 - bs_\mathrm{II}). \quad (15)$$

Similarly, by premultiplying (8) by $(v_\mathrm{II}, -c_\mathrm{II})$, we can eliminate $y_\mathrm{II}(t)$:

$$c_\mathrm{II}(1 - bs_\mathrm{II}) y_\mathrm{II}(t) = (v_\mathrm{II} + bs_\mathrm{I} c_\mathrm{II}) y_\mathrm{I}(t) + (c_\mathrm{II} v_\mathrm{I} - c_\mathrm{I} v_\mathrm{II}) y_\mathrm{I}(t+1).$$

Substituting for y_II from this, the first equation of (8) becomes

$$a_0 y_\mathrm{I}(t+2) + a_1 y_\mathrm{I}(t+1) + a_2 y_\mathrm{I}(t) = 0. \quad (16)$$

We now define the net output of the society in terms of labour-time as

$$y(t) = y_\mathrm{II}(t) + [y_\mathrm{I}(t) - c_\mathrm{I} y_\mathrm{I}(t) - c_\mathrm{II} y_\mathrm{II}(t)],$$

which is consumption *plus* net investment. Then we obtain from (14) and (16) an equation of the same type concerning net output, i.e.

$$a_0 y(t+2) + a_1 y(t+1) + a_2 y(t) = 0, \quad (17)$$

which may be compared with Hicks' basic difference equation of the theory of the trade cycle and which can be handled as Hicks did his.[7]

First, the general solution to (17) is obtained in the usual way. Solving the characteristic equation,

$$a_0 \nu^2 + a_1 \nu + a_2 = 0, \qquad (18)$$

we obtain ν_1 and ν_2. Then the general solution is given as

$$y(t) = \xi_1 \nu_1^t + \xi_2 \nu_2^t,$$

and constants ξ_1 and ξ are determined by the initial conditions, i.e. the values of y in periods 0 and -1. It can be shown that the characteristic equation (18) of the aggregated system (17) is identical with the characteristic equation (12) of the original two sector model (9). We can show $\nu_i = 1/\mu_i$, $i = 1, 2$, so that we have $\nu_1 = 1 + g_1$ and $\nu_2 = 1 + g_2$. Then the particular solution $\xi_1 \nu_1^t$ gives the steadily progressive moving equilibrium, which is unstable because $\mu_1 > |\mu_2|$ or $1 + g_1 < |1 + g_2|$, as has been shown before. Also, we have explosive oscillations around the moving equilibrium if department II is higher in the composition of capital than I, and explosion without fluctuations in the converse case.

If he is provided with all the arrangements which he requires, Hicks can guide Marx further. We may complicate the simple model (17) by introducing the 'Full Employment' ceiling with an upward trend, autonomous investment increasing at a regular rate, the asymmetry of the working of the accelerator on the downswing and upswing, and so on. These elaborations, together with the fundamental result from the original free system, that the moving equilibrium is unstable if no ceiling is set, enable us to derive constrained cycles. If the initial position of the economy is given off the equilibrium growth path, output diverges from it, either by tracing out oscillations or in a monotonic way. The expansion in output will finally hit the ceiling at some point; then the path will bounce off it, after a little while during which the

[7] J. R. Hicks, *A Contribution to the Theory of the Trade Cycle* (Oxford, 1950), p. 69. In its simplest form, his equation can also be written as (17) with $a_0 = 1$, $a_1 = -(c+v)$, and $a_2 = v$, where c and v are Hicks'; that is, c is the marginal propensity to consume and v the investment coefficient, i.e. the ratio of the induced investment to the change in output. Hicks assumed time lags of one period in consumption and investment decisions.

economy creeps along the ceiling. In the downward movement the strong acceleration which we had on the upswing will cease to work. We shall have a multiplier process towards the floor, corresponding to the level of autonomous investment. The floor inclines upwards because of the assumed trend of autonomous investment. Along the floor output will be increased, so that the acceleration principle will start to work again – a second upswing is inevitable.

This Hicksian view might not satisfy Marx, because our equations (8) and (17) do not take Marx's view of crisis properly into account. Marx was unsuccessful in formulating a mathematical model of the trade cycle, but he was quite explicit about how he viewed industrial fluctuation. In his words, 'a crisis could...be explained as the result of a disproportion of production in various branches of the economy, and as a result of a disproportion between the consumption of the capitalists and their accumulation. But as matters stand, the replacement of the capital invested in production depends largely upon the consuming power of the non-producing classes, while the consuming power of the workers is limited partly by the laws of wages, partly by the fact that they are used only as long as they can profitably be employed by the capitalist class. The ultimate reason for all real crises always remains the poverty and restricted consumption of the masses as opposed to the drive of capitalist production to develop the productive forces.' (III, p. 485.) However, Hicks' theory could be extended, by replacing the second equation of (8) and by an inequality, so as to allow over-production of consumption goods.

CHAPTER 11

The reserve army and the falling rate of profit

It is evident that the rate of employment is the ratio of the population of labourers actually employed to the total number of people who want to work; therefore its movement is investigated by comparing the rate of increase of employed workers to the rate of increase of the total population (if a constant fraction of the total population remains 'unproductive' through time). However, it is not clear what Marx assumed about the absolute or proportional increase in the labouring population, or about the natural rate of growth of the labour force. Leaving this unclear, he concentrated his attention on the relative surplus population or 'the varying proportions in which the working-class is divided into active and reserve army'. He affirmed: 'every special historic mode of production has its own special laws of production, historically valid within its limits alone'; and he claimed to have found 'a law of population peculiar to the capitalist mode of production' (I, p. 632).

What Marx assumed about the population growth is vague, but his model of reproduction is clearly distinct from the model which Samuelson called 'von Neumann–Malthus',[1] though very similar to the one that I have called 'Marx–von Neumann'.[2] In the von Neumann–Malthus model, Samuelson assumes that the rate of growth of population is a rising function of the real wage rate which takes on a value of zero when the real wage rate is fixed at the subsistence level; so we have a persistent balanced growth of capital and labour, or a von Neumann–Malthus golden age, only at an equilibrium real wage rate above the subsistence level. It is, however, clear that Marx rejected such a view, that a simultaneous equilibrium of capital and labour could be established by adjusting the real wage rate. He wrote: 'According to them [i.e. the dogmatic economists] wages rise in consequence of accumulation of capital. The higher wages stimulate the working population to more rapid multiplication, and this goes on until the labour-market becomes too full, and therefore

[1] P. A. Samuelson, 'Understanding the Marxian Notion of Exploitation: A Summary...', *Journal of Economic Literature*, IX, June 1971, p. 406.
[2] See my *Equilibrium, Stability and Growth* (Oxford, 1964), ch. 5.

capital, relatively to the supply of labour, becomes insufficient. Wages fall, and now we have the reverse of the medal. The working population is little by little decimated as the result of the fall in wages, so that capital is again in excess relatively to them, or, as others explain it, falling wages and the corresponding increase in the exploitation of the labourer again accelerates accumulation, whilst, at the same time, the lower wages hold the increase of the working-class in check. Then comes again the time, when the supply of labour is less than the demand, wages rise, and so on. A beautiful mode of motion this for developed capitalist production!' (I, p. 637.)

It is of course true that Marx was a subsistence-wage theorist. In his words, the 'value of labour-power [hence, the real wage rate] is determined by the value of the necessaries of life habitually required by the average labourer. The quantity of these necessaries is known at any given epoch of a given society, and can therefore be treated as a constant magnitude.' (I, p. 519.) Thus, 'there enters into the determination of the value of labour-power a historical and moral element' (I, p. 171). He also admitted that for the majority of the working-class life at the subsistence wage level was tragic and horrible. He wrote: 'in this "Paradise of Capitalists" there follows, on the smallest change in the price of the most essential means of subsistence, a change in the number of deaths and crimes!' (I, p. 672.) 'The minimum limit of the value of labour-power is determined... by the value of those means of subsistence that are physically indispensable. If the price of labour-power fall to this minimum, it falls below its value, since under such circumstances it can be maintained and developed only in a crippled state.' (I, p. 173.) 'The owner of labour-power is mortal. If then his appearance in the market is to be continuous,... the seller of labour-power must perpetuate himself, "in the way that every living individual perpetuates himself, by procreation". The labour-power withdrawn from the market by wear and tear and death, must be continually replaced by, at the very least, an equal amount of fresh labour-power. Hence the sum of the means of subsistence necessary for the production of labour-power must include the means necessary for the labourer's substitutes, i.e., his children, in order that this race of peculiar commodity-owners may perpetuate its appearance in the market.' (I, pp. 171–2.)

On the other hand, however, Marx wrote: 'The over-work of the employed part of the working-class swells the ranks of the reserve, whilst conversely the greater pressure that the latter by its competition exerts on the former, forces these to submit to over-work and to subjugation under the dictates of capital. The condemnation of one part of the working-class to enforced idleness by the over-work of the other part, and the converse, becomes a means of enriching the individual capitalists and accelerates at the same time the production of the industrial reserve army on a scale corresponding with the advance of social accumulation. How important is this element in the formation of the relative surplus-population, is shown by the example of England. Her technical means for saving labour are colossal.' (I, pp. 636–7.) 'We have explained...that labour-power is always available under the capitalist system of production, and that more labour can be rendered fluent, if necessary, without increasing the number of labourers or the quantity of labour-power employed. We...assume that the portion of the newly created money-capital capable of being converted into variable capital will always find at hand the labour-power into which it is to transform itself.' (II, p. 505.) Thus, from the evidence of these statements we may say that Marx assumed, though not explicitly, a high rate of growth of the labour force (that is, high in relation to the rate of growth of the demand for labour) even at the subsistence-wage rate, for biological, sociological, technical and other reasons, i.e. the natural increase in the labour force, the arrival of new-comers from the backward areas or the non-capitalistic sectors, technical improvements of the labour-saving type. Therefore the economy can grow at the minimum real wage rate, producing a relative surplus population which is ever growing. It is a Marx–von Neumann golden age! 'Accumulation of capital is, therefore, increase of the proletariat.' (I, p. 614.)

Throughout the following, we are concerned with an economy where the natural rate of growth of the total population or the labour force is kept unchanged; we explicitly assume that it is a positive constant. Under this assumption, we shall confirm in this chapter the following three propositions concerning employment which are stated by Marx: (i) Under the condition that the value composition of capital remains the same, growth of capital gives rise to a proportional increase in the employment of labour, and 'their [the labourers'] relation of dependence upon capital takes on a form endurable'. 'Instead of becoming more intensive with the growth of capital, this relation of dependence only becomes more extensive.' (I, p. 617.) (ii) 'The course characteristic of modern industry, viz. a decennial cycle (interrupted by smaller oscillations), of periods of average activity, production at high pressure, crisis and stagnation, depends on the constant formation, the greater or less absorption, and the re-formation of the industrial reserve army or surplus-population.' (I, pp. 632–3.) (iii) '[The] change in the technical composition of capital, the growth in the mass of means of production, as compared with the mass of the labour-power that vivifies them, is reflected...in its value-composition, by the increase of the constant constituent of capital at the expense of its variable constituent.' (I, p. 622.) 'Since the demand for labour is determined not by the amount of capital as a whole, but by its variable constituent alone, that demand falls progressively with the increase of the total capital, instead of...rising in proportion to it. It falls relatively to the magnitude of the total capital, and at an accelerated rate, as this magnitude increases.' (I, p. 629.)

Marx derived these conclusions from a one-department model in volume I; in this chapter we shall try to re-establish them in the two-department model. These conclusions are important not only for their own sake but also because Marx derived from them his view of the breakdown of capitalism. In his words, along with the constantly or periodically increasing reserve army, will grow 'the mass of misery, oppression, slavery, degradation, exploitation; but with this too grows the revolt of the working-class, a class always increasing in numbers, and disciplined, united, organised by the very mechanism of the process of capitalist production itself. The monopoly of capital becomes a fetter upon the mode of production, which has sprung up and flourished along with, and under it. Centralisation of the means of production and socialisation of labour at last reach a point where they become incompatible with their capitalist integument...The knell of capitalist private property sounds. The expropriators are expropriated.' (I, p. 763.)

The most important factor in the following analysis is, as Marx said, 'the composition of capital and the changes it undergoes in the course of the process of accumulation'. 'The many individual

THE RESERVE ARMY

capitals invested in a particular branch of production have, one with another, more or less different compositions. The average of their individual compositions gives us the composition of the total capital in this branch of production. Lastly, the average of these averages, in all branches of production, gives us the composition of the total social capital of a country, and with this alone are we, in the last resort, concerned in the following investigation.' (I, pp. 612–13.)

We start again with our basic demand–supply equations for the outputs of the two departments:

$$y_{\mathrm{I}}(t) = c_{\mathrm{I}} y_{\mathrm{I}}(t) + c_{\mathrm{II}} y_{\mathrm{II}}(t) + c_{\mathrm{I}} \Delta y_{\mathrm{I}}(t) + c_{\mathrm{II}} \Delta y_{\mathrm{II}}(t), \quad (1)$$

$$y_{\mathrm{II}}(t) = v_{\mathrm{I}} y_{\mathrm{I}}(t) + v_{\mathrm{II}} y_{\mathrm{II}}(t) + v_{\mathrm{I}} \Delta y_{\mathrm{I}}(t)$$
$$+ v_{\mathrm{II}} \Delta y_{\mathrm{II}}(t) + b s_{\mathrm{I}} y_{\mathrm{I}}(t) + b s_{\mathrm{I}} y_{\mathrm{I}}(t) + b s_{\mathrm{II}} y_{\mathrm{II}}(t), \quad (2)$$

where y_{I} is the output of department I in terms of value, for one unit of which c_{I} constant capital and v_{I} variable capital are required to yield s_{I} surplus value; similarly for department II; and b represents the ratio of the capitalists' consumption (in terms of value) to the total surplus value. Let the rate of growth of the total value of capitals utilized be defined as

$$g_K(t) = \frac{(c_{\mathrm{I}} + v_{\mathrm{I}}) \Delta y_{\mathrm{I}}(t) + (c_{\mathrm{II}} + v_{\mathrm{II}}) \Delta y_{\mathrm{II}}(t)}{(c_{\mathrm{I}} + v_{\mathrm{I}}) y_{\mathrm{I}}(t) + (c_{\mathrm{II}} + v_{\mathrm{II}}) y_{\mathrm{II}}(t)}. \quad (3)$$

As $c_i + v_i + s_i = 1$, $i = $ I, II, we have from (1) and (2)

$$s_{\mathrm{I}} y_{\mathrm{I}}(t) + s_{\mathrm{II}} y_{\mathrm{II}}(t) = (c_{\mathrm{I}} + v_{\mathrm{I}}) \Delta y_{\mathrm{I}}(t)$$
$$+ (c_{\mathrm{II}} + v_{\mathrm{II}}) \Delta y_{\mathrm{II}}(t) + b[s_{\mathrm{I}} y_{\mathrm{I}}(t) + s_{\mathrm{II}} y_{\mathrm{II}}(t)], \quad (4)$$

which implies that the total surplus value equals the value of investment *plus* the value consumed by the capitalists' families. This can be further rewritten in the familiar form of the equality between savings and investment,

$$a[s_{\mathrm{I}} y_{\mathrm{I}}(t) + s_{\mathrm{II}} y_{\mathrm{II}}(t)]$$
$$= (c_{\mathrm{I}} + v_{\mathrm{I}}) \Delta y_{\mathrm{I}}(t) + (c_{\mathrm{II}} + v_{\mathrm{II}}) \Delta y_{\mathrm{II}}(t), \quad (5)$$

where $a = 1 - b$ denotes the ratio of the value of investment in constant and variable capitals to the total surplus value, which is called the rate of accumulation and is assumed to be constant unless otherwise stated. As $s_{\mathrm{I}} = e v_{\mathrm{I}}$ and $s_{\mathrm{II}} = e v_{\mathrm{II}}$, where e is the rate of exploitation, we obtain from (5) by dividing it by the value of total capital, $(c_\mathrm{I}+v_\mathrm{I})y_\mathrm{I}(t) + (c_\mathrm{II}+v_\mathrm{II})y_\mathrm{II}(t)$, and bearing the definition of the rate of growth of capital in mind

$$g_K(t) = ae\frac{V(t)}{C(t)+V(t)} = ae\frac{1}{k(t)+1}, \qquad (6)$$

where $C(t)$ and $V(t)$ denote the total constant capital and the total variable capital respectively, and $k(t)$ the value-composition of the total social capital in period t, that is $C(t)/V(t)$. It is noted that as $C(t)$ and $V(t)$ are weighted sums of $y_\mathrm{I}(t)$ and $y_\mathrm{II}(t)$, the value-composition of the social capital may change when $y_\mathrm{I}(t)$ and $y_\mathrm{II}(t)$ fluctuate from period to period, provided that departments I and II are different in the value-composition of capital.

Next, let us define the rate of growth of the demand for labour as

$$g_L(t) = \frac{l_\mathrm{I}\Delta y_\mathrm{I}(t) + l_\mathrm{II}\Delta y_\mathrm{II}(t)}{l_\mathrm{I}y_\mathrm{I}(t) + l_\mathrm{II}y_\mathrm{II}(t)}, \qquad (7)$$

where l_I and l_II are labour directly required per unit of y_I and y_II respectively. Obviously, $l_i = v_i + s_i = (1+e)v_i$, $i = \mathrm{I}, \mathrm{II}$; we have, therefore,

$$g_L(t) = \frac{v_\mathrm{I}\Delta y_\mathrm{I}(t) + v_\mathrm{II}\Delta y_\mathrm{II}(t)}{v_\mathrm{I}y_\mathrm{I}(t) + v_\mathrm{II}y_\mathrm{II}(t)} = \frac{v_\mathrm{I}y_\mathrm{I}(t+1) + v_\mathrm{II}y_\mathrm{II}(t+1)}{v_\mathrm{I}y_\mathrm{I}(t) + v_\mathrm{II}y_\mathrm{II}(t)} - 1.$$

Hence,

$$1 + g_L(t) = \left\{\frac{V(t+1)}{C(t+1)+V(t+1)}[C(t+1)+V(t+1)]\right\}$$
$$\div \left\{\frac{V(t)}{C(t)+V(t)}[C(t)+V(t)]\right\}$$
$$= \frac{k(t)+1}{k(t+1)+1}\frac{C(t+1)+V(t+1)}{C(t)+V(t)}$$
$$= \frac{k(t)+1}{k(t+1)+1}(1+g_K(t)), \qquad (8)$$

which plays a role of fundamental importance in the following discussion.

From (8) Marx's first result mentioned above follows at once. From the definition of $k(t)$ as

$$k(t) = \frac{C(t)}{V(t)} = \frac{c_\mathrm{I}y_\mathrm{I}(t) + c_\mathrm{II}y_\mathrm{II}(t)}{v_\mathrm{I}y_\mathrm{I}(t) + v_\mathrm{II}y_\mathrm{II}(t)}, \qquad (9)$$

it is seen that the composition of the total social capital remains the same, if $y_I(t)$ and $y_{II}(t)$ grow in balance.[3] Then from (8) we have $g_L(t) = g_K(t)$, since $k(t) = k(t+1)$. Thus, 'the demand for labour and the subsistence-fund of the labourers clearly increase in the same proportion as the capital, and the more rapidly, the more rapidly the capital increases' (I, p. 613). If the rate of growth of the demand for labour, $g_L(t)$, thus determined is equal to the natural rate of growth of the labour force ρ, the rate of unemployment will remain constant through time. In particular, if there is full employment at the outset it will persist forever. On the other hand, if $g_L(t)$ is greater than ρ, the economy will suffer from persistent shortage of labour, while in the opposite case of the former being smaller than the latter, full employment growth becomes impossible. Of the last two possibilities Marx remarked as follows: 'In the first case, it is not the diminished rate either of the absolute, or of the proportional, increase in labour-power, or labouring population, which causes capital to be in excess, but conversely the excess of capital that makes exploitable labour-power insufficient. In the second case, it is not the increased rate either of the absolute, or of the proportional, increase in labour-power, or labouring population, that makes capital insufficient; but, conversely, the relative diminution of capital that causes the exploitable labour-power, or rather its price, to be in excess.' (I, pp. 619–20.) It must also be remarked that it is extremely difficult to keep the rate of unemployment constant. The steadiness of the rate of employment at a high level, however desirable it is for both workers and capitalists, may be realized only in a state of balanced growth; and vicious fluctuations or cumulative changes (in either direction) in the employment ratio will easily be generated by the slightest shock since, as we have seen in the last section, the balanced growth path is definitely unstable.

Next we turn to Marx's second result. We assume now that the value-composition of capital is higher in department II, producing wage and luxury goods, than in I, producing capital goods. Then we shall generally have oscillations around the balanced growth path; and moreover, they will be explosive.

---

[3] If departments I and II are identical in the composition of capital, $k(t)$ remains unchanged even though $y_I(t)$ and $y_{II}(t)$ do not grow in balance. However, the two-department model analysis excludes this case, because the two departments are assumed to be distinct in composition.

That is to say, the relative output, $y_I(t)/y_{II}(t)$, oscillates around a stationary level which it takes on in the state of balanced growth and the amplitude of oscillations will become larger and larger as time goes on. Such fluctuations in relative output will be reflected in the movement of the value composition of the total social capital. As $k_I = c_I/v_I$ and $k_{II} = c_{II}/v_{II}$, we have from (9)

$$k(t) = \frac{k_I v_I y_I(t) + k_{II} v_{II} y_{II}(t)}{v_I y_I(t) + v_{II} y_{II}(t)}, \quad (10)$$

which means that $k(t)$ is an average of the departmental compositions of capital, with departmental variable capitals as weights. These weights fluctuate when relative output fluctuates; and as $k_{II} > k_I$, oscillations of the relative output with growing amplitude bring about oscillations of $k(t)$, with its eventual greatest and least values, k_{II} and k_I.[4]

Let us now substitute (6) into the extreme right-hand side of (8); then we obtain

$$1 + g_L(t) = \frac{k(t) + 1 + ae}{k(t+1) + 1} \quad \text{or} \quad g_L(t) = \frac{k(t) - k(t+1) + ae}{k(t+1) + 1}, \quad (11)$$

from which we find that oscillations of $k(t)$ with growing amplitude generate similar oscillations of the rate of growth of the demand for labour, $g_L(t)$. If k_{II} differs sufficiently from k_I so $k_I + ae < k_{II}$, then $g_L(t)$ will eventually take on negative values periodically, though it remains positive during the earlier part of the history, when the amplitude of oscillations of $k(t)$ is small (i.e. less than ae). Thus we have alternate attractions and repulsions of workers by capital, which become greater and greater in their extent with the progress of time. It is evident from the above analysis that the alternate contraction and expansion of the reserve army produced in this way should ultimately be ascribed to the periodic changes in industrial activities; and this view led Marx to the following conclusions: 'For Modern Industry with its decennial cycles and periodic phases, which, moreover, as accumulation advances, are complicated by irregular oscillations following each other more and more quickly, that would indeed be a beautiful law, which pretends to make the action of capital dependent on the absolute variation of the population,

[4] If we ignore the conditions for feasibility, $y_I(t) \geq 0$ and $y_{II}(t) \geq 0$, $k(t)$ will oscillate in an explosive way.

instead of regulating the demand and supply of labour by the alternate expansion and contraction of capital, the labour market now appearing relatively under-full, because capital is expanding, now again over-full, because it is contracting. Yet this is the dogma of the economists. According to them...' This quotation is followed by the one quoted on p. 129, from volume I, p. 637.

We have so far assumed that the value-composition of capital remains the same in each department, so that changes in the value composition of the total social capital have only reflected changes in the relative output. We are next concerned with the effects on the rates of growth of capital and labour of a particular type of technical improvement in which Marx was interested. According to him, 'the degree of productivity of labour, in a given society, is expressed in the relative extent of the means of production that one labourer, during a given time, with the same tension of labour-power, turns into products'. 'The increase of some [means of production] is a consequence, that of the others a condition of the increasing productivity of labour. E.g. with the division of labour in manufacture, and with the use of machinery, more raw material is worked up in the same time, and, therefore, a greater mass of raw material and auxiliary substances enter into the labour-process. That is the consequence of the increasing productivity of labour. On the other hand, the mass of machinery, beasts of burden, mineral manures, drain-pipes, etc., is a condition of the increasing productivity of labour.' 'But whether condition or consequence, the growing extent of the means of production, as compared with the labour-power incorporated with them, is an expression of the growing productiveness of labour.' (I, p. 622.)

Such changes in the technical composition of capital present themselves as changes in the technical coefficients, such as the capital-input coefficients a_{ij} and labour-input coefficients l_j. They also generally give rise to changes in the values of commodities, λ_r, $r = 1, ..., m$, since they depend on the technical coefficients. However, an increase in a_{ij} will bring about an increase in λ_r, whereas a decrease in l_j will bring about a decrease; they may be compensated by each other, so that λ_r may remain unaffected. Throughout the following, we are concerned for the sake of simplicity only with such a class of changes in the technical composition of capital, whose various effects on the values of individual commodities are neutralized. As λ_r is constant, a change in the technical composition of capital will be reflected correctly in its value-composition; therefore we assume that the value-composition of capital k_i of each department rises from year to year. Marx called 'the value composition of capital, in so far as it is determined by its technical composition and mirrors the changes of the latter, the organic composition of capital' (I, p. 612). Thus a kind of neutral technical change is assumed by a rise in the value-composition.

When k_i increases, v_i and s_i decrease if the rate of exploitation is kept constant, because we have by definition the identity: $c_i + v_i + s_i = (k_i + 1 + e) v_i = 1$, $i =$ I, II. Now the rate of growth of capital is defined as

$$g_K(t) = \frac{(c_\mathrm{I} + v_\mathrm{I})_{t+1} y_\mathrm{I}(t+1) + (c_\mathrm{II} + v_\mathrm{II})_{t+1} y_\mathrm{II}(t+1) - (c_\mathrm{I} + v_\mathrm{I})_t y_\mathrm{I}(t) - (c_\mathrm{II} + v_\mathrm{II})_t y_\mathrm{II}(t)}{(c_\mathrm{I} + v_\mathrm{I})_t y_\mathrm{I}(t) + (c_\mathrm{II} + v_\mathrm{II})_t y_\mathrm{II}(t)}, \quad (3')$$

where $(c_\mathrm{I} + v_\mathrm{I})_t$ and $(c_\mathrm{II} + v_\mathrm{II})_t$ represent the sums of the coefficients for production of $y_\mathrm{I}(t)$ and $y_\mathrm{II}(t)$; i.e. $(c_\mathrm{I})_t + (v_\mathrm{I})_t$ and $(c_\mathrm{II})_t + (v_\mathrm{II})_t$ respectively. Similarly, the rate of growth of the demand for labour (7) is rewritten as

$$g_L(t) = \frac{l_{\mathrm{I},t+1} y_\mathrm{I}(t+1) + l_{\mathrm{II},t+1} y_\mathrm{II}(t+1) - l_{\mathrm{I},t} y_\mathrm{I}(t) - l_{\mathrm{II},t} y_\mathrm{II}(t)}{l_{\mathrm{I},t} y_\mathrm{I}(t) + l_{\mathrm{II},t} y_\mathrm{II}(t)}. \quad (7')$$

Furthermore, a similar amendment is made on the right-hand side of (5), which should now read:

$$a[s_{\mathrm{I},t} y_\mathrm{I}(t) + s_{\mathrm{II},t} y_\mathrm{II}(t)] = (c_\mathrm{I} + v_\mathrm{I})_{t+1} y_\mathrm{I}(t+1) + (c_\mathrm{II} + v_\mathrm{II})_{t+1} y_\mathrm{II}(t+1) - (c_\mathrm{I} + v_\mathrm{I})_t y_\mathrm{I}(t) - (c_\mathrm{II} + v_\mathrm{II})_t y_\mathrm{II}(t). \quad (5')$$

From these equations we derive the equations concerning the rates of growth of capital and labour in exactly the same way as before.

As the composition of the total social capital $k(t)$ is, needless to say, an average of the departmental compositions, it is between $k_\mathrm{I}(t)$ and $k_\mathrm{II}(t)$. Let us denote the larger and the smaller of $k_\mathrm{I}(t)$

and $k_{\mathrm{II}}(t)$ by $k^*(t)$ and $k_*(t)$ respectively. We then have, from (6) and (8),

$$g_K(t) \leqslant \frac{ae}{k_*(t)+1}, \tag{6'}$$

$$1+g_L(t) \leqslant \frac{k^*(t)+1}{k_*(t+1)+1}\left[1+\frac{ae}{k_*(t)+1}\right]. \tag{8'}$$

Therefore, when $k_{\mathrm{I}}(t)$ and $k_{\mathrm{II}}(t)$ increase more or less proportionately, the ratio $[k^*(t)+1]/[k_*(t)+1]$ is reasonably stable, while $k_*(t)$ increases; hence, we find from (6') and (8') that both $g_K(t)$ and $g_L(t)$ are bounded by declining ceilings. Marx then derived his third conclusion under the assumption that changes in k_{I} and k_{II} are accelerated with the advance of accumulation. In his words, 'This [assumed] accelerated relative diminution of the variable constituent, that goes along with the accelerated increase of the total capital...produces...a relatively redundant population of labourers, i.e., a population of greater extent than suffices for the average needs of the self-expansion of capital and therefore a surplus-population.' (I, p. 630.)

'Up to this point it has been assumed that the increase or diminution of the variable capital corresponds rigidly with the increase or diminution of the number of labourers employed.' (I, p. 635.) Marx then made the assumption of wage adjustment: 'the general movements of wages are exclusively regulated by the expansion and contraction of the industrial reserve army' (I, p. 637). Then an increase in the reserve army induces a decrease in real wages, so that capitalists are now exploiting workers at a greater rate. It is therefore seen from (6) and (8) that the decrease in the rate of growth of capital will be mitigated and some reserve forces will be mobilized. However, such a lull cannot prevail over a long period. As long as k_{I} and k_{II} have an inherent tendency to increase, or as long as cyclic fluctuations of outputs are unavoidable and explosive, a large reserve army will sooner or later be formed and wages will tend to diminish again. The real wage rate will at last reach its minimum level, below which it is impossible to maintain capitalist production because there will be a rebellion of organized workers. There is thus an upper bound to the rate of exploitation. Similarly an increase in the rate of accumulation, a, will encourage the rate of growth of capital and hence the rate of growth of the demand for labour; but this too is no more than a temporizing policy, because a is bounded by one. The means adopted to overcome crises diminish the means whereby crises can be prevented. At last, capitalists will be at the end of their tether; 'we have the expropriation of a few usurpers by the mass of the people' (I, p. 764). And 'capitalist production begets, with the inexorability of a law of Nature, its own negation. It is the negation of negation' (I, p. 763).

I should now draw the reader's attention to the fact that the rate a at which capitalists reserve the surplus value for accumulation has so far been assumed to be determined exogenously. This is, however, a very unrealistic assumption, because in any economy where commodities are traded through the medium of money no capitalist makes a decision about accumulation in terms of the surplus value measured in labour-time. Marx wrote: 'By the conversion of the commodity-capital into money the surplus product, in which the surplus-value is represented, is also turned into money. The capitalist reconverts the so metamorphosed surplus-value into additional natural elements of his productive capital. In the next cycle of production the increased capital furnishes an increased product.' (II, p. 493.) Thus capitalists can at best decide a proportion of the profit or 'the so metamorphosed surplus-value' which is re-invested in the process of annual reproduction of society. Let s_c be the ratio of capitalists' savings to the total amount of profit. The assumption that s_c is a constant fraction which is determined by the capitalists' propensity to save is economically meaningful and might be accepted (or at worst refutable) as a first approximation to reality, but the parallel assumption concerning the rate of accumulation a in terms of value could not claim such a commanding position, even in Marx's system, as the constancy of s_c occupies in the orthodox theory. The ratio a is not a directly 'operationally meaningful' concept in the sense of Samuelson's definition.[5]

If it is thus illegitimate to assume that the rate of accumulation a is given, we must expand the system so as to be able to determine it endogenously. Assume that capitalists exploit workers as much as possible, as Marx thought they really were doing in the Victorian era. Then the actual length of the working day T is

[5] P. A. Samuelson, *Foundation of Economic Analysis* (Harvard University Press, 1947), pp. 3–5.

prolonged to the maximum $\overline{T}$, so that the rate of exploitation takes on its maximum value $\bar{e}$. Also, assume that the departmental composition of capital $k_\mathrm{I}(t)$ and $k_\mathrm{II}(t)$ change in an autonomous way. Then the identities,

$$c_i(t) = k_i(t)v_i(t), \quad s_i(t) = \bar{e}v_i(t),$$
$$c_i(t) + v_i(t) + s_i(t) = 1 \quad (i = \mathrm{I}, \mathrm{II})$$

fully determine all the parameters of Marx's reproduction scheme except the rate of accumulation a. Now if we could extend the model so that it could determine outputs $y_\mathrm{I}(t)$ and $y_\mathrm{II}(t)$ and their growth rates independently of a, then $g_K(t)$ and $k(t)$ would be determined by (3) and (9) respectively. Therefore, (6) contains only one unknown variable a to be determined. The crux will thus be resolved if we succeed in determining departmental outputs and growth rates outside the reproduction model in terms of value. This problem is not so difficult; by re-stating the equations between the demand and supply of commodities, not in terms of value but in terms of physical quantities and the capitalists' propensity to save out of profits, we can determine departmental outputs and growth rates, as we shall see in the next chapter, without any reference to the rate of accumulation defined in terms of value.

There is one more problem, which is postponed to the next chapter. In the above analysis of the effects of an accelerating increase in the value-composition of capital, we have assumed that the values of commodities remain unaffected in spite of changes in capital and labour-input coefficients. It is evident that this assumption is non-vacuous, but there are of course some technical improvements which bring forth changes (perhaps decreases) in the values of commodities and result in a higher composition of capital. If values of wage goods decrease, there will be a decrease in the value of labour-power and hence an increase in the rate of exploitation, the latter in turn having a favourable effect on the rate of growth of the demand for labour, through its favourable effect on the rate of growth of capital. Thus if an upward shift of the exploitation curve may accompany technical improvements, it may be possible for a capitalist society to avoid the crises pointed out by Marx. Then we must ask: Can technological development play the role of the saviour of the regime?

Before going on to discuss this problem in the next chapter, the rest of the present chapter is devoted to a brief examination of the 'law of the tendency of the rate of profit to fall'. Marx wrote: 'the average rate of profit in the various branches of production is determined not by the particular composition of each individual capital, but by the average social composition' (III, p. 220). Although it is clear that he took the average social composition as the actual one, it should in fact be interpreted as the average of the industrial compositions weighted by the golden equilibrium industrial outputs y_i, $i = 1, ..., m$. We have the Morishima–Seton formula,

$$\pi = \frac{e \sum_{i=1}^{m} V_i y_i}{\sum_{i=1}^{m} (C_i + V_i) y_i}, \qquad (12)$$

which is one of the conclusions of the transformation problem. As all the followers of Marx as well as his critics have discussed the falling rate of profit by taking the average social composition as the actual average, the following treatment based on the true formula (12) may be claimed as the first rigorous proof of the law. Nevertheless, it is true that there is no significant difference between the previous proofs by other authors and our new proof, except that we have the golden-equilibrium total constant capital and the golden-equilibrium total variable capital in place of their actual total constant capital and actual total variable capital.[6]

For the sake of simplicity, we proceed in terms of the two-departmental model. Let y_I and y_{II} be the golden-equilibrium outputs of departments I and II. Then the departmental equivalent of the formula (12) may be written as

$$\pi = e \frac{v_I y_I + v_{II} y_{II}}{(c_I + v_I) y_I + (c_{II} + v_{II}) y_{II}} = e \frac{1}{k+1}, \qquad (13)$$

where k is the average of the departmental value-composition of capital:

$$k = \frac{c_I y_I + c_{II} y_{II}}{v_I y_I + v_{II} y_{II}} = \frac{k_I v_I y_I + k_{II} v_{II} y_{II}}{v_I y_I + v_{II} y_{II}}. \qquad (14)$$

Now we assume that there is an increase in the capital-input coefficients a_{ij}, $i = 1, ..., n$, in each industry j, which is accom-

[6] See Morishima and Seton, 'Aggregation', p. 209.

panied by a decrease in the labour-input coefficient l_j, so as to have no effect on the values λ_i, $i = 1, \ldots, m$. We also assume that before and after the technical change industries within each department are identical in the value composition of capital. Marx did not specify the technical change in such a restrictive way, but the following weak specification made by Marx is insufficient for deriving the law of the falling rate of profit rigorously. He wrote: 'owing to the distinctive methods of production developing in the capitalist system the same number of labourers, i.e. the same quantity of labour-power set in motion by a variable capital of a given value, operate, work up and productively consume in the same time span an ever-increasing quantity of means of labour, machinery and fixed capital of all sorts, raw and auxiliary materials – and consequently a constant capital of an ever-increasing value. This continual relative decrease of the variable capital *vis-à-vis* the constant, and consequently the total capital, is identical with the progressively higher organic composition of the social capital in its average.' (III, p. 212.) This 'gradual change in the composition of capital is not confined only to individual spheres of production, but... it occurs more or less in all, or at least in the key spheres of production, so that it involves changes in the average organic composition of the total capital of a certain society.' (III, p. 212.)

By the assumptions c_I and c_{II} increase, while v_I and v_{II} decrease, so that k_I and k_{II} increase at some rate which may possibly differ from each other. As y_I and y_{II} are the golden-equilibrium outputs, we have

$$\left. \begin{array}{l} y_I = (1+g)(c_I y_I + c_{II} y_{II}) \\ y_{II} = (1+g)(v_I y_I + v_{II} y_{II}), \end{array} \right\} \quad (15)$$

where g is the golden equilibrium rate of growth, which is equal to the rate of profit π. Therefore, (14) and (15) together yield

$$k = \frac{y_I}{y_{II}} = \frac{c_I y_I + c_{II} y_{II}}{v_I y_I + v_{II} y_{II}},$$

from which we obtain

$$v_I k^2 + (v_{II} - c_I) k - c_{II} = 0. \quad (16)$$

Since it is assumed that each coefficient of this equation decreases, its positive solution k must increase. Thus the technical change induces a change in the average *equilibrium* (but not necessarily the *actual*) organic composition of the total capital of the society. We may then conclude from (13), as Marx did: 'the gradual growth of constant capital in relation to variable capital must necessarily lead to *a gradual fall of the general rate of profit*, so long as the rate of surplus-value, or the intensity of exploitation of labour by capital, remain the same' (III, p. 212; italics by Marx). 'The immediate result of this is that the rate of surplus-value, at the same, or even a rising, degree of labour exploitation, is represented by a continually falling general rate of profit' (III, p. 213).

Finally, it is noted that the growth paths discussed in chapters 10 and 11 (and also those which will be obtained in chapter 12) are no more than 'warranted' growth paths, if we may use Harrod's terminology. Marx, like Harrod, was also concerned with temporary or more persistent deviations of the actual path from the corresponding warranted path. However, it is very difficult to formulate these parts of *Capital* in a rigorous way by means of simple mathematical models, though they supply interesting and important material.

CHAPTER 12

The dynamic transformation problem

One of Marx's main purposes in *Capital* was to examine the conditions of production and exchange corresponding to the capitalist mode of production. In the theory of exchange, Marx's purpose was to recognize the social character of human labour, or the relation of each individual's labour to the aggregate labour of society, behind the exchange ratios between commodities. Blind citizens in society, however, are not aware of this fundamental condition, or its inevitable consequences, and demand commodities simply because of their perceptible properties – values in use. When individuals make an exchange, their practical concern is with the proportions in which commodities are exchanged. At first sight the ratio appears to reflect the natural usefulness of commodities, but eventually the scientific conviction arises that the labour-time socially necessary for the production of commodities ultimately regulates the ratios of exchange. As has been made clear by the static transformation problem, it is of course true that the law of value asserts itself in a capitalist economy only in an extended form, allowing some deviations of prices from values; but what is important is that the law in the extended sense has been fulfilled, in spite of the fact that the members of society are ignorant of it.

Similarly, in the theory of reproduction, Marx's purpose was to study the process of reproduction from the point of view of the replacement of value. In Marx's words, the problem is: 'How is the *capital* consumed in production replaced in value out of the annual product and how does the movement of this replacement intertwine with the consumption of the surplus-value by the capitalists and of the wages by the labourers?' (II, p. 397.) This problem was discussed by Marx, for the case of simple reproduction in a form more or less similar to chapter 9 above, and for the case of extended reproduction in a form more or less similar to chapters 10 and 11 above. In the latter case the rate of accumulation, i.e. the ratio of the value of investment to the total surplus value, is one of the central concepts of the theory. It is defined in terms of value and is regarded as given exogenously. (In literary terms, Marx assumed that the rate of accumulation of the capitalists of department I was an exogenous factor, to which that of the capitalists of department II was adjusted.) In an actual economy, however, capitalists are not aware of the scientific law of reproduction; capitalists' decisions about investment are made, as are traders' decisions about exchange, not in terms of value, but in terms of prices. Why does 'the general law of capitalist accumulation' forcibly assert itself like a law of Nature, in spite of the fact that all the members of the society are ignorant of it? Marx asked the same question about the law of value and was led to extend it. Similarly, as will be seen below, in a society where capitalists are responsive to prices but not to values, the law of capitalist accumulation cannot assert itself in its original version; it is transformed into a more realistic law, just as values are transformed into prices in the static transformation problem.

Let us reformulate the theory of reproduction under the new assumption that capitalists spend a portion of their profits for consumption and the rest for investment. Obviously the new version is expected to have many parts in common with the previous theory developed in chapters 10 and 11, but we shall repeat some of our description, so that this chapter can be self-contained. The most fundamental equations in the theory of reproduction are those describing the physical replacement of the constant and variable capitals which are consumed in the process of reproduction; they are the demand–supply equations for capital, wage and luxury goods. Let $x_I(t)$ and $x_{II}(t)$ be the output vectors of capital, wage and luxury-goods industries produced at time t. They are n and $m-n$ dimensional column vectors. As the production processes are assumed to be of unit time duration, the production processes of $x_I(t+1)$ and $x_{II}(t+1)$ start at time t. It is also assumed that capital goods last only for one period. Then, to produce outputs $x_I(t+1)$ and $x_{II}(t+1)$ capital goods of the amounts $A_I x_I(t+1)$ and $A_{II} x_{II}(t+1)$ are demanded, at time t, by the capital-good industries and wage or luxury-good industries respectively. As outputs of capital goods are available in the amounts $x_I(t)$, the equations between demand and supply of capital goods are written as:

$$x_I(t) = A_I x_I(t+1) + A_{II} x_{II}(t+1). \qquad (1)$$

As for workers, let us assume that each worker is paid wages at

THE DYNAMIC TRANSFORMATION PROBLEM   147

a level at which he can purchase only the minimum amounts of goods biologically required for subsistence for one period. As before, let B represent a column vector of necessities of life in these amounts. If a worker is not capable of choosing commodities and has to work T hours per period, then by working one hour he is enabled to consume only $\omega \, (= 1/T)$ units of B. As $L_I x_I(t+1) + L_{II} x_{II}(t+1)$ man-hours of labour are employed by industries at time t, workers' demands for wage goods amount to
$$\omega B[L_I x_I(t+1) + L_{II} x_{II}(t+1)]$$
at time t, since it is assumed that wages are paid before work and that there is no consumption lag.

Next, $F(t)$ denotes a column vector of the quantities of wage or luxury goods consumed by capitalists at time t. As capitalists spend $c_c \times 100\%$ of their income (i.e. profits) on wage or luxury goods, we have

$$p_{II} F(t) = c_c \pi[(p_I A_I + w L_I) x_I(t) \\ + (p_{II} A_{II} + w L_{II}) x_{II}(t)], \qquad (2)$$

where p_I and p_{II} are price vectors of capital goods and wage or luxury goods respectively, π is the rate of profit, w the wage rate per man-hour, and c_c the capitalists' average propensity to consume. We assume that c_c is constant through time. Capitalists' demands for wage and luxury goods $F(t)$ must be fulfilled at every point of time. Although c_c (like the rate of accumulation a in the last two chapters 10 and 11) is an exogenous factor to be determined subjectively by capitalists, this assumption is more admissible than the previous one. Capitalists can decide the value of c_c by themselves, even though they live on the surface of the capitalist society, so that they are unconscious of 'values' and are interested only in prices, whilst they do not pay any attention to the value of a, unless they are well-trained Marxists! As will be seen later, the constancy of c_c does not imply that of a.

We now have the equations between demand and supply of wage goods and luxury goods. They are written as

$$x_{II}(t) = \omega B[L_I x_I(t+1) + L_{II} x_{II}(t+1)] + F(t). \qquad (3)$$

These, together with (1), form a Leontief-like dynamic input–output system in physical terms. If 'final demands' $F(t)$ are known for all t and initial outputs $x_I(0)$ and $x_{II}(0)$ are given, then physical industrial outputs are obtained by solving these difference equations. However, it has to be noticed that the consumption function (2) can determine only the aggregate value (in prices) of capitalists' consumption $p_{\mathrm{II}}F(t)$; it is unable to specify the elements of $F(t)$. In the case where a time profile is not available for each element of these vectors, the physical input–output system is unable to provide a determinate path of physical outputs. Thus the system is incomplete, unless it is supplemented by detailed consumption functions. Marx did not know the Walrasian idea of micro-behavioural functions. He did not want to develop a theory which might be subject to the casual properties of capitalists' demands for individual wage and luxury goods. So he was content to establish an aggregate theory which was invariantly true, so long as capitalists' individual demand functions fulfilled condition (2).

We now introduce Marx's aggregation conditions: All the industries producing capital goods are identical in the value-composition of capital, as are all those producing wage or luxury goods. Then the capital-goods industries may be aggregated into one department and the wage and luxury-goods industries into another. We also have a proportionality between prices and values within each department, i.e. between p_I and Λ_I and between p_II and Λ_II, so that we may write

$$p_\mathrm{I} = \alpha_\mathrm{I}\Lambda_\mathrm{I}, \qquad (4)$$

$$p_\mathrm{II} = \alpha_\mathrm{II}\Lambda_\mathrm{II}, \qquad (5)$$

where α_I and α_II are scalars which are referred to as the prices of the aggregate outputs of the departments. Throughout the following, we assume that the rate of exploitation is constant and that long-run equilibrium prices always prevail. The former implies that ω remains unchanged, so that from the factor-price frontier we obtain π, which corresponds to ω. Prices p_I and p_II are the long-run equilibrium prices associated with π thus determined.

Let us now aggregate industries in terms of *value*; i.e., premultiply (1) by Λ_I, and add (3) premultiplied by Λ_II. We then obtain

$$y_\mathrm{I}(t) = c_\mathrm{I} y_\mathrm{I}(t+1) + c_\mathrm{II} y_\mathrm{II}(t+1), \qquad (6)$$

$$y_\mathrm{II}(t) = v_\mathrm{I} y_\mathrm{I}(t+1) + v_\mathrm{II} y_\mathrm{II}(t+1) + \Lambda_\mathrm{II} F(t), \qquad (7)$$

THE DYNAMIC TRANSFORMATION PROBLEM 149

where, as before, $y_I(t) = \Lambda_I x_I(t)$, $y_{II}(t) = \Lambda_{II} x_{II}(t)$; and

$$\left.\begin{aligned} c_I &= \sum_{i=1}^{n} \lambda_i a_{ij}/\lambda_j & (j = 1, \ldots, n), \\ c_{II} &= \sum_{i=1}^{n} \lambda_i a_{ij}/\lambda_j & (j = n+1, \ldots, m), \\ v_I &= \omega \left(\sum_{i=n+1}^{m} \lambda_i b_i \right) l_j \Big/ \lambda_j & (j = 1, \ldots, n), \\ v_{II} &= \omega \left(\sum_{i=n+1}^{m} \lambda_i b_i \right) l_j \Big/ \lambda_j & (j = n+1, \ldots, m). \end{aligned}\right\} \quad (8)$$

It is noted that equations (8) result from the aggregation condition that the organic composition of capital is the same for all industries belonging to the same department. Taking $w = \omega p_{II} B$ into account and considering (2), (4) and (5), we can further rewrite (7) in the form,

$$y_{II}(t) = v_I y_I(t+1) + v_{II} y_{II}(t+1)$$
$$+ c_c \pi \left(\frac{\alpha_I}{\alpha_{II}} c_I + v_I \right) y_I(t) + c_c \pi \left(\frac{\alpha_I}{\alpha_{II}} c_{II} + v_{II} \right) y_{II}(t). \quad (9)$$

We now have simultaneous difference equations (6) and (9), which determine the path of aggregate outputs in terms of value, $y_I(t)$ and $y_{II}(t)$.

Equations (6) and (9) above are mathematically of the same family as equations (6) and (7) in chapter 10. They are different only in the coefficients of capitalists' consumption. In equation (9) these coefficients are

$$c_c \pi \left(\frac{\alpha_I}{\alpha_{II}} c_I + v_I \right) \quad \text{and} \quad c_c \pi \left(\frac{\alpha_I}{\alpha_{II}} c_{II} + v_{II} \right),$$

whereas in equation (7) of chapter 10 they are bs_I and bs_{II}. Therefore the path determined by (6) and (9) has the same properties as the one which we examined in that chapter. That is to say, there is a ray of outputs along which both $y_I(t)$ and $y_{II}(t)$ grow at the same rate. This balanced growth path is definitely unstable, so that if the economy is initially moved off the balanced growth ray it will diverge further from it as time goes on; we have explosive oscillations around the balanced growth ray if the value-composition of capital is higher in department II than in department I, and monotonic divergence from the ray in either direction if the capital intensity condition is reversed.

Let us now define K^* as the aggregate total capital (including variable capital) measured in terms of prices and g_{K^*} as the rate of growth of K^*. We then have

$$g_{K^*}(t) = \frac{(\alpha_I c_I + \alpha_{II} v_I) \Delta y_I(t) + (\alpha_I c_{II} + \alpha_{II} v_{II}) \Delta y_{II}(t)}{(\alpha_I c_I + \alpha_{II} v_I) y_I(t) + (\alpha_I c_{II} + \alpha_{II} v_{II}) y_{II}(t)}. \quad (10)$$

$g_{K^*}(t)$ can easily be calculated. Multiply (6) and (9) by α_I and α_{II} respectively, and add them up. Considering the price–cost equations,

$$\alpha_i y_i(t) = (1+\pi)(\alpha_I c_i + \alpha_{II} v_i) y_i(t) \quad (i = I, II),$$

and the definition of the average propensity to save, $s_c = 1 - c_c$, we obtain

$$(\alpha_I c_I + \alpha_{II} v_I)(y_I(t+1) - y_I(t))$$
$$+ (\alpha_I c_{II} + \alpha_{II} v_{II})(y_{II}(t+1) - y_{II}(t))$$
$$= s_c \pi [(\alpha_I c_I + \alpha_{II} v_I) y_I(t) + (\alpha_I c_{II} + \alpha_{II} v_{II}) y_{II}(t)].$$

Hence, $$g_{K^*}(t) = s_c \pi. \quad (11)$$

This equation, recently confirmed by growth theorists, implies that the aggregate total capital K^* increases at a constant rate, $s_c \pi$, irrespective of the initial point from which the economy starts to expand. When we have balanced growth, departmental outputs also grow at the same rate. On the other hand, if the initial point is set off the balanced growth ray, either $y_I(t)$ or $y_{II}(t)$ grows at a higher rate than the other. The total capital consumed by one of the departments increases more rapidly than the total capital consumed by the other department, so that (11) means that total capital in the whole economy (aggregated in terms of prices) grows at a steady rate which is a product of capitalists' average propensity to save and the rate of profit.

Now we transform the growth formula (11) into a formula in terms of value. We aggregate the total capital in terms of value and denote it by $K = (c_i + v_I) y_I(t) + (c_{II} + v_{II}) y_{II}(t)$. The rate of growth of K is given by

$$g_K(t) = \frac{(c_I + v_I) \Delta y_I(t) + (c_{II} + v_{II}) \Delta y_{II}(t)}{(c_I + v_I) y_I(t) + (c_{II} + v_{II}) y_{II}(t)}. \quad (12)$$

THE DYNAMIC TRANSFORMATION PROBLEM 151

To obtain $g_K(t)$ we first aggregate the balance equation in physical terms, (1) and (3), in terms of value. Adding (6) and (7) simply, we get the investment–saving equation in terms of value,

$$(c_\mathrm{I} + v_\mathrm{I})\Delta y_\mathrm{I}(t) + (c_\mathrm{II} + v_\mathrm{II})\Delta y_\mathrm{II}(t)$$
$$= [s_\mathrm{I} y_\mathrm{I}(t) + s_\mathrm{II} y_\mathrm{II}(t)] - \Lambda_\mathrm{II} F(t), \quad (13)$$

because of
$$y_i(t) = (c_i + v_i + s_i) y_i(t) \quad (i = \mathrm{I}, \mathrm{II}).$$

On the right-hand side of (13), the part in the first set of brackets represents the total surplus value, while the last term denotes the total value of wage and luxury goods consumed by capitalists. After subtracting the latter from the former, the rest is devoted to accumulation; therefore the rate of accumulation is defined as

$$a = \frac{s_\mathrm{I} y_\mathrm{I}(t) + s_\mathrm{II} y_\mathrm{II}(t) - \Lambda_\mathrm{II} F(t)}{s_\mathrm{I} y_\mathrm{I}(t) + s_\mathrm{II} y_\mathrm{II}(t)}. \quad (14)$$

Then (13) at once yields

$$g_K(t) = a \frac{S(t)}{C(t) + V(t)}, \quad (15)$$

where $S(t)$ represents the aggregate surplus value and $C(t) + V(t)$ the aggregate total capital K. On the other hand, bearing (2) and (5) in mind, we may rewrite (14) in the form,

$$a = \frac{\left[s_\mathrm{I} - c_c \pi \left(\frac{\alpha_\mathrm{I}}{\alpha_\mathrm{II}} c_\mathrm{I} + v_\mathrm{I}\right)\right] y_\mathrm{I}(t) + \left[s_\mathrm{II} - c_c \pi \left(\frac{\alpha_\mathrm{I}}{\alpha_\mathrm{II}} c_\mathrm{II} + v_\mathrm{II}\right)\right] y_\mathrm{II}(t)}{s_\mathrm{I} y_\mathrm{I}(t) + s_\mathrm{II} y_\mathrm{II}(t)},$$

which may further be rewritten as

$$a = s_c$$
$$+ \frac{c_c \left[\left\{s_\mathrm{I} - \pi \left(\frac{\alpha_\mathrm{I}}{\alpha_\mathrm{II}} c_\mathrm{I} + v_\mathrm{I}\right)\right\} y_\mathrm{I}(t) + \left\{s_\mathrm{II} - \pi \left(\frac{\alpha_\mathrm{I}}{\alpha_\mathrm{II}} c_\mathrm{II} + v_\mathrm{II}\right)\right\} y_\mathrm{II}(t)\right]}{s_\mathrm{I} y_\mathrm{I}(t) + s_\mathrm{II} y_\mathrm{II}(t)}$$
(16)

since $c_c + s_c = 1$.

We now have two transformation problems: one of transforming capitalists' average propensity to save s_c into the rate of accumulation a, and the other of transforming the rate of growth of the aggregate total capital in terms of prices $g_{K*}(t)$ into the corresponding rate in terms of value $g_K(t)$. The equation (16) is the formula for the first problem. It must, however, be remembered that s_c is a parameter of our problem, on the prescribed value of which the solutions $y_\mathrm{I}(t)$ and $y_\mathrm{II}(t)$ to the dynamic system, (6) and (9), depend. In the general case where the coefficients of $y_\mathrm{I}(t)$ and $y_\mathrm{II}(t)$ in the numerator of the fraction on the right-hand side of (16) are *not* proportional to those in the denominator, the rate of accumulation a will not only differ from s_c, but will also change from period to period unless the departmental outputs $y_\mathrm{I}(t)$ and $y_\mathrm{II}(t)$ grow proportionally. We have only three special cases where a is equated with s_c.

First, it is obvious that when capitalists do not consume, the entire profit or the entire surplus value is saved for accumulation, so that the propensity to save in terms of prices equals the rate of accumulation in terms of values. In fact we get, from (16), $a = s_c = 1$ if $c_c = 0$. Secondly, as has been seen, if there is no exploitation s_I and s_II are zero, and there are also no profits (i.e. $\pi = 0$), because exploitation is necessary for positive profits. Therefore the parts in the sets of curled parentheses on the right-hand side of (16) vanish, so that $a = s_c$ is obtained formally. However, in this case there are no profits, no savings, and no consumption by capitalists. Thus no accumulation is possible, so that a and s_c are equated at zero. Finally, we have the case where the value-composition of capital is equalized between the two departments. We have in this case $\alpha_\mathrm{I} = \alpha_\mathrm{II}$ and $s_i = \pi(c_i + v_i)$, $i = \mathrm{I}, \mathrm{II}$. Then the parts in the curled parentheses on the right-hand side of (16) again vanish; hence $a = s_c$.

For the second problem of transforming the rate of growth $g_{K*}(t)$ into $g_K(t)$, we have three sufficient conditions for identical transformation. First, when we have balanced growth of outputs both $g_{K*}(t)$ and $g_K(t)$ are equal to $\Delta y_i(t)/y_i(t)$, $i = \mathrm{I}, \mathrm{II}$, because they are weighted averages of the rates of growth of departmental outputs and weights are irrelevant in this case, since departmental outputs expand at the same rate. Secondly, no exploitation implies no deviation of prices from values. It is therefore evident that the aggregate total capital in terms of values is identical with that in terms of prices, so that they grow at a common rate. Thirdly, if the two departments have the same value-composition of capital, all prices are proportional to the corresponding values, or $\alpha_\mathrm{I} = \alpha_\mathrm{II}$. Accordingly, $g_{K*}(t) = g_K(t)$ follows at once from (10) and (12).

We thus have three cases where $a = s_c$ and three cases where $g_{K*}(t) = g_K(t)$. As $g_{K*}(t)$ is the product of s_c and π and $g_K(t)$ is

THE DYNAMIC TRANSFORMATION PROBLEM 153

the product of a and $S(t)/[C(t)+V(t)]$, we now have the following three cases in which $S(t)/[C(t)+V(t)]$ is identified with π. Case (i): There is balanced growth in an economy with no capitalists' consumption. Case (ii): There is no exploitation. Case (iii): All industries are homogeneous in their value structure. The last two cases are familiar to us in the static transformation problem. One of these, case (ii), does hold for all societies with 'simple commodity production' but is never realized in capitalist societies, whilst the other, case (iii), is possible under the capitalist mode of production, although it is a very restrictive case and contradicts Marx's idea of disaggregating the economy into two major departments.

The condition of equal value composition of capital can be weakened into the 'linear dependence of industries' which has been discussed in chapter 7. As the latter is reduced to the former in the case of Marx's aggregation conditions into two departments being fulfilled, we are concerned, in the following, with an economy whose industries cannot be aggregated into the two Marxian departments, so that there are at least two capital-good industries or two wage or luxury-good industries which are different from each other in the value composition of capital. Let

$$M = \begin{bmatrix} A_\mathrm{I} & A_\mathrm{II} \\ \omega BL_\mathrm{I} & \omega BL_\mathrm{II} \end{bmatrix},$$

then the 'linear dependence of industries' implies[1]

$$\pi(C+V)M = SM,$$

so that $\quad (1+\pi)(C+V)M = (C+V+S)M = \Lambda M,$

where Λ is the vector of values $(\Lambda_\mathrm{I}, \Lambda_\mathrm{II})$, C the vector of constant capitals, V the vector of variable capitals, and S the vector of surplus values, all of them being per unit of output. As $C+V = \Lambda M$, we have

$$(1+\pi)\Lambda MM = \Lambda M,$$

which implies that ΛM gives a set of solutions to the price equations, so that ΛM is proportional to the production-price vector $p = (p_\mathrm{I}, p_\mathrm{II})$. This in turn means that ΛM is proportional to pM

---

[1] See pp. 77–8 above.

154   THE REPRODUCTION SCHEME

because the production-price vector p is equal to $(1+\pi)pM$, by definition. Hence we have

$$\frac{\Lambda M\Delta x(t)}{\Lambda Mx(t)} = \frac{pM\Delta x(t)}{pMx(t)}.$$

As the left-hand side of this equation represents the rate of growth of the total capital in terms of value, $g_K(t)$, and the right-hand side the one in terms of prices, $g_{K*}(t)$, we thus have $g_K(t) = g_{K*}(t)$.

We also have, from the assumption of the 'linear dependence of industries'

$$\pi(C+V)Mx(t+1) = SMx(t+1),$$

which may be rewritten as

$$\pi(C+V)(x(t) - F^*(t)) = S(x(t) - F^*(t))$$

because of the input–output equation, $x(t) = Mx(t+1) + F^*(t)$, where $F^*(t)$ stands for the column vector of capitalists' consumption of goods, so that their elements are zero for capital goods and $F(t)$ for wage and luxury goods. Hence, if we additionally assume that the value composition of the capitals required for producing those goods which are consumed by capitalists is equal to the average value composition of capital along the golden, balanced growth equilibrium path, we obtain, from the above equation,[2]

$$\pi = \frac{S(t)}{C(t) + V(t)},$$

where $S(t)$ represents the aggregate surplus value, $Sx(t)$, and $C(t) + V(t)$ the aggregate total capital used, $(C+V)x(t)$. We can now find $a = s_c$ easily from the formulas (11) and (15), because $g_K(t) = g_{K*}(t)$.

Thus we have the identical transformation of s_c into a, providing the industries are 'linearly dependent' and the additional assumption mentioned above is satisfied. One might conclude

[2] The additional assumption states

$$CF^*(t)/VF^*(t) = Cy/Vy,$$

where y represents the vector of the golden equilibrium relative outputs. This implies

$$\frac{SF^*(t)}{(C+V)F^*(t)} = \frac{Sy}{(C+V)y},$$

because the uniform rate of exploitation prevails throughout industries, $S = eV$. The right-hand side of this equation equals the equilibrium rate of profit π, as we have seen in chapter 6. Hence we obtain the result.

from this fact and the fact that the assumption of 'linearly dependent industries' is necessary and sufficient for the validity of Marx's peculiar algorithm for calculating the production prices,[3] that Marx's static and dynamic transformation problems can be solved consistently under the assumption of 'linear dependence of industries', so that it should be regarded as one of his implicit assumptions. However, on the other hand, we must recognize that it is an assumption which is still very restrictive and unjustifiable, although it is weaker than the traditional condition of the equal value composition of capital.

The remaining case, case (i), is a new member of the team of solutions to the transformation problem. Clearly the condition of no capitalists' consumption can hardly be considered as realistic. But it may be legitimate, since capitalists' consumption is not only negligible in amount but also has to be neglected when we want to draw only a rough and hyperbolic picture of the capitalist economy. Marx wrote: 'Accumulate, accumulate! That is Moses and the prophets! "Industry furnishes the material which saving accumulates." Therefore, save, save, i.e., reconvert the greatest possible portion of surplus-value, or surplus-product into capital!' (1, p. 595.) From this point of view, s_c is considered as being equal to one, at least approximately. Therefore Marx's model of reproduction is reduced to von Neumann's model, that is the model of 'accumulation for accumulation's sake, production for production's sake', in Marx's words (1, p. 595); the state established in case (i) is no more than the von Neumann growth equilibrium discussed by many contemporary growth theorists. We obtain

$$\pi = \frac{Sy}{(C+V)y} = \frac{e}{k+1} \quad (17)$$

in case (i), where e is the rate of exploitation and k is the value-composition of capital for the entire economy. From (17) we can derive Marx's proposition that when e is constant and k rising, π is falling. We might thus interpret Marx's proposition of a falling tendency in profits as a law of comparative growth-equilibria which would be obtained by comparing von Neumann equilibria established under different sets of techniques of production.

It is seen that (17) may be consistent with capitalists'

[3] Established in chapter 7 above.

consumption in some special cases. For example, assume that capital goods and wage and luxury goods are not distinct and that an identical proportion of each output is consumed by capitalists.[4] Then we have, in place of (1) and (3),

$$x(t) = Ax(t+1) + \omega BLx(t+1) + \gamma x(t), \qquad (18)$$

where $x(t)$ denotes the vector of outputs of all commodities in period t, $\gamma x(t)$ the vector of capitalists' consumption (γ being a scalar), and A and L are the matrix of capital-input coefficients and the vector of labour-input coefficients of all commodities. Premultiply (18) by the vector of the equilibrium production prices p and the vector of values Λ respectively, and we have

$$px(t) = pAx(t+1) + p\omega BLx(t+1) + \gamma px(t) \qquad (19)$$

and $\qquad \Lambda x(t) = \Lambda Ax(t+1) + \Lambda \omega BLx(t+1) + \gamma \Lambda x(t). \qquad (20)$

Note that $p\omega B = w$ in (19). Then, in view of the price and value equations
$$px = (1+\pi)(pAx + wLx),$$
$$\Lambda x = \Lambda Ax + \Lambda \omega BLx + S(x),$$

for all x, where $S(x)$ denotes the total surplus value of x, we obtain, from (19) and (20),

$$\pi = g + \gamma \frac{px^0}{pAx^0 + wLx^0} = g + \gamma(1+\pi), \qquad (21)$$

$$\frac{S^0}{C^0 + V^0} = g + \gamma \frac{\Lambda x^0}{\Lambda Ax^0 + \Lambda \omega BLx^0} = g + \gamma \left(1 + \frac{S^0}{C^0 + V^0}\right) \qquad (22)$$

in the state of balanced growth $x(t) = x^0(1+g)^t$; C^0, V^0 and S^0 in (22) represent constant and variable capitals and surplus value in the state of balanced growth. Therefore, from (21) and (22), we have

$$\pi = \frac{S^0}{C^0 + V^0},$$

which implies that total profits equal total surplus value, provided that the equilibrium production prices are normalized in such a way that the total costs are equal to the total value of capital, i.e.
$$(pA + wL)x^0 = (\Lambda A + \Lambda \omega BL)x^0.$$

[4] As was noted in chapter 6, this assumption would not have been accepted by Marx, because he assumed that capital goods and wage and luxury goods were distinct and that capitalists as well as workers never consumed capital goods.

Thus Marx's formula for converting the surplus value into profits holds if capitalists consume an identical fraction of each output; hence $s_c = a$ from (11] and (15).

We are now in a position to assign to the dynamic transformation problem the part which it has to play in Marx's theory of reproduction. To convince the reader of the importance of the subject, we begin by reminding him of the reason why the dynamic transformation problem is a problem in Marxian economics, in spite of the fact that Marx did not fully recognize it as such. Marx assumed that the rate at which capitalists reserved the surplus value for accumulation had already been determined at the outset of the reproduction process. It must be emphasized, unfortunately, that this is a very unrealistic assumption, because in any economy where commodities are traded through the medium of money no capitalist makes a decision about accumulation in terms of the surplus value measured in labour-time. On the other hand Marx himself wrote: 'By the conversion of the commodity-capital into money the surplus-product, in which the surplus-value is represented, is also turned into money. The capitalist reconverts the so-metamorphosed surplus-value into additional natural elements of his productive capital.' (II, p. 493.) 'One part of the capitalists is continually converting its potential money-capital, grown to an appropriate size, into productive capital i.e. with the money hoarded by the conversion of surplus-value into money they buy means of production, additional elements of constant capital. Another part of the capitalists is meanwhile still engaged in hoarding its potential money capital.' (II, p. 496.) These quotations are sufficient to show that Marx recognized that capitalists made their decisions on saving and investment in terms of money. Then the rate of accumulation a Marx assumed in his reproduction theory must be founded on the actually observable propensity to consume s_c. The dynamic transformation problem asks: How is the ratio a determined? What relationship is there between a and s_c?

The accumulation rate a is determined in a roundabout way. First we assume that capitalists exploit workers as much as possible. Then the actual length of the working-day T is prolonged to the maximum $\overline{T}$, so that the rate of exploitation takes on its maximum value $\bar{e}$, and the real wage rate is determined at $\overline{\omega} = 1/\overline{T}$. The last enables us to find the rate of profit $\bar{\pi}$, by reading the ordinate of a point on the factor–price frontier corresponding to $\bar{w}$. We are also provided with the values of v_I, v_II, s_I and s_II, in addition to the values of c_I and c_II, which are taken as the coefficients of the Marxian input–output equations (6) and (9).

Next we assume that capitalists save a constant proportion of total profits, whereas workers cannot save at all. We may then determine the rate of growth of the aggregate total capital (measured in terms of prices) by the growth formula $g_{K^*}(t) = s_c \bar{\pi}$, which is sometimes referred to as the Cambridge formula.[5] $g_{K^*}(t)$ is a weighted average of the rates of growth of the two departmental outputs, which are determined by the two departmental input–output equations.

Here we have the dynamic transformation problem. As we know $y_\mathrm{I}(t)$, $y_\mathrm{II}(t)$, $\Delta y_\mathrm{I}(t)$ and $\Delta y_\mathrm{II}(t)$, as well as the value coefficients c_I, c_II, v_I and v_II, we can easily calculate the aggregate total capital in terms of value, $C(t) + V(t)$, and its growth rate, $g_K(t)$. We can also calculate the total surplus value $S(t)$. Therefore the formula (15) determines the rate of accumulation. It has been seen that without restrictive conditions on technology and capitalists' consumption, s_c can equal a only in the case where (i) capitalists do not consume and (ii) a balanced growth of outputs prevails in the economy. The condition (i) is not very harmful, at least in Marx's world, because the capitalists' propensity to save may be considered to be very high. On the other hand, condition (ii) is problematic, because the balanced growth equilibrium has been proved to be unstable. We may thus conclude as follows: Marx's transformation formula, that the ratio of the surplus value to the aggregate total capital equals the rate of profits, holds true as a relationship along the Marx–von Neumann golden equilibrium path, but it must be replaced in all other circumstances by the general relationship which is implied by the two growth formulas (11) and (15), linked by the definitions of the two rates of growth, (10) and (12).

However, this rather negative conclusion does not injure Marx much, because the theory of the relative surplus population, which may be considered one of the most important parts of

[5] L. Pasinetti extended the applicability of this formula to the case of the workers' propensity to save being positive. This invited the Pasinetti–anti-Pasinetti controversy, but we need not become involved in it here. Instead we confine ourselves to the original simplest case with which Marx was concerned. See my *Theory of Economic Growth* (Oxford, 1969), pp. 34–43.

Marxian economics, can be shown to hold true *mutatis mutandis* under the assumption of capitalists' propensity to save being constant. This is evident and no independent argument is needed, since the system of equations (6) and (9) in this chapter is formally similar to that of (1) and (2) in chapter 11, from which Marx derived his 'law of population peculiar to the capitalist mode of production'. We can thus derive similar conclusions concerning growth of outputs and the movement of the relative surplus population from either of the two sets of reproduction equations, one consisting of the equations based on the assumption that a is constant and the other based on the assumption that s_c is constant. The first system ought to be rejected because of its operational meaninglessness, while the second may be acceptable because it is refutable. Without the notion of values we may still construct the second set of equations, which are aggregated in terms of the von Neumann equilibrium production-prices (see the last part of chapter 8). Thus we finally obtain a Marxian growth theory without the labour theory of value. Some Marxian economists may feel that this a deplorable conclusion, but I venture to say that it is the most important consequence of the dynamic transformation problem. Moreover, it is extremely important in Marxian economics to distinguish those theories which are independent of the labour theory of value from those which cannot dispense with it. This is especially so because there are still many unsolved problems relating the labour theory of value, as will be seen in the last chapter of this book.

There are two more points which must be discussed here. First, we have so far assumed that the workers' position is very weak, so that each of them has to work for the maximum number of hours per period. When workers become sufficiently powerful to escape from Victorian conditions, they will no longer be exploited at the maximum rate $\bar{e}$. Then the actual rate of exploitation will be less than $\bar{e}$; and it is clear that Marx's theory will collapse, unless we have a theory which can satisfactorily explain the prevailing level of the rate of exploitation. An easy way of getting out of this difficulty is to make a compromise with the neo-classical school. It is obvious that the solutions $y_I(t)$ and $y_{II}(t)$ to equations (6) and (9) depend on the actual rate of exploitation e, since their coefficients, v_I, v_{II}, c_I, c_{II}, π, α_I, α_{II}, all depend on e. It then follows that the rate of growth of the demand for labour is a function of e. On the other hand, the rate of growth of the labour force (or the supply of labour) may be considered as depending on the real wage rate, which in turn depends on the rate of exploitation. When full employment of labour persists for a long period, the growth rate of the demand for labour has to be equated with that of the supply. The rate of exploitation is determined at the point where the two growth-rate curves intersect.

But this compromised Marxian theory is no more than a paper tiger. It is incompatible with the theory of the relative surplus population, which is one of the mainstays of Marxian ideology. Certainly, true Marxists will continue to struggle with the dilemma and will never submit to a solution based on the neo-classical principle. In any case, it is certain that models assuming some kind of wage rigidity[6] form the subject-matter of non-neoclassical economics and provide conclusions about economic growth which are quite different from the optimistic predictions of the neo-classics.

Finally, let us look at the problem which was raised at the end of the last chapter but held over for consideration here. In chapter 11 we confirmed Marx's assertion of the mortality of capitalism, for a particular class of changes in the technological composition of capital which have no effects on the values of individual commodities. For the case of a technical improvement being non-neutral in the sense that it gives rise to a disturbance in the value system, nothing definite has yet been established. The rest of this chapter is devoted to showing that we can find a counter-example to Marx's 'breakdown' theory, when the assumption of neutral technical changes is removed.

For the sake of simplicity, we assume that (i) there is only one capital good and one wage good; (ii) the two industries have the same capital-input and labour-input coefficients before the technical change, i.e. $A_\mathrm{I} = A_\mathrm{II}$ and $L_\mathrm{I} = L_\mathrm{II}$ (it is noted that As and Ls are not matrices and vectors but numbers), (iii) the working day is fixed at $\overline{T}$, so that the real wage rate ω is set at $1/\overline{T}$; (iv) no technical change takes place in the capital-good industry, but the method of production of the wage-good industry is improved in such a way that its capital-input and labour-input coefficients decrease at a common, constant rate,

---

[6] They might be called 'fixwage' models, imitating Hicks; see his *Capital and Growth*, pp. 76–127. Also see my *Theory of Economic Growth*, ch. 4.

THE DYNAMIC TRANSFORMATION PROBLEM 161

$1-r$, per period. The A_I and L_I remain unchanged through time, but the capital-input and labour-input coefficients of the wage-good industry decay through time, according to the formulas $r^t A_\text{II}$ and $r^t L_\text{II}$ respectively. It is then seen that the value of the capital good is constant at Λ_I and the value of the wage good decreases as $r^t \Lambda_\text{II}$.[7] We then have the following coefficients of the reproduction equations:

$$c_\text{I}(t) = \frac{\Lambda_\text{I} A_\text{I}}{\Lambda_\text{I}} = c_\text{I}(t-1), \quad v_\text{I}(t) = \frac{\omega(r^t \Lambda_\text{II}) B L_\text{I}}{\Lambda_\text{I}} = r v_\text{I}(t-1),$$

$$c_\text{II}(t) = \frac{\Lambda_\text{I}(r^t A_\text{II})}{(r^t \Lambda_\text{II})} = c_\text{II}(t-1), \quad v_\text{II}(t) = \frac{\omega(r^t \Lambda_\text{II}) B(r^t L_\text{II})}{(r^t \Lambda_\text{II})}$$

$$= r v_\text{II}(t-1),$$

$$l_\text{I}(t) = \frac{L_\text{I}}{\Lambda_\text{I}} = l_\text{I}(t-1), \quad l_\text{II}(t) = \frac{r^t L_\text{II}}{r^t \Lambda_\text{II}} = l_\text{II}(t-1),$$

$$(23)$$

where B is the consumption coefficient at the subsistence level.[8] As $A_\text{I} = A_\text{II}$ and $L_\text{I} = L_\text{II}$, we have $\Lambda_\text{I} = \Lambda_\text{II}$; therefore

$$c_\text{I}(t) = c_\text{II}(t), \quad v_\text{I}(t) = v_\text{II}(t), \quad l_\text{I}(t) = l_\text{II}(t) \quad \text{for all } t, \quad (24)$$

to the effect that the two industries have the same value composition of capital. It is noticed that the value composition of capital is increasing through time in both industries.

Now the departmental demand–supply equations are written as

$$x_\text{I}(t-1) = A_\text{I} x_\text{I}(t) + r^t A_\text{II} x_\text{II}(t), \tag{25}$$

$$x_\text{II}(t-1) = \omega B [L_\text{I} x_\text{I}(t) + r^t L_\text{II} x_\text{II}(t)] + F(t), \tag{26}$$

where $F(t)$ is the capitalist's demand for the consumption good. These equations are translated into value by multiplying them by Λ_I and $r^{t-1} \Lambda_\text{II}$ respectively. As the two industries are always identical in the value-composition of capital, prices are always proportional values. Therefore we have the capitalists' budget equation

$$r^{t-1} \Lambda_\text{II} F(t) = c_c \pi [(c_\text{I}(t-1) + v_\text{I}(t-1)) y_\text{I}(t-1)$$
$$+ (c_\text{II}(t-1) + v_\text{II}(t-1)) y_\text{II}(t-1)]$$

---

[7] Λ_II denotes the initial value of the wage good.
[8] It is noted that l_II should not be confused with L_II. $r^t L_\text{II}$ is the labour required for one physical unit of the wage good, while l_II is the labour required for producing one unit of value of output of the wage good.

at the beginning of period $t-1$, where $y_I(t) = \Lambda_I x_I(t)$, $y_{II}(t) = r^t \Lambda_{II} x_{II}(t)$, and c_c is the capitalists' average propensity to consume, which is assumed to be constant through time. In view of this, the demand–supply equation can be written as

$$y_I(t-1) = c_I(t-1)y_I(t) + c_{II}(t-1)y_{II}(t), \qquad (27)$$

$$\begin{aligned}y_{II}(t-1) &= v_I(t-1)y_I(t) + v_{II}(t-1)y_{II}(t) \\ &\quad + c_c \pi [(c_I(t-1) + v_I(t-1))y_I(t-1) \\ &\quad + (c_{II}(t-1) + v_{II}(t-1))y_{II}(t-1)]. \end{aligned} \qquad (28)$$

It must be noticed that, because of the change in the value of the wage good, these equations have $v_I(t-1)$ and $v_{II}(t-1)$, instead of $v_I(t)$ and $v_{II}(t)$, as coefficients of $y_I(t)$ and $y_{II}(t)$.[9]

On the other hand, we have

$$1 = c_i(t) + v_i(t) + s_i(t) \quad (i = \text{I, II}) \qquad (29)$$

from the value-determining equations, and

$$\alpha_I = (1+\pi)(\alpha_I c_i(t) + \alpha_{II} v_i(t)) \quad (i = \text{I, II}) \qquad (30)$$

from the price-determining equations. In our particular case of the two departments having the same organic composition of capital, α_I equals α_{II}, so that (29) and (30) yield

$$s_i(t) = \pi(c_i(t) + v_i(t)) \quad (i = \text{I, II}).$$

Then we have from (11) and (12), in view of $g_{k*}(t) = g_k(t)$,

$$s_c \pi = \frac{[c_I(t-1) + v_I(t-1)]y_I(t) + [c_{II}(t-1) + v_{II}(t-1)]y_{II}(t)}{[c_I(t-1) + v_I(t-1)]y_I(t-1) + [c_{II}(t-1) + v_{II}(t-1)]y_{II}(t-1)} - 1,$$

which is compared with the rate of growth of the demand for labour,

$$\begin{aligned} g_L &= \frac{L_I x_I(t) + r^t L_{II} x_{II}(t)}{L_I x_I(t-1) + r^{t-1} L_{II} x_{II}(t-1)} - 1 \\ &= \frac{l_I(t-1)y_I(t) + l_{II}(t-1)y_{II}(t)}{l_I(t-1)y_I(t-1) + l_{II}(t-1)y_{II}(t-1)} - 1. \end{aligned}$$

Taking (24) into account, we finally obtain a simple equation,

$$g_L = s_c \pi. \qquad (31)$$

[9] (27) and (28) are derived from (25) and (26) by taking (23) into account.

THE DYNAMIC TRANSFORMATION PROBLEM 163

We are now provided with a counter-example which excites 'usurpers'. Because of the decrease in v_I and v_II, the rate of profit π is *increasing* from period to period, as we see from (30). Capitalists are assumed to save a constant proportion of profits, so that s_c remains constant. Therefore (31) tells us that the rate of growth of the demand for labour is increasing through time, a result which is contrary to Marx's prediction. This shows how difficult it is to investigate the effects of biased technological development. The greatness of Marx as an economist lies in the fact that he was one of the pioneers in this adventurous subject, which is now so popular among economists. His breakdown theory shows that he had imperfections as a philosopher of revolution, but he has bequeathed us a great academic problem.

PART V

Capital and Value

CHAPTER 13

The turnover of capital

The theory of reproduction developed in chapters 9–12 differs from Marx's own formulation in one important respect. I have made this modification deliberately. Our formulation, which is a special case of Marx's, is valid only when capital goods can serve for one period. At first sight it might be thought that this is an absurd treatment of capital, because capital goods which are non-durable are hardly considered as proper capital goods. But, as will be shown later in this chapter, this assumption, in spite of its *prima facie* inadequacy, has to be made in order to solve the problems which Marx called 'peculiar difficulties' (II, p. 459) concerning the replacement of constant capital made necessary by wear and tear.

'Only by treating capital goods at different stages of wear and tear as *qualitatively* different goods, so that each capital good newly defined can serve only for one period, can we adequately deal with the age structure of capital stock.'[1] Marx almost came up with this 'golden rule' way of treating depreciation of capital goods which was later developed by von Neumann,[2] but he did not follow through with it. Like neo-classical economists, he distinguished the part of the value representing the constant

[1] Morishima, *Theory of Economic Growth*, p. 89. I hope the reader will read chapter VI of that book (on the von Neumann revolution) in parallel with this chapter.
[2] See von Neumann, 'General Economic Equilibrium'. Surprising as it may be, Marx was almost in a position to discover the von Neumann idea. He pointed out two alternative methods of accounting. One is the usual neoclassical accounting, according to which the item of constant capital includes the sum which the machinery loses by wear and tear in use, as well as the value of raw material and auxiliary material consumed; while the other is the von Neumann accounting, according to which the total value of the machinery employed is included in the item of constant capital and the remaining value, which remains in the machinery after the process, is included in the value of output (as a by-product of the process). See I, p. 213. Marx quoted the following sentence from Malthus: 'If we reckon the value of fixed capital employed as a part of the advances, we must reckon the remaining value of such capital at the end of the year as a part of the annual returns.' (I, p. 213.) But unfortunately Marx used the neoclassical accounting.

capital *consumed* in production from the value of the constant capital *employed* in production. Then he met the following capital age-structure difficulties. 'True, the materials of production are entirely consumed and their values completely transferred to the product. But only a portion of the employed *fixed* capital is wholly consumed and its value thus transferred to the product.' (II, p. 400.) But 'an aliquot part of their value – equal to the wear and tear, or the value depreciation of the fixed capital that is to be replaced – must first be precipitated in the form of money that will not function any more as a medium of circulation during the current period of annual reproduction, which alone we are examining' (II, p. 458). Thus, after the sale of its products, department II, producing consumption goods 'would not reconvert an aliquot portion of [the value of its output] during the current period of annual reproduction from money into the bodily form of fixed components of its constant capital' (II, pp. 458–9). 'But then we would have an over-production of means of production...on the other side, the side of I [i.e. the department producing capital goods], and the basis of our scheme would be destroyed.' (II, p. 459.)

Marx resolved this dilemma by introducing 'the seemingly still more absurd hypothesis that II itself was throwing the money into circulation, by which that constituent portion of the value of its commodities is converted into money which has to compensate the wear and tear of its fixed capital' (II, p. 462). He wrote: 'But the absurdity is only apparent. Class II consists of capitalists whose fixed capital is in the most diverse stages of its reproduction. In the case of some of them it has arrived at the stage where it must be entirely replaced in kind. In the case of the others it is more or less remote from that stage. All the members of the latter group have this in common, that their fixed capital is not actually reproduced, i.e., is not renewed *in natura* by a new specimen of the same kind, but that its value is successively accumulated in money. The first group is in quite the same (or almost the same, it does not matter here) position as when it started in business, when it came on the market with its money-capital in order to convert it into constant (fixed and circulating) capital on the one hand and into labour-power, into variable capital, on the other. They have once more to advance the money-capital to the circulation, i.e., the value of constant fixed capital as well as that of the circulating and variable capital.' (II, p. 463.) The case of simple reproduction was examined by Marx along these lines, but the hypothesis is useless when the activities of the departments are expanding, so that Marx left the case of extended reproduction unexamined.

Marx's failure was mainly due to the fact that he ignored the von Neumann 'golden rule'. If he had developed the idea of treating capital goods at different stages of wear as different goods, he could have solved the depreciation problem in a different and more convenient way, like that developed by von Neumann. According to this treatment there can be no distinction between the circulating and fixed elements of constant capital. The entire value of constant capital is transferred to its products. However, except in some special cases, the products are no longer single but multiple, because a production process using a fixed capital good at the stage of wear t produces the same capital good at the stage of wear $t+1$ as a by-product, at the end of the production period. Then the total cost of production, including the surplus value, must be distributed between the main product and the 'by-products'. We can thus avoid the depreciation problem by reducing it to the 'imputation' problem and continue to use the equations of valuation and reproduction, based on the unit period of production and the unit period of servicability of capital goods, which we used in chapters 9–12, although it is necessary to extend the output matrix so that it includes the by-products now legitimated.

Thus Marx was tackling the same economic problems as von Neumann, but unfortunately he was not so mathematically able as von Neumann. The last part of his life was a series of hard struggles with algebra, differential calculus and numerical examples. Engels was unable to refrain from adding an editorial note on Marx's behalf in *Capital*, volume II: 'Firmly grounded as Marx was in algebra, he did not get the knack of handling figures, particularly commercial arithmetic, although there exists a thick batch of copybooks containing numerous examples of all kinds of commercial computations which he had solved himself. But knowledge of the various methods of calculation and exercise in daily practical commercial arithmetic are by no means the same and consequently Marx got so tangled up in his computations.' (II, p. 287.) It is almost certain that he could not have solved mathematical problems of joint production, if he had got the idea of treating capital goods left over for production in the future as by-products of the current production process. Nevertheless, his analysis of the process of reproduction does him great credit, because it may be considered as a seedling of the von Neumann-type growth theory. If Marx had been more mathematical and had thought of the von Neumann golden rule, he could have developed the whole of the von Neumann model independently and a huge short cut might have been made in the history of economic theory.

It has been emphasized by many economists that there are similarities between Marx and von Neumann.[3] But the formal similarities which economists have pointed out are not very interesting. In fact, it is not surprising to find that a model of economic growth is *formally* a special case of von Neumann's, because the latter is so general. What I want to establish here is a deeper or economic similarity between these two thinkers. I want to present literary evidence to support my assertion that Marx had a view of the structure of production which is now ascribed to von Neumann.[4] I want to convince the reader of my opinion, that many von Neumann-like ideas recognized by Marx could have been well developed if he had stuck to his prototype, assuming that all capital goods are available only for one period and that all goods are produced in one period, and if he had decided to adopt the von Neumann accounting. He would then have obtained the model of reproduction which I called 'Marx–von Neumann' in my *Equilibrium, Stability and Growth*. Although I was not aware of all of them when I wrote the book, this model is supported by enough bibliographical justifications to be described as a perfected mathematization of Marx's theory of simple and extended reproduction.[5]

[3] For example, see András Bródy, *Proportions, Prices and Planning, A Mathematical Restatement of the Labour Theory of Value* (North-Holland Publishing Co., 1970).
[4] It is no wonder that von Neumann was an 'Austrian', but it is rather surprising to find that Marx was one as well.
[5] One of the main results obtained by von Neumann is the equality between the rate of growth and the rate of profit. But the so-called Marx–von Neumann model has been constructed so as to extend the formula to: the rate of growth = the rate of profit multiplied by capitalists' propensity to save. (See my *Equilibrium, Stability and Growth*, Oxford, 1964, p. 145.) Marx's analysis of simple reproduction is a special case of the capitalsts' propensity to save being zero, so that the rate of profit is positive in spite of the absence of growth.

Let us begin by collecting the literary evidence. Marx first directed his attention to the *durability of capital goods*. He wrote: 'in relation to the products toward the creation of which it contributes, a portion of the constant capital retains the definite use-form in which it enters into the process of production. Hence it performs the same functions for a longer or shorter period, in ever repeated labour-processes. This applies for instance to industrial buildings, machinery, etc. – in short to all things which we comprise under the name of *instruments* of labour.' (II, p. 161.) 'If a machine worth £10,000 lasts for, say, a period of ten years... [it] need not be renewed and continues to function in its bodily form until this period has expired.' (II, pp. 166–7.) 'The value-part of the productive capital, the part invested in fixed capital, is advanced in one lump sum for the entire period of employment of that part of the means of production of which the fixed capital consists. Hence this value is thrown into the circulation by the capitalist all at one time. But it is withdrawn again from the circulation only piecemeal and gradually by realising the parts of value which the fixed capital adds piecemeal to the commodities. On the other hand the means of production themselves, in which a component part of the productive capital becomes fixed, are withdrawn from the circulation all at one time to be embodied in the process of production for the entire period in which they function. But they do not require for this period any replacement by new samples of the same kind, do not require reproduction. They continue for a longer or shorter period to contribute to the creation of the commodities thrown into circulation without withdrawing from circulation the elements of their own renewal. Hence they do not require from the capitalist a renewal of his advance during this period.' (II, p. 171.)

Next, Marx noticed that the *production period*, i.e. the time during which capital was held fast in the sphere of production, might vary with the goods to be produced. In his words: 'Let us take two branches of business with working-days of equal length, say, of ten hours each, one of them a cotton spinning-mill, the other locomotive works. In one of these branches a definite quantity of finished product, cotton yarn, is turned out daily or weekly; in the other, the labour-process has to be repeated for perhaps three months in order to manufacture a finished product, a locomotive. In one case the product is discrete in nature, and each day or week the same labour starts over again. In the other case the labour-process is continuous and extends over a rather great number of daily labour-processes which, in their inter-connection, in the continuity of their operation, bring forth a finished product only after a rather long period of time. Although the duration of the daily labour-process is the same here, there is a very marked difference in the duration of the productive act, i.e. in the duration of the repeated labour-processes required to get out a finished product.' (II, p. 232.)

The time structure of production was analysed in the same way by Marx as by the Austrian economists. On the assumption that the manufacture of a machine requires 100 consecutive separate ten-hour working days, Marx wrote: 'these 100 working-days form a continuous magnitude, a working-day of 1,000 working-hours, one single connected act of production. I call such a working-day which is composed of a more or less numerous succession of connected working-days a *working period* [italicized by Marx]. When we speak of a working-day we mean the length of working time during which the labourer must daily spend his labour-power, must work day by day. But when we speak of a working period we mean the number of connected working-days required in a certain branch of industry for the manufacture of a finished product. In this case the product of every working-day is but *a partial one, which is further worked upon from day to day and only at the end of the longer or shorter working period receives its finished form, is a finished use-value.*' (My italics, II, p. 234.) Thus at the beginning of every working-day workers operate on products at some intermediate stage with the help of machines as well as raw and auxiliary materials, and at the end of the day produce intermediate products which are nearer to the final products. 'One layer of labour after another is piled up on the product. It is not alone the value of the extended labour-power that is continually being transferred to the product during the labour-processes, but also surplus-value. This product, however, is unfinished, it has not yet the form of a finished commodity, hence it cannot yet circulate.' (II, p. 235.)

Marx was thus concerned with capitalist production, under the assumption that it took a number of periods to produce commodities by using capital goods which were serviceable for several periods. As the above quotations prove, he analysed every complete production process of longer duration into elementary production processes of unit duration, in the same way as von Neumann did, by introducing intermediate products as additional goods. On the other hand, Marx differed from von Neumann in his treatment of durable capital goods. Instead of treating capital goods at different stages of wear and tear as different goods and reckoning the remaining value of such capital goods at the end of the year as a part of the annual returns, Marx included only the value of the portions of the capital goods which were worn out, in the price of the product. He wrote: 'by the wear and tear of the instruments of labour, a part of their value passes on to the product, while the other remains fixed in the instruments of labour and thus in the process of production... The longer an instrument lasts, the slower it wears out, the longer will its constant capital-value remain fixed in this use-form. But whatever may be its durability, the proportion in which it yields value is always inverse to the entire time it functions. If of two machines of equal value, one wears out in five years and the other in ten, then the first yields twice as much value in the same time as the second.' (II, p. 161.)

The inconsistency between the replacement of the value and the replacement of the substance of the components of the commodity-capital in this neo-classical depreciation caused Marx great difficulty. 'A part of capital has been advanced in the form of constant capital, i.e. of means of production, which function as factors of the labour-process so long as they retain the independent use-form in which they enter this process. The finished product, and therefore also the creators of the product, so far as they have been transformed into product, is thrust out of the process of production and passes as a commodity from the sphere of production to the sphere of circulation. But the instruments of labour never leave the sphere of production, once they have entered it.' (II, p. 160.) They function as means of production from the moment they enter into the process of production to the moment when they cease to serve and must therefore be replaced by new capital goods of the same kinds. Fixed capital goods lose their exchange-value continuously (by neo-classical depreciation), while they are physically replaced at intervals as 'a horse cannot be replaced piecemeal', and this fact may give rise to a discrepancy between replacement investment and depreciation.

THE TURNOVER OF CAPITAL

This is seen in the following way. Let k_{ij} be the quantity of capital good i required for the production of one unit of good j. Good j is a capital good if $1 \leq j \leq n$, a wage or luxury good if $n+1 \leq j \leq m$, as before. We assume, for the sake of simplicity, that production of every good takes only one period. Let τ_{ij} be the lifetime of capital good i when it is used for production of good j. It takes on a positive integral value when i is a fixed capital good, while it is unity if i is a circulating capital good (such as fuel, material, and so on). Defining a current-input coefficient a_{ij} as k_{ij}/τ_{ij} ($i = 1, ..., n$; $j = 1, ..., m$) and matrices

$$A_{\mathrm{I}} = \begin{bmatrix} a_{11} & \cdots & a_{1n} \\ \vdots & & \vdots \\ a_{n1} & \cdots & a_{nn} \end{bmatrix}, \quad A_{\mathrm{II}} = \begin{bmatrix} a_{1n+1} & \cdots & a_{1m} \\ \vdots & & \vdots \\ a_{nn+1} & \cdots & a_{nm} \end{bmatrix},$$

we can write the cost-price equations in the form:

$$p_{\mathrm{I}} = (1+\pi)(p_{\mathrm{I}} A_{\mathrm{I}} + w L_{\mathrm{I}}), \tag{1}$$

$$p_{\mathrm{II}} = (1+\pi)(p_{\mathrm{I}} A_{\mathrm{II}} + w L_{\mathrm{II}}), \tag{2}$$

where p_{I} and p_{II} denote the price vector of capital goods and the price vector of wage and luxury goods respectively, w the wage rate, π the profit rate, and L_i the vector of labour-input coefficients. Next, let $x_{\mathrm{I}}(t)$ be the output vector of capital goods and $x_{\mathrm{II}}(t)$ of wage and luxury goods, t representing the period when the production is carried out. Let R_{t+1} and I_{t+1} be the vector of replacement demand for capital goods and the vector of net investment respectively, in period $t+1$. Finally, C_{t+1} and D_{t+1} represent the vector of workers' consumption of wage goods and the vector of capitalists' consumption of wage and luxury goods respectively, in period $t+1$. We then have the demand-supply equations:

$$x_{\mathrm{I}}(t) = R_{t+1} + I_{t+1}, \tag{3}$$

$$x_{\mathrm{II}}(t) = C_{t+1} + D_{t+1}, \tag{4}$$

because $x_{\mathrm{I}}(t)$ and $x_{\mathrm{II}}(t)$ are available for supply at the beginning of period $t+1$.[6]

[6] There is a difference in notation between the preceding chapters and this chapter. In the former $x_{\mathrm{I}}(t)$ and $x_{\mathrm{II}}(t)$ represent the outputs available at t (hence their production is carried out in period $t-1$), while here they denote the outputs available at $t+1$.

After having spent $p_I I_{t+1}$ and $p_{II} D_{t+1}$ on capital goods and wage and luxury goods, capitalists devote the remainder of profits, i.e.

$$\pi \sum_{i=1}^{II} (p_I A_i + w L_i) x_i(t) - p_I I_{t+1} - p_{II} D_{t+1}$$

to an increase in the employment of workers,[7] so that the total wages in period $t+1$ will be

$$\sum_{i=1}^{II} w L_i x_i(t) + \pi \sum_{i=1}^{II} (p_I A_i + w L_i) x_i(t) - p_I I_{t+1} - p_{II} D_{t+1},$$

which equals $p_{II} C_{t+1}$, the total consumption of workers, because they cannot save. Hence

$$\sum_{i=1}^{II} w L_i x_i(t) + \pi \sum_{i=1}^{II} (p_I A_i + w L_i) x_i(t) = p_I I_{t+1} + p_{II}(C_{t+1} + D_{t+1}). \tag{5}$$

On the other hand, the sum of (1) and (2), postmultiplied by $x_I(t)$ and $x_{II}(t)$ respectively, equals the sum of (3) and (4) premultiplied by p_I and p_{II} respectively. Therefore,

$$(1+\pi) \sum_{i=1}^{II} (p_I A_i + w L_i) x_i(t) = p_I (R_{t+1} + I_{t+1}) + p_{II}(C_{t+1} + D_{t+1}). \tag{6}$$

Equations (5) and (6) yield

$$\sum_{i=1}^{II} (p_I A_i) x_i(t) = p_I R_{t+1}, \tag{7}$$

that is to say, the depreciation, or the part of constant capital which passes on to the products, must equal the replacement investment.

This equality is, however, not necessarily satisfied unless some special conditions are fulfilled. To see this clearly, we assume, for the sake of convenience of explanation, that all capital goods last for two periods and that those which are available in period t are all new. There is then no replacement demand for capital goods in period $t+1$, whereas the depreciation in period t amounts to

---

[7] Or more naturally, we may say that a part of profits is spent for an increase in constant and variable capitals and the rest on wage and luxury goods for capitalists' personal consumption.

half of the money value of the existing stock of capital goods in period t. Thus $p_I R_{t+1} = 0$ and

$$\sum_{i=1}^{II} (p_I A_i) x_i(t) > 0;$$

we have a contradiction to (7); therefore equations (1)–(6) cannot hold simultaneously. Marx puzzled over this paradox seriously and eventually, in order to avoid it, reluctantly introduced a stringent condition that the age structure of fixed capital is stationary. Under this assumption, the $1/\tau_{jr} \times 100$ per cent of the stock of capital good j, $k_{jr} x_r(t)$, held by industry r in period t must be replaced in kind at the beginning of period $t+1$, so that the total replacement demand for capital goods of all industries amounts to

$$R_{t+1} = \sum_{i=1}^{II} A_i x_i(t),$$

and hence the total value of replacement demand, $p_I R_{t+1}$, equals the total amount of depreciation,

$$\sum_{i=1}^{II} (p_I A_i) x_i(t).$$

It is evident, however, that consistency is not assured when the age structure of fixed capital is no longer stationary. There will not be universal consistency between 'the replacement of the wear and tear portion of the value in the form of money' and 'the replacement of fixed capital in kind', unless we can get rid of the neo-classical method of depreciation and obey the von Neumann golden rule in the valuation of capital costs.

If we treat capital goods at different stages of wear and tear as qualitatively different goods and capital goods remaining at the end of the production period as by-products of the current production process, we have no possibility of inconsistency. Every capital good can now last for only one period, so that it must be fully replaced in every period in kind as well as in value. Thus the problem which afflicted Marx disappears as soon as we accept the von Neumann golden rule. Moreover, we can effectively resolve many problems related to the age composition of capital, such as the differences in productivity and transferability between new and old capital goods, the determination of the economic lifetime of each capital good as a length of time which may possibly be different from its physical lifetime, and so on. There is no reason to suppose that Marx would not have adopted von Neumann's approach if he could have discovered or learned it.

By including intermediate products and old capital goods in the list of goods, we can analyse the existing concrete processes of production into abstract processes which are standardized so that each is of unit time duration. Every good can last for only one period; new and old capital goods become qualitatively different goods after one period, so that every good of the same quality has a lifetime of one period, i.e., $\tau_{ij} = 1$ for all i and j. Then the capital coefficient k_{ij} and the current-input coefficient a_{ij} are not distinguishable, so that in the following we denote the quantity of good j technically required per unit intensity of 'process' i by a_{ji}. Let l_i be the labour-time consumed per unit intensity of i and b_{ji} the quantity of good j produced per unit intensity of i. Each process converts a bundle of n commodities and labour $(a_{1i}, ..., a_{ni}, l_i)$ into a different bundle of n commodities $(b_{1i}, ..., b_{ni})$ after one period.

An entire production process over t periods is analysed into t abstract processes by introducing $t-1$ intermediate products, which together with the final product of the process give t products. Thus multi-period production does not affect the balance between the number of goods and the number of processes. On the other hand, however, the von Neumann treatment of durable capital goods leads us to a completely different conclusion. Let there be $n-1$ goods in the ordinary sense, the first $n-2$ being perishable, while the last can serve for two periods. Let us call a one-year-old unit of good $n-1$ good n, in order to distinguish it from the new good $n-1$. To produce each ordinary good j, $j = 1, ..., n-1$, there are available two processes, one using the new capital good $n-1$, and the other the one-year-old capital good n. Good n is only a by-product of those processes which utilize the new capital good $n-1$, and there is no additional process to produce n, so that the total number of 'processes' is $2(n-1)$, which is greater than the total number of 'goods' n, unless $n = 2$. Moreover, the list of processes may include the processes of carrying new or old goods over to the next period. Hence there is no need for the number of processes m to be identical with the number of goods n. In general, we now have rectangular input and output matrices:

$$A = \begin{bmatrix} a_{11} & \cdots & a_{1m} \\ \vdots & & \vdots \\ a_{n1} & \cdots & a_{nm} \end{bmatrix}, \quad B = \begin{bmatrix} b_{11} & \cdots & b_{1m} \\ \vdots & & \vdots \\ b_{n1} & \cdots & b_{nm} \end{bmatrix}.$$

Once we get rid of the world where $n = m$, the Marxian analysis of value and production in terms of simultaneous equations loses its foundations entirely. If $n < m$, we would have a negative degree of freedom (i.e. an over-determination) in price determination, and a positive degree of freedom (i.e. an under-determination) in output determination. It is obvious, even for hard-line Marxian economists, that the valuation and production systems should now be formulated, as they were by von Neumann, in terms of dual sets of inequalities.

Let L be the labour-input coefficient row vector, ω the real wage rate representing the number of baskets a worker can consume by working one hour, π_t the maximum rate of profit in period t, P_t the price vector in period t, c the vector representing a unit of the standard consumption basket, and x_t the vector of intensities of operation of processes in period t.[8] Like von Neumann, our Marx may assume that ω is a constant to be determined sociologically by the power of capitalists to exploit workers, and that the hourly money-wage rate w_t actually paid in period t is equal to the hourly living cost, so that

$$w_t = P_t \omega c. \tag{8}$$

Outputs are evaluated at prices P_{t+1} instead of P_t, as one period is needed for production, and the total value of outputs $P_{t+1}B$ cannot exceed the total cost plus the profit at the maximum rate, $(1 + \pi_t)(P_t A + w_t L)$. We have a set of weak inequalities:

$$P_{t+1} B \leqslant (1 + \pi_t) P_t (A + \omega c L), \tag{9}$$

because of (8).

In a capitalist economy, production in period t is guided by this cost–price inequality. If (9) holds with strict inequality ' $<$ ' for a particular process i, then i cannot yield profits at the rate π_t. Capitalists will not invest any money in such a process, so that it

---

[8] In our present notation, A corresponds to the previous $(A_\mathrm{I}, A_\mathrm{II})$, L to $(L_\mathrm{I}, L_\mathrm{I})$, c to B, P to $(p_\mathrm{I}, p_\mathrm{II})$, and x to $(x_\mathrm{I}, x_\mathrm{II})$. The present B, the output matrix, should not be confused with the previous B, the subsistence consumption vector.

will operate at null intensity. This rule of choice of processes, the rule of profitability, is stated by the equation,

$$P_{t+1} Bx_t = (1+\pi_t) P_t (A+\omega cL) x_t, \qquad (10)$$

because, as $x_t \geqslant 0$, (10) implies that unprofitable members of (9) are multiplied by null members of x_t.

The x_t thus determined makes outputs of the amount Bx_t available at the beginning of period $t+1$, and these are partly consumed by workers, the rest being devoted to further production. In period $t+1$ industrial demands and workers' demands for goods are proportional to the activity levels, x_{t+1}, and the employment of labour, Lx_{t+1}, in that period respectively; the proportionality coefficients are the input coefficients A in the case of the industrial demands and the consumption coefficients ωc, in the case of the individual demands. The total demands cannot exceed the amounts of goods available for supply, so that we have

$$Bx_t \geqslant (A+\omega cL) x_{t+1}. \qquad (11)$$

The activity levels x_{t+1} are adjusted so that the equality between supply and demand holds for as many goods as possible. If, in spite of all possible adjustments of x_{t+1}, there remain some goods for which (11) holds with strict inequality ' > ', then their prices in period $t+1$ are set at zero, that is to say, they are free goods. This pricing rule of free goods may be stated, like the rule of profitability, in terms of an equation, as

$$P_{t+1} Bx_t = P_{t+1}(A+\omega cL) x_{t+1}, \qquad (12)$$

because the strict inequalities which may remain in (11) are ruled out by multiplying them by the corresponding prices, which are zero.

As the careful reader may already have noticed, the P_{t+1}s appearing in (9) and (10) should be distinguished from those in (12). Those in (9) and (10) are the prices which are expected in period t to prevail in period $t+1$, while those in (12) are the prices which actually prevail in period $t+1$. They are identical only when entrepreneurs can correctly foresee the prices in the next period. Furthermore, they can be equated to the P_ts as well, in the state of stationary price equilibrium. In that state the rate of profit π_t will also be kept unchanged; the subscript t or $t+1$, therefore, may be deleted from P_t, P_{t+1} and π_t. It can then be seen that such a price equilibrium may be compatible with a balanced growth of outputs; $x_{t+1} = (1+g)x_t$. In fact, substituting from this, the system (9)–(12) can be written as:

$$PB \leq (1+\pi) P(A+\omega cL), \qquad (13)$$

$$PBx = (1+\pi) P(A+\omega cL) x, \qquad (14)$$

$$Bx \geq (1+g) (A+\omega cL) x, \qquad (15)$$

$$PBx = (1+g) P(A+\omega cL) x, \qquad (16)$$

after deleting subscripts t and $t+1$ from x_t and x_{t+1}; and von Neumann and others have shown that the system (13)–(16) has, under appropriate economic assumptions concerning the sign patterns of A, B and L, an economically meaningful set of solutions $(\bar{\pi}, \bar{g}, \bar{x}, \bar{p})$ fulfilling $\bar{P}B\bar{x} > 0$. The growth equilibrium thus established corresponds to Marx's state of extended reproduction, if $\bar{g} > 0$; and we have $\bar{g} = \bar{\pi}$ in the state of balanced growth equilibrium since we have ruled out capitalists' consumption.[9]

It is interesting to see that the above system can provide a rule for determining the *economic* life span of capital goods. As I have emphasized, our list of goods includes old capital goods at various stages of wear and tear in addition to new final goods and intermediate products. If there is an s-year-old capital good available in period $t+1$ for which there is no demand, its price in $t+1$ will be set at zero according to the rule of free goods. If it is zero, then the profit accruing from the process of carrying this old capital good over to the next period is also zero (because the rate of profit is finite).[10] Then there is no incentive for capitalists to carry such capital goods over, and they will be discarded as soon as they become free. Thus the rule of free goods enables us endogenously to determine the economic lifetime of capital goods, as distinct from the physical lifetime.

Although Marx recognized that the time taken to turn over invested capital (determined by the lifetime of capital goods), the

---

[9] This simple von Neumann system has been extended into the generalized von Neumann system of the Marx–von Neumann type so as to include capitalists' consumption as well as workers' savings. See my *Equilibrium, Stability and Growth*, pp. 131–53, and *Theory of Economic Growth*, pp. 89–114.
[10] It is assumed that a capital good can be stored for one period without labour and other goods. The cost of carrying over is zero since the capital good has no value, so that only zero profit can be expected.

production period and so on were changeable, he treated them as if they varied exogenously; he examined the effects of an autonomous change in the period of circulation and thus in the period needed for the turnover of capital. (II, p. 291.) But, as has been seen above by reformulating Marx's theory in the von Neumann way we can derive an economic criterion for entrepreneurs' decisions not to use a capital good of a particular age any longer. Similarly the production period may also be chosen. If there are a number of methods of production with different production periods, entrepreneurs will choose one from among them according to the rule of profitability. In this case the list of processes has to be extended so that it includes all the alternative methods of production, which have been analysed into abstract 'processes'. This generalization in no way changes the fundamental characteristics of the model. It is still a Marx–von Neumann model. Thus Marx can be saved from becoming obsolete and may continue to be the most important contributor to the most crucial area of economic theory, as long as he is willing for his model to be dissolved into a new and more powerful one, the Marx–von Neumann. That Marx would not object to this proposal is suggested by the fact that the part of *Capital* which discusses the turnover of capital (particularly chapters VIII, XII and XIII of volume II), which I regard as one of the best parts of the three volumes, is surprisingly close to von Neumann.

CHAPTER 14

The labour theory of value revisited

It was seen in the previous chapter that if a von Neumann revolution broke out in Marxian economics it would bring about great structural changes, particularly in the price-determination equations. First of all, the output-coefficient matrix can no longer be an identity matrix, since old capital goods are treated as by-products of the processes which use one-period younger capital goods. Secondly, the output-coefficient matrix can no longer be a square matrix because, for instance, if capital goods last for several periods and those at different stages of wear and tear are treated as different goods, it is possible to produce the same new goods by different processes, by utilizing 'different' capital goods. The existence of alternative production processes tends to make the number of processes larger than the number of goods, whereas the possibility of joint production tends to reverse the inequality. In any case, it is not necessary that goods and processes should be equal in number. Thirdly, as a consequence of the inequality between the number of goods and the number of processes, the price-determination equations will generate over- or under-determination of prices according as the number of processes is greater or smaller than the number of goods. It is then found that the strict equations between prices and costs (including profits at the uniform rate) for all goods are too restrictive; they are therefore replaced by inequalities which state that prices do not exceed costs *plus* profits at the maximum rate. The inequalities are supplemented by the rule of profitability, which states that those processes whose rates of profits are not as high as the maximum rate are not utilized. This is, however, an evident generalization (or a correctly formulated version) of Marx's law of equalization of the general rate of profits through competition (III, pp. 173–99), because it rules out discrepancies among the rates of profits of the *active* manufacturing processes chosen by capitalists and implies that the processes not chosen by entrepreneurs can yield profits only at rates which do not exceed the rate of profit of the processes actually adopted.

Obviously, such great changes cannot but affect the system of value-determination equations, which is also a dual of the physical reproduction (or input–output) system in Marx's model. In fact, as will be seen later, they shake and destroy the foundations of the labour theory of value, in the original form in terms of simultaneous equations which was developed by Marx. Thus the recognition of joint production and alternative manufacturing processes, as a result of which the von Neumann revolution arises, encourages us to sacrifice Marx's own formulation of the labour theory of value and to extend (or modify) it to meet the spirit of the von Neumann revolution. Indeed, one of the main purposes of this final chapter is to show that values of commodities are not necessarily determined as non-negative and unique if we stick to the equation approach after having admitted joint production and alternative processes, while the other is to reformulate the theory of value in an inequality form which is analogous to von Neumann's price–cost inequality system. It will be seen that the values determined by the inequality system are non-negative and play the role of shadow prices in economies which maximize the productivity of labour by utilizing labour efficiently. In the capitalist mode of production where the price-guided (or profit-guided) choice of techniques prevails, equilibrium prices determined competitively are different from values except in certain very special cases, but the values may still have some normative relevance in capitalist economies, because they enable us to find those techniques by the use of which the amount of labour needed to produce given amounts of commodities can be minimized.

Thus it looks at first sight as if the labour theory of value can survive the von Neumann revolution so long as it is content with its weakened position as well as its reformulation and modification. However the classical criticism which originated with Böhm–Bawerk applies to the labour theory of value, not only in its original version but also in the revised one. That is to say, as soon as the heterogeneity of labour is allowed for, the value of theory is seen to conflict with Marx's law of the equalization of the rate of exploitation through society, unless the different sorts of labour are reduced to the homogeneous abstract human labour in proportion to their wage rates. This is a serious dilemma from the point of view of Marxian economists, because on the one hand different rates of exploitation among different classes of workers obviously are not compatible with Marx's view of the polarization of society into two classes, capitalists and workers, and on the other, if different sorts of labour are converted into the abstract human labour in proportion to their wages, then the resulted value system depends on relative wages and hence Marx's intention of obtaining an intrinsic value system completely independent of markets is not fulfilled. There is no easy way out of this predicament. Our solution, a Marxian economics without the labour theory of value, is unlikely to be accepted by Marxists, but I shall nevertheless strongly recommend it to them at the end of this final chapter.

It has been seen that in Marx's economics the theory of value has to provide a system of values of commodities which can serve as weights for the aggregation of many industries, or primitive sectors, into two or several major 'departments'. It is then required that the system of values be (*a*) non-negative, (*b*) unique and (*c*) independent of what happens in the market. The reasons for (*a*) and (*b*) need no explanation, while the requirement (*c*) cannot be avoided, as it was Marx's aim to develop a long-run macro-dynamic theory. The other purpose of Marx's theory of value is to provide a theoretical foundation for his two-class view of the capitalist society. Therefore each worker has to be shown to be equally exploited by the capitalists, so that (*d*) a uniform rate of exploitation must be established throughout the society when the values of commodities are determined so as to fulfil the equations (or inequalities) of the value theory. We shall now see how the introduction of joint production, alternative processes, or heterogeneous labour will conflict with the above four requirements.

Let us deal first with the problem of joint production. It has been seen by Samuelson, Arrow, Koopmans and others that the static input–output equation system may result in negative outputs or negative prices if joint production processes are allowed for.[1] The same argument applies to the value-determination system of Marx, as the following numerical example shows. Suppose there are two kinds of capital goods, circulating and fixed. The circulating capital good, labelled as good 1, is not durable, while the fixed capital good can serve for two periods.

---

[1] See, for example, T. C. Koopmans, 'Maximization and Substitution in Linear Models of Production', *Input–Output Relations*, ed. by The Netherlands Economic Institute (Leiden: H. E. Stenfert Kroese N.V., 1953).

The new fixed capital good is distinguished from the old by calling them goods 2 and 3 respectively. The fixed capital goods are not used for producing themselves but for producing the circulating capital good, so that the latter can be produced by processes 1 and 2, utilizing the new and old fixed capital goods respectively. By the von Neumann convention the old capital good is a by-product of process 1 using the new capital good. The process which produces the fixed capital good is called process 3.

TABLE 1

	Process 1		Process 2		Process 3	
	Input	Output	Input	Output	Input	Output
Good 1	0.7	1	0.9	1	0.9	0
Good 2	0.5	0	0	0	0	1
Good 3	0	0.5	0.5	0	0	0
Labour	1	–	1	–	1	–

Input–output coefficients are given in table 1. It is noted that process 2 is assumed to require a greater amount of the circulating capital good than process 1, because the former uses the old fixed capital good and the latter the new. We then have the value-determination equations:

$$\left. \begin{array}{l} \lambda_1 + 0.5\lambda_3 = 0.7\lambda_1 + 0.5\lambda_2 + 1, \\ \lambda_1 = 0.9\lambda_1 + 0.5\lambda_3 + 1, \\ \lambda_2 = 0.9\lambda_1 + 1. \end{array} \right\} \quad (1)$$

Solving we obtain negative values: $\lambda_1 = -50$, $\lambda_2 = -44$, $\lambda_3 = -12$. Thus when the von Neumann treatment of old capital goods as by-products of those processes which use younger capital goods is adopted, a negative value may be attributed to each good.

However, it has to be noticed that the case of all goods having negative values is obtained only when the system does not satisfy the condition of productiveness. In fact, if we adopt the Marxian or the neo-classical depreciation procedure, the process of production of good 1 is characterized as follows: As half a unit of the fixed capital good brings forth two units of good 1 during its lifetime (i.e. in two periods), by consuming 0.7 units of good 1 and one unit of labour in the first period and 0.9 units of good 1 and one unit of labour in the second, so the process produces one unit of good 1 per period, by using 0.8 units of good 1, 0.25 units of good 2 (the fixed capital good) and one unit of labour per period. On the other hand, good 2 is produced by 0.9 units of good 1 and one unit of labour as before. Therefore, the value-determination equations are now written as

$$\left.\begin{aligned}\lambda_1 &= 0.8\lambda_1 + 0.25\lambda_2 + 1,\\ \lambda_2 &= 0.9\lambda_1 + 1,\end{aligned}\right\} \quad (2)$$

which give negative values $\lambda_1 = -50$ and $\lambda_2 = -44$, because the input-coefficient matrix is not 'productive'. It is noted that the first equation of the neo-classical system (2) is no more than the average of the first two equations of the von Neumann system (1). Hence the productiveness of the neo-classical system is necessary and sufficient for the positiveness of the values of the circulating and new fixed capital goods.

However, this condition is not sufficient to assure positive values for the old capital goods. This is illustrated by replacing the input coefficient 0.9 and the labour-input coefficient 1 of process 3 by 0.2 and 0.5 respectively. We then have the von Neumann system:

$$\left.\begin{aligned}\lambda_1 \phantom{{}={}} + 0.5\lambda_3 &= 0.7\lambda_1 + 0.5\lambda_2 + 1,\\ \lambda_1 \phantom{{}+ 0.5\lambda_3} &= 0.9\lambda_1 + 0.5\lambda_3 + 1,\\ \lambda_2 \phantom{{}+ 0.5\lambda_3} &= 0.2\lambda_1 + 0.5,\end{aligned}\right\} \quad (1')$$

and the neo-classical counterpart:

$$\left.\begin{aligned}\lambda_1 &= 0.8\lambda_1 + 0.25\lambda_2 + 1,\\ \lambda_2 &= 0.2\lambda_1 + 0.5.\end{aligned}\right\} \quad (2')$$

It is at once seen that the neo-classical system is 'productive' and determines λ_1 and λ_2 at 7.5 and 2.0 respectively. But the value of the old capital good in the von Neumann system depends on the magnitudes of λ_1 and λ_2 and may be negative; in the present case, $\lambda_3 = -0.5$. We have thus obtained an example which enables us to conclude that negative values are not ruled out in the von Neumann system, unless restrictive assumptions are imposed in addition to the productiveness of the prevailing technology.

In order for the values of all commodities to be determined to be non-negative, we have to reformulate the theory of value in the same way as von Neumann formulated the theory of prices, not in terms of equations but in terms of inequalities. In the following we do not classify industries into capital-goods, wage-goods and luxury-goods industries, because a process producing say, a wage good may jointly produce a capital good as a by-product. However, we continue to classify goods into the two groups, capital-goods and wage or luxury-goods, so that we may partition the output-coefficient matrix into

$$B = \begin{bmatrix} B_\mathrm{I} \\ B_\mathrm{II} \end{bmatrix},$$

where the submatrix B_I lists outputs of capital goods produced by various processes, and B_II is a similar submatrix of outputs of wage and luxury goods. As wage and luxury goods are not directly used for production, the input-coefficient matrix is written as

$$\begin{bmatrix} A \\ 0 \end{bmatrix},$$

and L stands for the labour-input coefficient vector. To obtain an inequality version of the labour theory of value, we consider a linear programming problem: To minimize

$$Lx \qquad (3)$$

subject to $\qquad B_\mathrm{I} x \geqslant Ax + Y_\mathrm{I}, \qquad (4)$

$$B_\mathrm{II} x \geqslant Y_\mathrm{II}, \qquad (5)$$

$$x \geqslant 0, \qquad (6)$$

where x denotes the vector of activity levels and Y_I and Y_II are the vector of net outputs of capital goods and that of wage goods and luxury goods respectively. Net outputs are taken as given; the total amount of labour employed, (3), is minimized with respect to x. It is evident that the programme of efficient employment of labour given as a solution to the problem maximizes the productivity of human labour.

It is well known that each linear programming problem has

its dual. With the above minimizing problem is coupled a problem: To maximize

$$\Lambda_I Y_{II} + \Lambda_{II} Y_{II} \quad (7)$$

subject to $\quad \Lambda_I B_I + \Lambda_{II} B_{II} \leqslant \Lambda_I A + L, \quad (8)$

$$\Lambda_I \geqslant 0, \quad \Lambda_{II} \geqslant 0. \quad (9)$$

Λ_I and Λ_{II} may be interpreted as vectors of the 'shadow prices' of the commodities grouped into the two classes. The dual problem maximizes the value of net outputs evaluated at the shadow prices. By virtue of the fundamental duality theorem of linear programming, we have

$$Lx = \Lambda_I Y_I + \Lambda_{II} Y_{II}, \quad (10)$$

which states that the total value of net outputs equals the total amount of labour required, directly or indirectly, for their production, so that by Marx's *second* definition of value (see chapter 1) $\Lambda_I Y_I + \Lambda_{II} Y_{II}$ can be interpreted as the value of the composite commodity, $Y = (Y_I, Y_{II})$.

When only a particular element, y_j, of Y is positive, all the other elements being zero, λ_j may be interpreted as the value of the single commodity j. We may then ask whether the values of commodities are independent of the final demand Y. This is the problem of the (static) non-substitution theorem. Georgescu-Roegen, Samuelson, Arrow, Koopmans and others have shown that if there is no joint production, a change in the final demand does not affect the values.[2] This non-substitution theorem has been extended by Mirrlees to a class of cases allowing for by-products, including some von Neumann cases.[3] But in the general case of joint production the theorem does not remain true; Λ_I and Λ_{II} depend on Y. Therefore the λ_j obtained for the final demand being set at some Y may be different from the λ_j which is obtained for a particular Y with $y_j = 1$ and $y_i = 0$, for all $i \neq j$. As the latter is the value of commodity j, this means that the elements of the solution vector $(\Lambda_I, \Lambda_{II})$ to the dual linear programming problem do not give the values of individual commodities; nevertheless, as

---

[2] See, for example, P. A. Samuelson, 'Abstract of a Theorem Concerning Substitutability in Open Leontief Models', *Activity Analysis of Production and Allocation*, ed. by T. C. Koopmans (New York, 1951); and T. C. Koopmans, 'Maximisation and Substitution'.

[3] J. A. Mirrlees, 'The Dynamic Non-substitution Theorem', *Review of Economic Studies*, XXXVI (1), 1969, pp. 67–76.

has been seen, it is true that the sum, $\Lambda_{\text{I}}Y_{\text{I}}+\Lambda_{\text{II}}Y_{\text{II}}$, can be interpreted as the value of the composite commodity Y.

The duality result (10) is equivalent with the following two rules. First, the 'rule of valuation' associates the null shadow price, i.e. $\lambda_j = 0$ (where λ_j is an element of Λ_{I} or Λ_{II}), with the jth condition in (4) or (5), if the latter holds with strict inequality ' > ', i.e. if there is over-production of commodity j. Secondly, the 'rule of efficiency' associates the null activity level, i.e. $x_i = 0$ (where x_i is an element of x), with the ith condition of (8), if the latter holds with strict inequality ' < '; that is to say, the ith process is not utilized when the value of outputs of the ith process does not reach its value of inputs. In fact, we have from (4), (5) and (9)

$$(\Lambda_{\text{I}}B_{\text{I}}+\Lambda_{\text{II}}B_{\text{II}})x \geqslant \Lambda_{\text{I}}Ax+\Lambda_{\text{I}}Y_{\text{I}}+\Lambda_{\text{II}}Y_{\text{II}}, \quad (11)$$

which holds with equality if and only if the rule of valuation holds. On the other hand, we have from (8) and (6)

$$(\Lambda_{\text{I}}B_{\text{I}}+\Lambda_{\text{II}}B_{\text{II}})x \leqslant \Lambda_{\text{I}}Ax+Lx, \quad (12)$$

which holds with equality if and only if the rule of efficiency prevails. Furthermore, it is seen that the duality result (10) is obtained if and only if both (11) and (12) are fulfilled with equality. Hence the identity of the two rules with the duality result is established.

These rules are obviously analogous to the rule of free goods and the rule of profitability, which have been familiar among non-Marxian economists since von Neumann. There is, however, an evident difference between them, in that one deals with values and the other with prices. In the case of prices the rule of valuation (or the rule of free goods) is acceptable because the competitive prices will be set at zero for those goods which are in excess supply; whereas in the case of values one might think that the value of a good should be positive even if it is free, except in the extreme case where no labour is needed, directly or indirectly, to produce that good. But Marx's definition of value is not so simple as the one which has been stylized as his definition. Marx had, in addition to the usual main definition which is valid in the ordinary case of all commodities being useful, a supplementary rule which is applied to the degenerate case including some free goods. He wrote: 'Nothing can have value, without being an object of utility. If the thing is useless, so is the labour contained in it; the labour does not count as labour, and therefore creates no value.' (I, p. 41.) There can be no more explicit statement of the 'rule of valuation' than this quotation, which states that if a good is useless, so that the demand for it does not match its supply and the corresponding condition in (4) or (5) is therefore satisfied with strict inequality, then, in spite of the fact that a positive amount of labour is contained in it, its value has to be set at zero. It is indeed surprising to find in *Capital* a foretaste of the modern inequality approach to the determination of values or prices.

In a centralized economy where labour is the sole scarce factor of production, techniques of production would be chosen so as to minimize the employment of labour. On the other hand in an economy where the capitalist mode of production prevails individual entrepreneurs are not interested in minimizing total employment, but adopt those techniques which maximize the rate of profit, calculated in terms of equilibrium prices. Thus, in a capitalist economy we have a price-guided choice of techniques, so that the techniques actually chosen may be different from those which are optimal from the viewpoint of the above linear programming problem. Consequently the values of commodities calculated on the basis of the adopted techniques are not necessarily the same as the values theoretically determined by linear programming. Thus the 'actual' values may differ from the 'optimum' values. Since Marx was interested in the former, but not the latter, we next devote ourselves to examining the 'actual' values for uniqueness.[4]

Let π be the maximum rate of profit which prevails when prices and the wage rate are set at $P = (p_\text{I}, p_\text{II})$ and w, where p_I and p_II are row vectors of prices of capital goods and prices of wage and luxury goods respectively. By definition π must fulfil

$$PB \leqslant (1+\pi)(p_\text{I}A + wL) \qquad (13)$$

with at least one process satisfying this price–cost condition with equality. The money-wage rate w is adjusted so as to enable each worker to consume ω units of the normalized consumption vector c, so that we have

$$w = p_\text{II}\omega c. \qquad (14)$$

---

[4] It is well known that solutions to a linear programming problem may not be unique; therefore there may be two or more optimum value systems.

Substituting for w from this, (13) can be written as

$$PB \leqslant (1+\pi)(p_I A + p_{II} \omega c L). \qquad (15)$$

By adjusting P we can find a maximum of the maximum rate of profit π^0, corresponding to a given real wage rate (or a given level of consumption) ω^0. When the real wage rate is fixed at ω^0 and prices are flexible, entrepreneurs adopt only those processes which satisfy (15) at ω^0 and π^0 with equality, since the others are found to be unprofitable.

Suppose now that the total number of production processes available in the economy, m, is greater than the number of goods, h. Suppose, say, that $h+1$ processes are found to be profitable when the real-wage rate is set at ω^0, so that the rate of profit is maximized at π^0. Let P^0 be the long-run equilibrium prices associated with ω^0 and π^0. Processes are re-numbered, if necessary, in such a way that the first $h+1$ processes are profitable and the others unprofitable. We denote the input and output matrices consisting of the first h processes by A_1 and B_1 respectively, L_1 being the corresponding labour-input coefficient vector. A_2 and B_2 represent the input and output matrices obtained by replacing process h in A_1 and B_1 by process $h+1$; L_2 is the labour-input coefficient vector generated by the replacement. We then have the following two sets of equations,

$$P^0 B_1 = (1+\pi^0)(p_I A_1 + p_{II}{}^0 \omega^0 c L_1), \qquad (16)$$

$$P^0 B_2 = (1+\pi^0)(p_I{}^0 A_2 + p_{II}{}^0 \omega^0 c L_2). \qquad (17)$$

Let us furthermore suppose that processes h and $h+1$ are alternative ways of producing the same commodities and that either of the two sets of processes $(1, ..., h)$ and $(1, ..., h-1, h+1)$ can produce all h kinds of goods. Then entrepreneurs can adopt either, or any convex combination of them; they are, in fact, indifferent from the point of view of the entrepreneurs, because they are equi-profitable. The values of the commodities are determined by

$$\Lambda B_1 = \Lambda_I A_1 + L_1, \qquad (18)$$

or

$$\Lambda B_2 = \Lambda_I A_2 + L_2, \qquad (19)$$

according as the first or the second set of processes is chosen. In the general case of using the first and second sets in the

proportion of q to $1-q$, where $0 \leqslant q \leqslant 1$, the value formula may be written as
$$\Lambda B_q = \Lambda_I A_q + L_q, \qquad (20)$$
where $B_q = qB_1 + (1-q)B_2$ and similarly for A_q and L_q. Although the two sets of processes are associated with the same long-run equilibrium prices, as (16) and (17) show, it can be seen that the Λ derived from (18) is not necessarily identical with the one from (19), and either of them may further differ from the Λ determined by (20). This simple but important fact violates the uniqueness of the value system, because when there are alternative processes, it is possible for the same sorts of commodities to be produced simultaneously by different processes and therefore to have different values. Moreover, when a process is mixed with another equally profitable process the values may depend on the proportions in which these processes are mixed; and the proportions may easily fluctuate since the processes are indifferent in profitability. Therefore the values may easily change, so that they cannot serve as solid weights for aggregation.

The above argument can be illustrated by a simple numerical example. Consider a one-commodity economy having two alternative processes whose production coefficients are given as follows:

TABLE 2

	Process 1		Process 2	
	Input	Output	Input	Output
Commodity	0.25	1	0.5	1
Labour	0.5	–	0.25	–

These processes are equally profitable at $\pi = \frac{1}{3}$, when the ratio of the price of the commodity to the wage rate, p/w, is unity. To produce the commodity by process 1, $\frac{2}{3}$ hour of labour is required, since $\lambda = 0.25\lambda + 0.5$, instead of the $\frac{1}{2}$ hour needed by process 2. When half the total output of the commodity is produced by process 1 and the other half by 2, then the average capital and labour-input coefficients are equalized at 0.375, so that the value is calculated at $\frac{3}{5}$ hour. Finally, consider the case where the two processes are simultaneously utilized to produce the commodity in the following manner. Process 1 uses a_{11} units of the commodity produced by process 1 and a_{21} units of the commodity produced by process 2, together with labour of 0.5, for the production of one unit of the commodity. Similarly, process 2 combines a_{12} units of the commodity produced by process 1 and a_{22} units of the commodity produced by process 2 with labour of 0.25 to produce one unit of the commodity. The conditions which are required technologically are only $a_{11}+a_{21} = 0.25$ and $a_{12}+a_{22} = 0.5$, so that a_{ij}s may be taken as:

$$a_{11} = 0.25, \quad a_{21} = 0, \quad a_{12} = 0.25, \quad a_{22} = 0.25.$$

Then we have the value-determination equations

$$\lambda_1 = 0.25\lambda_1 \qquad\qquad + 0.5,$$
$$\lambda_2 = 0.25\lambda_1 + 0.25\lambda_2 + 0.25,$$

where λ_1 denotes the value of the commodity produced by process 1 and λ_2 the value of that produced by process 2. If the value ought to be determined uniquely for each commodity, λ_1 and λ_2 should be equalized. However, solving the above equations, we have $\lambda_1 = \frac{2}{3}$ and $\lambda_2 = \frac{5}{9}$. Obviously, $\lambda_1 \neq \lambda_2$; thus a situation contradicting the uniqueness postulate is generated, as the same commodity has different actual values simultaneously.

We have so far assumed that all labour is homogeneous. In recognizing its heterogeneity, however, Marx wrote: 'As the coat and the linen are two qualitatively different use-values, so also are the two forms of labour that produce them, tailoring and weaving. Were these two objects not qualitatively different, not produced respectively by labour of different quality, they could not stand to each other in the relation of commodities. Coats are not exchanged for coats, one use-value is not exchanged for another of the same kind.' (I, pp. 41–2.) He also said: 'Some people might think that if the value of a commodity is determined by the quantity of labour spent on it, the more idle and unskilful the labourer, the more valuable would his commodity be, because more time would be required in its production.' (I, p. 39.)

In the calculation of values, these different varieties of labour embodied in the different kinds of commodities are reduced to their common quality of 'human labour in the abstract'. 'It is the expenditure of simple labour-power, i.e. of the labour-power which, on the average, apart from any special development, exists in the organism of every ordinary individual. Simple average labour, it is true, varies in character in different countries and at different times, but in a particular society it is given. Skilled labour counts only as simple labour intensified, or rather, as multiplied simple labour, a given quantity of skilled being considered equal to a greater quantity of simple labour.' (1, p. 44.) 'All are reduced to one and the same sort of labour, human labour in the abstract.' (1, p. 38.)

Marx admitted that the distinction commonly drawn between skilled and unskilled labour was ambiguous. In his words: 'The distinction between skilled and unskilled labour rests in part on pure illusion, or, to say the least, on distinctions that have long since ceased to be real, and that survive only by virtue of a traditional convention; in part on the helpless condition of some groups of the working-class, a condition that prevents them from exacting equally with the rest the value of their labour-power. Accidental circumstances here play so great a part, that these two forms of labour sometimes change places.' (1, pp. 197–8.) Therefore he proposed a scientific formula by which all kinds of actual labour could be reduced to their common character of being human labour generally: 'In order to modify the human organism, so that it may acquire skill and handiness in a given branch of industry, and become labour-power of a special kind, a special education or training is requisite, and this, on its part, costs an equivalent in commodities of a greater or less amount. This amount varies according to the more or less complicated character of the labour-power. The expenses of this education (excessively small in the case of ordinary labour-power), enter pro tanto into the total value spent in its production.' (1, p. 172.)

In spite of this formula, Marx assumed every kind of labour to be unskilled, simple labour. However, it is not difficult to revise his value-determination equations so as to allow for different kinds of labour. For the sake of simplicity, we assume that there are no joint products and no alternative processes. We also do not group commodities into capital goods, wage goods and luxury goods, and assume that there are h goods and $n+1$ kinds of labour. To produce a unit of good j ($j = 1, ..., h$), a_{ij} units of good i ($i = 1, ..., h$) and l_{kj} units of labour k ($k = 1, ..., n+1$) are required, while to produce a unit of labour j ($j = 1, ..., n$), q_{ij} units of good i ($i = 1, ..., h$) and m_{kj} units of labour k ($k = 1, ..., n+1$) are required. We take labour $n+1$ as the standard labour, i.e., the unskilled, simple labour or human labour in the abstract. Then the values of the commodities $\Lambda = (\lambda_1, ..., \lambda_h)$ and the conversion ratios of skilled into unskilled labour $\Theta = (\theta_1, ..., \theta_n)$ are determined by the following equations:

$$\Lambda = \Lambda A + \Theta R + l, \qquad (21)$$

$$\Theta = \Lambda Q + \Theta T + m, \qquad (22)$$

where

$$A = \begin{bmatrix} a_{11} & \cdots & a_{1h} \\ \vdots & & \vdots \\ a_{h1} & \cdots & a_{hh} \end{bmatrix}, \quad Q = \begin{bmatrix} q_{11} & \cdots & q_{1n} \\ \vdots & & \vdots \\ q_{h1} & \cdots & q_{hn} \end{bmatrix},$$

$$R = \begin{bmatrix} l_{11} & \cdots & l_{1h} \\ \vdots & & \vdots \\ l_{n1} & \cdots & l_{nh} \end{bmatrix}, \quad T = \begin{bmatrix} m_{11} & \cdots & m_{1n} \\ \vdots & & \vdots \\ m_{n1} & \cdots & m_{nn} \end{bmatrix},$$

$$l = (l_{n+1,1} \cdots l_{n+1,h}), \quad m = (m_{n+1,1} \cdots m_{n+1,n}).$$

If the production of commodities and skilled labour is 'productive', the values and the conversion ratios are simultaneously determined to be positive. With the Θ thus obtained, (21) can be written as

$$\Lambda = \Lambda A + L, \qquad (23)$$

where $L = \Theta R + l$; (23) can further be partitioned into two sets of equations for capital goods and for wage and luxury goods, as has been done elsewhere in this book.

This generalization of Marx's labour theory of value might seem, at first sight, to give rise to no difficulty, as Marx believed. However, a closer examination enables us to see that it is in conflict with his theory of exploitation, unless the conversion ratios are determined to be proportional to the wage rates of the various kinds of labour. Let ω_i be the number of consumption baskets which the worker who offers a unit of labour i for one hour can buy by spending his hourly wages. Then a unit of the ith labour power is valued at $\omega_i \Lambda_{II} c$ in terms of unskilled labour, where Λ_{II} is the vector of the values of wage goods and c the vector of the quantities of wage goods contained in a unit of the basket. On the other hand, a unit of labour i counts as θ_i units of unskilled labour. Hence the worker i is exploited at the rate

$$e_i = \frac{\theta_i - \omega_i \Lambda_{\text{II}} c}{\omega_i \Lambda_{\text{II}} c} \quad (i = 1, \ldots, n+1),$$

where $\theta_i = 1$ for $i = n+1$. It is now seen that there prevails a uniform rate of exploitation throughout $n+1$ different kinds of labour, $e_1 = e_2 = \ldots = e_{n+1}$, if and only if $\omega_i/\omega_{n+1} = \theta_i$ for all $i = 1, \ldots, n$.

However, there is no reason why ωs should be proportional to θs. As the previous quotation from Marx shows, it is possible that a more skilled labourer with a larger θ_i may be paid a lower wage rate. Then we may have several groups of workers exploited at different rates, in contradiction to Marx's two-class view of the capitalist economy. To avoid this difficulty, we have to abandon the scientific determination of the conversion rates by the formulas (21) and (22), and simply convert different kinds of labour into unskilled labour in proportion to their wages. That is to say, the values of commodities are determined by

$$\Lambda = \Lambda A + L^*,$$

where $L^* = WR + l$ and $W = (w_1/w_{n+1}, \ldots, w_n/w_{n+1})$, w_i being the money-wage rate of labour. In this case, although the rate of exploitation is equalized throughout all kinds of labour, the values do not satisfy the postulate of independence from market conditions and may easily fluctuate from period to period as relative wages change.

We conclude by suggesting to Marxian economists that they ought radically to change their attitude towards the labour theory of value. If it has to determine the amounts of labour which the techniques of production actually adopted in a capitalist economy require, directly and indirectly, in order to produce commodities, it is not a satisfactory theory at all. As has been seen above, the value system may be determined to be negative, indefinite or even contradictory to the postulate of the uniform rate of exploitation. These findings urge us to abandon the theory.

For a thorough-going Marxist it would be impossible to conceive of Marxian economics without the labour theory of value. Since it provides the workers with an inspiring ideological rationale for their struggles against bourgeois regimes, Marxists would be greatly depressed by losing its authority. In addition to this emotional damage, the foundations of Marxian economics, as a two-department macro-dynamic theory, would be seriously shaken. If we refrain from aggregating the basic micro-model into a consolidated model of some manageable size, it is clear that we shall lose a number of the definite laws discovered by Marx, including the theory of the breakdown of capitalism; they would be either completely disproved or reduced to mere conjectures. Marxian economics would then suffer from the same kind of sterility as Walrasian general equilibrium theory – or at least it would certainly become less fruitful or more vacuous than it is. However, the most important task is of course to strengthen the foundations, for it is useless to build a palatial mansion on sand. One of the conclusions of this book is that Marx's economics can acquire citizenship in contemporary economic theory by detaching it from its root, the labour theory of value, and grafting it onto the von Neumann stock so as to produce the Marx–von Neumann flower! As has been seen in chapter 8, it is possible to construct an aggregate model by utilizing the equilibrium production prices (or the von Neumann prices) as weights of aggregation. The theory of aggregation is an uncultivated field in economics, both in orthodox economics and particularly in Marxian economics.

Finally, it is worth making an additional comment. Those economists who continue to use neo-classical aggregate production functions, in spite of the fact that their non-existence in the general case has been proved, must, by the principle of fairness admit their opponents' aggregation in terms of values, if these are approximately, though not exactly unique, not as a rigorous scientific method but as a practical procedure. We ought also to admit that the Marxian economists' 'surrogate' two-or-several-department model can often by suggestive and provide useful conjectures, such as their 'laws of motion of modern society'. It can supply a first approximation to reality, if the aggregation conditions are carefully examined and found to be approximately fulfilled. Thus the usefulness of the departmental analysis based on the concept of 'actual values' depends on the carefulness and skill of the economists who use it, though it cannot be provided with a full theoretical justification.

On the other hand, as has been seen above, the optimum labour theory of value determines the methods of production which minimize the amount of labour needed to produce given amounts of the final net outputs; the optimum values are firmly founded as the shadow prices to the problem and, therefore, contain no ambiguous element. The optimum value system can be taken as a norm of reference; the 'transformation problem', by measuring the distance of the actual or equilibrium price system from the optimum, can clarify how the techniques of production chosen under a capitalist regime deviate from the optimum state utilizing labour at its maximum productivity. From the formal point of view, this transformation problem is an extension of Marx's, not only in the sense that the former is formulated in terms of inequalities and the latter in terms of equations, but also in the sense that the former deals with the transformation of the *optimum* values under the optimum techniques into equilibrium production prices under the techniques actually chosen, while the latter is concerned only with the transformation of the *actual* values into these prices, taking no account of potential alternative methods of production.

Finally we show that the rate of exploitation holds true in terms of the optimum values in spite of the existence of joint products and alternative methods of production, provided that there is no heterogeneous labour. Let N be the number of workers actually employed. Specify $Y_I = 0$ and $Y_{II} = cN$ in (4) and (5), where c represents the subsistence consumption vector, as before. Then, by the duality theorem, the minimum value of Lx, subject to (4)–(6), equals $\Lambda_{II} cN$, which gives the amount of labour necessary to produce cN. The necessary labour is compared with the amount of labour actually consumed, TN, where T denotes the daily working hours per person, and the rate of exploitation may be defined as

$$e = \frac{\text{Surplus labour}}{\text{Necessary labour}} = \frac{TN - \Lambda_{II} cN}{\Lambda_{II} cN} = \frac{1 - \omega \Lambda_{II} c}{\omega \Lambda_{II} c}, \quad (24)$$

where $\omega = 1/T$, because only $\Lambda_{II} cN$ is required in 'socialist society' with no exploitation, while TN is actually consumed in capitalist society, so that the excess of TN over $\Lambda_{II} cN$ might be ascribed to exploitation by capitalists. It is at once seen that the rate of exploitation thus defined is identical with Marx's, because c in (24) above is nothing else than B in (2) in chapter 5. We may therefore conclude that Marx's theory of exploitation may survive the von Neumann Revolution in an economy with homogeneous labour.

Index

Aggregation
  non-distorting, 89–93
  in terms of wage units, 2, 10, 88
  in terms of value, 10
  into several departments, 98–104
  into two departments, 70, 82, 93–8, 109–12, 148
Arrow, K. J., 181, 185

Balanced-growth equilibrium
  instability of, 123–8, 135–7
Böhm-Bawerk, E., 6n, 180
Breakdown theory
  Marx's, 132–40
  a counter-example to, 160–3
Bródy, A., 1, 167n

Capital
  composition
    organic, 34, 138
    technical, 34, 137–8
    value, 34, 83–6, 137–8
    equal value composition, 37, 59, 74–6, 82, 95–6, 101–2, 152
    Samuelson's equal internal composition, 60–1
Capital goods
  economic life span, *see* Rule of free goods
  Marx's treatment of durability, 164–6, 168
Capital-input coefficient matrix
  indecomposability, 26
  productiveness, 22
Capitalist society
  conditions for its viability, 23–5, 54–5
Choice of techniques, *see* Rule of profitability

Dorfman, R., 115
Duality between physical and value systems, 4, 105–6

Effective demand
  Keynes' principle of, 19
Engels, F., 105n, 166
Exploitation frontier, 6, 55, 64
Exploitation rate
  condition of positive, 54–5

equalization of, 52, 193, 195
first definition, 47–8
second definition, 49–50
third definition, 50–1

Factor-price frontier, 6, 64–7
Frisch, R., 3, 9

General equilibrium theory
  two stage, 2
Georgescu-Roegen, N., 185
Golden-age equilibrium, 68, 80

Harrod, R. F., 144
Hicks, J. R., 2, 3, 8, 29, 34, 41, 127, 128, 160n

Jevons, W. S., 2

Kahn, R. F., 18
Kalecki, M., 3, 9
Keynes, J. M., 2, 3, 18, 19, 88–9, 102–4
Koopmans, T. C., 181, 185
Kuhn, H. W., 41

Labour
  heterogeneous, 180–1, 190–2
  necessary, 49
  paid and unpaid, 48
  surplus, 49
Labour power
  its value, 50
Lange, O., 8, 9
Leontief, W. W., 3, 12, 18, 30, 126
Linearly dependent industries, 77–82, 153–5

Malthus, T. R., 129, 164n
Marx–von Neumann model, 129–31, 158, 166–7, 174–8
Meade, J. E., 120
Menger, K., 2
Mirrlees, J. A., 185
Morishima, M., 6, 13n, 34n, 56n, 63, 65, 67, 71n, 105n, 129n, 142n, 158n, 160n, 164n, 167n, 177n
Morishima–Seton–Okishio theorem, 6, 63–8, 155

National product
  in terms of value, 19
von Neumann, J., 3–4, 8–9, 13, 42, 70–1, 117, 118n, 126, 129, 155, 158, 164, 166–7, 170, 173–5, 177n, 178–86, 194

Okishio, N., 6, 14n, 21n, 53, 63, 65, 67

Pasinetti, L., 158n
Production period
  Marx's treatment, 168–70
Profits
  Marx's view of, 57–8
  the rate of profit
    equalization of, 62–7
    its tendency to fall, 142–4

Quesnay, F., 5, 105

Relative surplus population, see Reserve army
Relative values
  Marx's laws, 29
  three Hicksian laws, 30–4
Reproduction
  extended
    Marx's scheme, 117–22
    a reformulation of the scheme, 122–8
    a scheme in terms of prices, 148–51
  simple, 106–9, 112–15
    Marx's view, 115–16
    orthodox view, 115–16
Reserve army, 131–9
Ricardo, D., 5, 74
Robinson, J., 46–7, 102
Rule of free goods, 176–7, 186
Rule of profitability, 176–7, 186

Samuelson, P. A., 6n, 29, 39n, 46–7, 56n, 59–61, 70, 72, 74, 78, 85, 115, 129, 140, 181, 185
Sato, R., 120n
Seton, F., 6, 63, 65, 67, 142n
Shinkai, Y., 125n
Simple commodity production, 28, 36
  general equilibrium of, 42–5
Smith, A., 5, 74
Solow, R. M., 115, 120
Sweezy, P. M., 46, 47

Technological change
  biased, 161–2
  Marxian neutral, see Capital, organic composition
Tinbergen, J., 3, 8
Transformation problem
  as a Markov chain problem, 77n
  dynamic, 145–6, 151–8
  Marx's algorithm, 59–60, 76–82
  static
    the first problem, see Morishima–Seton–Okishio theorem
    the second problem, 72–86
Tucker, A. W., 41

Use-value, 40–1
Uzawa, H., 120

Value
  actual, 187–90
  non-negativeness of, 22, 25–7, 181–3
  non-uniqueness, 188–90
  optimal, 184–6, 195
  two definitions, 11–12
    their identity, 17–18

Walras, L., 1–3, 29, 41–2, 105, 125

Zauberman, A., 1